WE STILL HERE

We Still Here

Hip Hop North of the 49th Parallel

Edited by
Charity Marsh and Mark V. Campbell

McGill-Queen's University Press
Montreal & Kingston ■ London ■ Chicago

ISBN 978-0-2280-0350-2 (cloth)
ISBN 978-0-2280-0483-7 (ePDF)
ISBN 978-0-2280-0484-4 (ePUB)

Legal deposit fourth quarter 2020
Bibliothèque nationale du Québec

Printed in Canada on acid-free paper that is 100% ancient forest free (100% post-consumer recycled), processed chlorine free

This book has been published with the help of a grant from the Canadian Federation for the Humanities and Social Sciences, through the Awards to Scholarly Publications Program, using funds provided by the Social Sciences and Humanities Research Council of Canada.

Funded by the Government of Canada | Financé par le gouvernement du Canada | Canada | Canada Council for the Arts | Conseil des arts du Canada

We acknowledge the support of the Canada Council for the Arts.

Nous remercions le Conseil des arts du Canada de son soutien.

Library and Archives Canada Cataloguing in Publication

Title: We still here : hip hop north of the 49th parallel / edited by Charity Marsh and Mark V. Campbell.
Other titles: Hip hop north of the 49th parallel | Hip hop north of the forty-ninth parallel
Names: Marsh, Charity, 1974– editor. | Campbell, Mark V., editor.
Description: Includes bibliographical references and index.
Identifiers: Canadiana (print) 20200287907 | Canadiana (ebook) 20200288032 | ISBN 9780228003502 (cloth) | ISBN 9780228004837 (ePDF) | ISBN 9780228004844 (ePUB)
Subjects: LCSH: Rap (Music)—Social aspects—Canada. | LCSH: Rap (Music)—Canada—History and criticism. | LCSH: Hip-hop—Canada.
Classification: LCC ML3918.R37 W361 2020 | DDC 782.4216490971—dc23

This book was typeset by True to Type in 10.5/13 Sabon

Contents

Acknowledgments

The seeds for the creation of this collection on hip hop were planted at the 2012 IASPM-Canada Conference entitled "Sounding the Nation? Diaspora, Indigeneity, and Multiculturalism." As part of a plenary discussion focusing on hip hop in Canada moderated by one of the founding hip hop studies scholars, Dr Murray Forman, Mark and I met for the first time, and since that day in Wolfville, Nova Scotia, we have worked together on a wide range of hip hop-based projects and academic/artistic collaborations.

During the past eight years, Mark and I have also embarked on many major changes in our lives, which have had an impact on how this collection has transformed over time – these life changes include growing our families, seeking out and taking up new positions in the academy, engaging in new forms of art making, and developing new research programs. Throughout all of these, it has been a pleasure to work alongside Mark on this project, as well as to encourage and support his significant and timely contributions to new and meaningful methods of digitally archiving often marginalized or overlooked hip hop voices and knowledges.

We Still Here: Hip Hop North of the 49th Parallel has been a long time in the making, and we want to acknowledge and thank all of the contributing authors for their patience and ongoing dedication to the collection. Over the years the creation of this work has been supported in part by the Social Sciences and Humanities Research Council and many of my SSHRC-funded undergraduate and graduate students, including Brett Wyatt, Ringo Jedlic, Elizabeth Bailey, and Ben Valiaho. For the final push to completion, Mark and I are deeply indebted to the hard work, perseverance, and diligence of doctoral candidate

Cassandra Ozog, who has formatted, copy edited, and communicated with the press on many of the final details. Cassie's infectious positivity and encouragement as we moved towards the completion of this project have been invaluable.

We would like to thank Jonathan Crago and the editorial board at McGill-Queen's University Press for their willingness to publish this work and their ongoing support throughout the process. We would also like to thank the reviewers who were involved at the beginning stages of our editing process prior to our sending the manuscript to the press, as well as the anonymous reviewers sought out by the press for their helpful comments and suggestions, which allowed for productive changes to the collection.

I am grateful for my friends and colleagues who have offered commentary, critique, and advice on much of my hip hop research, including Randal Rogers, Rebecca Caines, Carmen Robertson, Megan Smith, John Campbell, Susan Fast, Christina Baade, Line Grenier, Craig Jennex, Murray Forman, Mark Campbell, and Andreana Clay.

Over the past decade I have had the absolute privilege of collaborating with, and learning much about hip hop from, many artists and young people who have participated in the IMP Labs' hip hop projects and programming. I would also like to express my deep gratitude to those artists who have had a profound impact on the ways I think about and do hip hop research, particularly Lindsay Knight (aka Eekwol), Danny Fernandez (aka Def3), Tara Campbell (aka T-Rhyme), Alida Kinnie Starr, and Tania Willard.

I am grateful to Elaine Carol for her invitation to participate in the Raincity Rap Festivals. At these festivals I met, interviewed, and facilitated discussions with numerous hip hop folks who have made significant contributions to Canada's hip hop music culture, including Chin Injeti and Alida Kinnie Starr. During this time I had the honour of engaging in a critical discussion on intersectionality and hip hop with Jerilynn Webster, Kia Kadiri, Kim Sato, Tara Reeves, and Andrea Warner. I want to thank them for their generosity and openness while sharing with all of us stories about their hip hop lives, experiences, and knowledges. You are such powerful feminist, hip hop warriors!

Thank you to my family – mom and dad, my sisters Wendy, Tina, and Amber – for always believing in me and offering steadfast support. Thank you to Evie Ruddy, whose encouragement, love, and passion have brightened and reignited my world as this work finally comes to completion. My deepest gratitude and most powerful of loves is for my creative, thoughtful, intelligent, and curious little humans, Ilse and Aksel, who always bring me boundless joy, amusement, and courage.

We would also like to pay our respects to all of the hip hop folks who were interviewed for this collection throughout its many stages. Your contributions to hip hop in Canada are real and powerful and significant, and we are grateful for your input into Canada's vibrant hip hop communities and scenes. And finally, our heartfelt gratitude to JB The First Lady, for enthusiastically granting us permission to adapt the powerful lyrics from her song "Still Here" for the title of this collection. The lyrics – "they wanted us to disappear / but we still here" – speak clearly to the horrific and ongoing systemic violence of colonialism, while simultaneously celebrating the resilience and power of Indigenous peoples.

Charity Marsh

I would like to thank all the hip hop heads that inspire us to pursue the fifth element, especially my crew Bigger than Hip Hop. All of the scholars in this volume demonstrated enormous patience as the project evolved and were immensely generous. Thank you to Cassandra Ozog, True Daley, Sabra Ripley, and the Social Sciences and Humanities Research Council's Banting Postdoctoral Fellowship Program. To Gena, Kai, and Xavier, thank you for donating so many weekends, evenings, and trips to allowing this project to come to fruition. Rest in peace Rofromtheboro.

Mark V. Campbell

Figures

Foreword

Murray Forman

There was that time, circa 1988 or 1989, when a small crowd of us gathered in a muddy baseball field in Ottawa. Assembled in front of a makeshift stage that was erected at home plate, we eagerly awaited the appearance of a hip hop artist whose name has since receded from memory. Back then, live hip hop performances were still relatively new across Canada, and appearances – park jams or club shows – headlined by Canadian artists were even more rare. That early gig consequently attained event status among the local crews, the mud and threatening skies be damned.

In roughly the same period, Canada's first major rap sensation, Maestro Fresh Wes, was ascendant, riding the success of his album *Symphony in Effect*, featuring the hit singles, "Let Your Backbone Slide" and "Drop the Needle." While his Toronto-based hip hop peer Michie Mee was actually first to sign a major record deal in 1988 on the strength of her patois-inflected rap style and dynamic stage presence, Wes was out first with a full album. In an interview on CBC television in 1990 in which he discusses his early career trajectory, Wes explained that, up to that point, "no rap artist from Canada has really been that successful yet, so we must have been doing something wrong or maybe the Canadian music industry wasn't really opening their eyes or whatever."[1] The curious but timeworn Canadian tendency for self-deprecation and modesty shines through in the interview, as does the oblique reference to the nation that evidently gets it right, that cultural behemoth to the immediate south. Wes goes on to admit, perhaps somewhat sheepishly, that Canada was not even his main market at the start and that his primary focus was on the United States and England because, as he puts it, "that's where rap is alive."

Belying this comment, however, his second album, *The Black Tie Affair* (1991), features a profoundly Canada-centric track, "Nothin' At All," with its politically astute critique of neo-fascism and police state tactics (citing the "Oka Crisis" military siege at Quebec's Kanesatake Mohawk reserve), discriminatory government policy shaped within the weak discourses of multiculturalism, and the implicit and explicit biases against Black and Indigenous Canadians. With a flow that channels some of the best artists of the era (Rakim, Big Daddy Kane) and a lyrical potency equal to that of peers such as Chuck D of Public Enemy, Wes delivers a powerful invective that is forged in love, anger, and concern for his country, the memory of its past, its immediate present, and its future. That he ends with an extended tribute to under-acknowledged Black Canadian athletes and to artists across musical genres as well as shouting out a roster of the Toronto hip hop community confirms Wes's underlying positivity and his commitment to hip hop's presentational conventions.

We Still Here: Hip Hop North of the 49th Parallel captures and elaborates on the very themes that Maestro Fresh Wes raises in "Nothin' At All." The editors Charity Marsh and Mark V. Campbell have curated an impressive collection of chapters and assembled an array of smart and insightful authors who span the nation, encompassing a range of locales and communities at the macro and micro scales, and who fully embrace the wider scope of racial, ethnic, gender, and generational identities that inform this ongoing work in progress called Canada. With such a wide scope, it is to be expected that Canadian hip hop's distinct inner mechanics and contradictions will be exposed and, indeed, they are in this collection. But the editors and authors do not shy away from the tough issues, accepting the complexity of the nation's hip hop scenes and the socio-political fields within which they emerge and thrive, as if to say, "Yeah, Canadian hip hop can be messy. But these chapters are about *our* mess and how we understand and deal with it, how we nurture and grow with it." Ultimately, this book is fiercely aligned with that distinct hip hop expression "building," which articulates a collaborative and progressive approach to the establishment of communities of cause, to the enhancement of equal rights and social justice for all, and to the hip hop ethos of "peace, love, unity, and havin' fun" that spans the culture's entire existence.

Like Wes's track, the book's tone is equal parts critical engagement and a love letter to a nation that, for all of its imperfections, remains worthy of such care and attention. Marsh and Campbell plainly value the voices of people in the field, and throughout this book the anecdotes and testimonies of artists and hip hop activists come through loud and clear. Creative practices – the art and innovation of Canadian hip hop – are described in considerable detail, as are the lineages and social streams through which creativity flows. In this sense, the "diasporic reverberations" as discussed throughout and highlighted in the introductory chapter are palpable, and the tome itself serves as an amplifier of Canadian issues as they are felt and experienced in the nation's hip hop scenes, coast to coast and north to south.

With its theoretically rigorous emphasis on diaspora, the book offers a reminder that Canadian hip hop is part and parcel of a global flow of people and influences. Here, we see how hip hop's dispersed communities are forged within worldwide alliances and are shaped by the roots and heritage of homeland nations, by the shared linguistic traits of transnational anglophone or francophone scenes, and/or by the spiritual and political priorities of Indigenous peoples on every continent. In this regard, it is not just hip hop in Canada that is under analysis but Canada in hip hop, as the artists and scholars that advance the culture in these pages reposition their citizen status in recognition that, sometimes, one's love and responsibility to hip hop trumps national identity.

Moreover, Canada's reliance on the United States as its definitional Other (and, at times, as its definitional nemesis) has diminished over the years. For example, describing Canada's position sharing a border with the United States in a speech in 1969 at the Washington Press Club, Prime Minister Pierre Elliott Trudeau stated, "Living next to you is in some ways like sleeping with an elephant" where we are "affected by every twitch and grunt" (25 March 1969).[2] While such a perspective might have been realistic in Canadian hip hop's early years (as Maestro Fresh Wes himself indicates), this has not been the case for quite some time as artists and entrepreneurs more readily look within Canada itself for dope talent to emulate or for collaborative opportunities. As Canadian TV star cum rapper Drake has enjoyed untrammeled success at the peak of the global hip hop industry, Canadian producers, including Boi-1da, Chin Injeti, Wondagurl, and Tone Mason, are eagerly courted by some of the top hip hop artists from south of the border. *We Still Here: Hip Hop North of the 49th Parallel* offers an unambiguous and articulate denunciation of the notion that the United States still provides the standard by which quality and innovation are measured. As the book also makes abundantly clear, this also extends to hip hop studies.

A pronounced feature of the chapters included here is the general consensus among the authors that, in order to explore hip hop in Canada, it is essential to engage with plurality; this is to say that neither Canada *nor* hip hop culture is a singular entity but, rather, that each is the manifestation of multiple histories, sites, actions, discourses, languages, ideologies, skills, and techniques. A revelation in these pages is the ways in which many of the authors summon the nation's varied pasts, delving into the eighteenth, nineteenth, and twentieth centuries, encompassing colonial and postcolonial disputes, Indigenous treaty rights, and, coming into the early twenty-first century, tracing the emergence of a new politics of Indigenous struggle (including conditions associated with the 2008 Truth and Reconciliation Commission of Canada) as well as resistance to official and unofficial expressions of the subordination of and discrimination against Black Canadians and members of the country's LGBTQ+ communities. That the history recorded here substantially exceeds hip hop's nascence and evolution, at times by hundreds of years, is entirely significant and makes this a truly unique contribution to the study of roots and culture in hip hop studies.

Ultimately, it is to Marsh, Campbell, and the authors' credit that readers of this compendium will come away much better informed about Canada and its citizens and about the driving forces that are mobilized in and through Canadian hip hop culture's varied expressive art forms, its elements: Mcing, Djing, B-boying/B-Girling, and aerosol art/graffiti. To state it bluntly, this book is absolutely on hip hop's fifth element tip: *knowledge*.

Peace.
Murray Forman
Boston, MA

NOTES

1 See CBC (1990) for interview.

2 See a clip of this speech on CBC (n.d.).

WE STILL HERE

INDIGENOUS AND DIASPORA REVERBERATIONS

Hip Hop in Canada and Canadian Hip Hop. An Introduction

Charity **Marsh** and Mark V. **Campbell**

Writing about hip hop culture in Canada at the very moment when Canadian hip hop and pop artists dominate the billboards globally may appear as a curious endeavour. Why should we limit our discussion of hip hop to the borders of the Canadian nation-space? In the age of sophisticated algorithms and global discoverability on our hand-held devices that can ensure the latest Drake song can be obtained in places like New Zealand, why focus on hip hop culture in Canada? The global rise of Toronto-based emcee Aubrey Drake Graham, while wonderful news for music industry stakeholders, casts a huge market-oriented shadow on how we might think about hip hop culture as a social phenomenon. Focusing on the music industry is important for, as was clear in the lack of local radio airplay of the 2016 Polaris prize winner, Montreal's Kaytranada, and the 2017 Juno Award winner for hip hop, Toronto's Jazz Cartier, the Canadian music industry is not overly invested in supporting hip hop music in any sustained or significant way. We only have to think back to the majority of hip hop artists signed to record deals in the 1980s to recognize this pattern. Artists such as Rumble, Michie Mee, and Maestro Fresh Wes were all signed by non-Canadian record companies like Island Records in the United Kingdom, First Priority Records in the United States, and Germany's LMR Records, respectively. In various debates in the public sphere, significant and necessary attention is focused on thinking through the career ambitions of hip hop artists. But what happens when we are forceful in our desire to think about hip hop culture outside of market constraints and values?

Decidedly focusing on hip hop in Canada means we can be attentive to the myriad of beautiful ways in which culture evolves and transforms our society. Canada's ten provinces and three territories provide deeply varied ways in which hip hop culture is made to speak to its locality and to urgent social issues. Again, working within the borders of Canada means we can compare and contrast memories, significations, and creative production from diverse geographic and social regions governed by the same national discourses and cultural policies. Attention to the cultural innovations in hip hop cultures within these national borders means decentring the primacy of market-related analyses and, thus, a direct refusal to fetishize the financial implications of Drake's industry successes.

Since we initially sat down to conceptualize this edited volume, there have emerged three very formidable pop stars from Canada whose presence atop the Billboard Chart has become commonplace. Unlike Drake, Justin Bieber and the Weeknd are not considered hip hop artists, but their dress, dance, and vernacular clearly borrow heavily from hip hop culture. Hip hop culture's influence on pop music and youth cultures (even in the remotest regions) in Canada is undeniable;[1] yet, there exists no unified or concerted effort to articulate what might be unique about hip hop cultures north of the 49th parallel in North America. Shying away from a national hip hop identity, hip hop community members focus on their localities when digging up hip hop histories in cities like Halifax, Winnipeg, Saskatoon, Edmonton, and Vancouver, as well as smaller centres like Pangnirtung, Nunavut, and Prince Albert, Saskatchewan, as a way to articulate a sense of place.

To think about hip hop cultures within Canada is to necessarily struggle with the problem of the "nation" as hip hop's fluid and diasporic nature troubles some of the routine ways in which we understand culture, nation, and art. This collection of chapters was born out of a desire to make sense of the rich and diverse ways in which hip hop is taken up within Canadian national borders. From Angola to New Zealand, from Mexico to France, hip hop's global reach is undeniable, seeping through geographical borders to foster innovative and creative relationships. In Canada, this seepage and, subsequently, these unique kinds of relationships are audible and hyper-relevant within the contemporary lives of people living in urban centres such as Toronto, Vancouver, Montreal, Winnipeg, Halifax, and Edmonton as well as in the more rural and isolated communities found on Baffin Island, in the Northwest Territories, Yukon, and across the Prairie provinces.

Both the hyperlocal ways in which hip hop affects young people today and the global ways in which this subculture of style travels between national borders creates a productive friction. This friction forces us to continually reassess and re-evaluate some of the easy cognitive frames that suggest hip hop is simply the creative responses of African American youth to postindustrial American society. Drawing on numerous case studies, both Tony Mitchell (2001a) and Murray Forman (2002) have clearly outlined how hip hop, especially hip hop outside of the United States, cannot be understood within the limitations of cultural mimicry. Hip hop across the globe has common signifiers, arts practices, and, at times, political expressions, but it is through a localizing process that hip hop provides a dialogue that is filled with the complexities of place, space, and time. A sustained conversation between the global and the hyperlocal necessarily opens up generative spaces where the sometimes nefarious actions of the state and transnational corporations are illuminated, challenged, and deciphered in analytically astute creative expressions.

As a culture founded upon a mythology of resistance, emancipation, and revolt, hip hop has proven useful as a catalyst for strategic political action and social engagement around the world. As is evident within a number of chapters in this volume, hip hop cultures in Canada have at times enabled youth, especially Indigenous youth, to "mediate representations of themselves and their current lived experiences through mobile technologies and local networks, challenging common stereotypes and reified identities that continue to circulate in political, cultural, and national discourses" (Marsh 2009a, 110). Hip hop cultures in Canada have become ways in which the ongoing coloniality of both settler colonialism and diasporic wandering become central to analyses of our contemporary moment.

This collection of chapters is organized into three parts: Part 1: Remembering, Narrating, and Archiving Hip Hop in Canada; Part 2: Representation and Belonging; and Part 3: Politics, Poetics, and Potentials. Each part clusters important themes that, when read together, provide a way to think about the histories and herstories of hip hop in Canada, present-day concerns, and many possible futures of hip hop in this country. Embedded within each section are chapters, including interviews with individuals whose existence within hip hop culture is marginal or often overlooked by mainstream media outlets. We amplify marginalized voices to present a more polyvocal notion of hip hop in Canada as these individuals are either positioned or obscured as not your typical imagery associated with hip hop. More important, as scholars in the academy cognizant of our positionality, we want to ensure we make spaces for multiple voices in a lateral way that recognizes the importance of centring the margins of a culture already intimately aware of society's marginal spaces. Our desire is for these voices to interrupt the very structured and rigid way hip hop culture can get absorbed into academic work, reminding scholars and hip hop heads that we can operate on opposite sides of the same coin.

REMEMBERING, NARRATING, AND ARCHIVING HIP HOP IN CANADA

To remember hip hop culture, particularly before it was a polished consumer and global entity, is not merely a nostalgic activity demonstrating a serious generational divide. Rather, thinking about hip hop and its many histories and herstories is a political act, one that is juxtaposed to the conspicuous consumption and limited "shelf life" of music made for mass consumption. The historian of hip hop, if such an antiquated articulation of doing historical work can be applied to hip hop culture, is one whose work is never neutral, always producing ways of knowing and situated knowledges. Historical work in hip hop sits in direct contrast to the desires of the culture industry to enhance profit margins by exploiting the new markets. Hip hop's disposition towards newness and freshness makes the genre an attractive market for this kind of exploitation. Hip hop is still grappling with aging and what to do in a culture where newness, youth, and freshness are so deeply intertwined with representational strategies. While the newness embedded in the excessive styling of the culture continues to impressively innovate, the flip side is the work in double time one must do to capture, document, remember, celebrate, and disseminate. The work of Tania Willard, co-curator of the art exhibition *Beat Nation*, beautifully interrupts the overwhelming market-focused orientation of hip hop culture. Initially, Willard sought to curate an online exhibition of some of her Indigenous friends' engagement with hip hop. Willard, neither scholar nor hip hop head, provides useful ways of thinking about Indigeneity and hip hop, through hybridity, mixture, and fluidity. *Beat*

Nation brought to the fore a plethora of artworld stars like Corey Bulpitt, Kent Monkman, and Skeena Reece to deeply engage with what hip hop might mean from an Indigenous perspective.

Of course, whenever you have youthful creative expressions, struggle over representation and power exist: even if only circulating, hegemony is real. The narration of hip hop's social life and the discursive formations within which hip hop is inserted matter deeply to the sustainability of the culture in Canada. The earliest widely disseminated writing in hip hop in Canada came from the daily newspapers in major urban centres like Ottawa, Edmonton, Montreal, and Toronto. In short and pithy spurts of seven hundred words or less, journalists attempted to describe and make sense of hip hop culture for the wider world as early as 1984 in daily papers such as the *Toronto Star* and the *Montreal Gazette*. With condescending tones and flippant dismissals of the cultural inventiveness of hip hop, readers of daily newspapers were introduced to hip hop culture from journalists outside of that culture. Without taking up an old insider/outsider dichotomous debate, at the earliest stages of hip hop culture's existence in Canada, the writers who held the power to disseminate their views of hip hop to the masses also held the power to insert hip hop into specific discourses and so to shape public perception, reception, and consciousness.

Contentious historical records in the United States are slowly being augmented and rectified with an increasing number of hip hop archives. Institutional interest in archiving hip hop began with Marceylina Morgan's efforts at Harvard (unofficially in her office at UCLA) and continue with the subsequent development of other Ivy League homes for hip hop artefacts, such as Tulane and Cornell.[2] Archiving hip hop signals a dramatic shift in the way academic institutions take up a culture that has for the most part been excluded or, at best, granted sparse attention within cultural histories.

Within Canada, remembering, collecting, and archiving hip hop is being shaped by Mark Campbell's Northside Hip Hop Archive,[3] which focuses on local knowledges, interviews with artists and participants within the culture, as well as various cultural artefacts. Much of the work to be done in Canada concerns historiographic accounts of hip hop cultures in various cities. While somewhat accurately documented in the music, a general understanding of histories of hip hop cultures in Canada is only slowly beginning to emerge among mainstream media outlets.[4] Thus, Campbell's Northside Hip Hop Archive, an online archival project focusing on hip hop histories north of the

49th parallel, fills a major gap in Canadian hip hop. Moreover, the multi-media platform of an online archive presents a more complex system through which the diverse elements of hip hop can be documented. Particularly among the other elements, such as DJing, b-boying/b-girling, and aerosol art, media coverage and accurate historiographic accounts are critical to a better understanding and appreciation of the many diverse hip hop cultures produced and practised in Canada.

Like hip hop's excessive stylings, *We Still Here* is designed to trouble some of the comfortable ways in which we have become accustomed to understanding hip hop in Canada and Canadian hip hop. At play in the subtitle of this introduction and overall conception of the book is a necessary "loosening of knowledge," a poignant reminder of our agency and the utility of a diasporic frame (Gates 1988). Beyond simply being playful and postmodern, the option provided in the introduction subtitle, "Hip Hop in Canada and Canadian Hip Hop," signals our desire to rethink the normative ways in which we are complicit with the hegemony of the nation and of transnational corporations. From the perspectives of Indigenous, francophone, and diasporic Afro-Caribbean hip hoppers in Canada, this book would do a disservice if it did not illuminate and amplify the brilliant and continuous ways in which the nation is remapped, re-authored, and made both inclusive and accountable through hip hop music and cultures from Nova Scotia to Nunavut to British Columbia. Since the late 1990s, the works of Roger Chamberland, Murray Forman, Charity Marsh, Rinaldo Walcott, and others have opened up several ways in which we might understand the different facets of hip hop cultures in Canada. Now, since at least the late 2000s, digital culture has dramatically changed how we engage hip hop, influencing how we learn the art forms and how corporations operate in the era of peer-to-peer sharing, mash ups, and diasporic creative connections. The art of the DJ has been dramatically transformed with digital interfaces expanding the libraries and techniques of hip hop DJs (Campbell 2014). Yet, on the world stage, Canadian Turntablists continue to achieve, with DJ Vekked taking the World DMCs multiple times, following DJ Dopey's 2003 World DMCs win and DJ Atrak's 1997 win. Moreover, Canadian artist DJ SHE was the first female DJ in Canada to compete in the worldwide Red Bull 3 Style competition in 2010 and became a 2012 Pioneer DJ Stylus Award Nominee for Female DJ of the year.[5, 6]

By exploring various hip hop cultures in Canada, we find the physical geography and local influences of each region beautifully mapped onto the creative expressions of DJs, b-girls/b-boys, graph writers, producers, and emcees. Throughout the musical creations of hip hop cultures in Canada, Classified's sampling of a bagpipe from Maritimes folk music neatly contrasts French/English/Kreyol rhymes from Ottawa's D.L. Incognito, which also nicely contrasts with Nelson Tagoona's throat boxing in Nunavut – the heterogeneity found within Canadian borders is both mystifying and evidence of the importance and power of hip hop cultures. Within this heterogeneity is the mobility of young hip hoppers who search the country (and beyond) for fertile hip hop homes. It is not uncommon for aspiring artists to move to Montreal or Toronto or Vancouver early in their career, bringing their localized culture into contact with more diverse metropolitan spaces. It is through a lens of mobility that we begin to see how space and place, concepts integral to global hip hop discourse, are understood within Canada.

REPRESENTATION AND BELONGING

Even before hip hop as a concept and word entered our vocabulary, the politics of space was central to how graph writers made trains their public canvas. The erosion of the South Bronx, the abandoning of burned down apartment buildings, and the prominence of white flight all signify the interconnectedness and highly political concept of space. Robert Moses's "modernist catastrophe" of a freeway could not disentangle the politics of space and the emergence of hip hop culture, as Jeff Chang (2007,10) has documented so well. One cannot forget that in the United States, as well as in Canada, through the ideologies of settler colonialism and multiculturalism, the politics of space has always intersected the politics of race. From the Underground Railroad to present-day Southside Chicago, from the implementation of residential schools to today's Idle No More and Reconciliation movements, the entanglements of race, justice, oppression, negotiations, housing, and drugs force an extended consideration of how we imagine and understand the public interventions of hip hop cultures – interventions such as b-boy ciphers in Union Square to present-day city "beautification" (read: anti-graffiti) projects to hip hop videos of cultural identifications from the isolated communities of the far North posted to YouTube.[7]

Immediately, the politics of representation comes to mind when we think of the ways in which groups like Public Enemy, Warparty, A Tribe Called Red, and the Rascals intervene into dominant discourse, speaking truth to power in creative and thought-provoking ways. To "represent" is a key means by which hip hop cultures ensure creative "authenticity" and reproduce a canon of notions and ideas that remain core to how the culture reimagines itself in spite of place. For example, the centrality or originality (however mythical) and a sustained focus on style have been protective measures, ensuring "wackness and biting" do not become acceptable parts of the culture. Similarly, the canonization of 1520 Sedgwick, and New York City in general, has been a consistent spatial project that continually implicates space with the politics of representation. Urban centres such as Toronto and Vancouver tend to dominate discussions on hip hop in Canada, and yet regional hip hop identities and practices are represented throughout the nation, as is evident in a number of the chapters in *We Still Here*.

Prior to cinematic attempts such as *Wild Style* (1983), *Juice* (1992), and *Rhyme & Reason* (1997), representation was a key activity of the emcee. If we return to Grandmaster Flash and the Furious Five's "The Message" (1982), particularly the video, we find a thickly ethnographic snapshot of postindustrial life, with "broken glass everywhere" and people "pissing in the hallways." Even with a proliferation of films made within hip hop communities, to represent remains central to forms of empowerment and ethnography in conversation with the too often criminalizing efforts of dominant media outlets such as Fox News Network and, especially, regional and local news.[8]

Thinking back to Nas's seminal 1994 joint, "Represent," the track expresses significant dislike and concern for the formal education system while explaining some of the habits and customs of Nas's crew members as they attempt to survive in the "urban jungle." This speaking truth to neoliberal postindustrial power is the continued promise and potency of hip hop as racialized and marginalized communities work to demystify the systemic structures that nurture racial oppression. In the Canadian context, many of the same tactics are both necessary and frequently employed to ensure hip hop communities are empowered, often resulting in the dissemination of analytically astute observations. For example, tracks like Black-I's "Where I'm From," Warparty's "Feeling Reserved," Black Union's "Africville," Eekwol's "Apprento," and JB the First Lady's "Still Here" all speak to localized conditions of marginalization, disempowerment, and erasure. In naming this collection, we settled upon the hook from JB the First Lady's song "Still Here." *We Still Here* speaks on many levels to both the shared and diverse identities, experiences, motivations, politics, and activist strategies found within hip hop culture all over Canada. These tracks and others stand in stark contradistinction to dominant media reports, news stories, and articles that attempt to connect hip hop to crime, and racialized bodies to dysfunction. Thus, reading hip hop cultures in Canada and beyond is a useful practice in thinking through and analyzing the forms of life that challenge our dominant regimes of thought and open spaces for agency, analysis, and social consciousness.

POLITICS, POETICS, AND POTENTIALS

In multilingual cities like Montreal, Moncton, and Ottawa, there remain versions of the past and narrations of spatial politics that rely on and extend hip hop's historical embeddedness in the politics of space, particularly when we think of sites of anglophone blackness in Montreal or the historic black communities in North Preston. In Part 3 we include an interview with True Daley, a former Montreal resident whose anglophone heritage led her to Toronto. True was one of the three founders of the *Masters at Work* radio show on CKUT in 1991. Living at the intersection of race, gender, and language, True details her trials and tribulations with episodes of sexism and harassment fit for our current #MeToo movement. Speaking from the position of a racialized woman, anglophone radio host, and aspiring emcee, True's intersectionality adds a layer of complexity to how the politics of hip hop, despite its many liberatory moments, is not unequivocally emancipatory.

In many cities across the Prairies and in the Far North, identifications with mythic hip hop histories are reworked and even Indigenized, as young people participate in complex discussions concerning the ongoing effects of colonialism in the present day. As Marsh (2009a, 126) has argued, "Hip hop has become a place [for young people] to begin to dialogue about current crises within communities including fractures in relationships, social problems including drug addictions, depression, alcoholism, poverty, suicide, crime, cultural trauma, environmental degradation – and the ongoing legacies of colonialism."

Many of the chapters in *We Still Here* work, then, to elaborate ways in which we might come to fully appreciate the intersections of race and the spatial politics of localized hip hop communities. Too often we think of urbanized spaces when we imagine the location and impact of hip hop, but, as many of the authors demonstrate, we must also consider spaces like the university and non-urban spaces that often provide fertile ground for Indigenous hip hop artists. Thinking across space and time, examining hip hop cultures with a consideration of the creative potential and representational possibilities of space, the probability for hip hop to motivate remapping revisions and reconsiderations of the "naturalness" of Western spatial constructs and offer something different is both real and relevant.

By way of documented histories/herstories of Canadian hip hop cultures, there exist very few published writings that explicitly attempt to historicize hip hop in Canada nationally. Several regional writings, both popular and academic, have provided windows onto the earliest days of hip hop in Canada. Street zines in the 1990s and documentaries in the late 1990s and early 2000s have done well to continue to piece together a number of hip hop narratives in Canada. Documentaries such as the 1994 release of *Make Some Noise!*, CBC's *Love Props and the T-Dot* (2011), and *Hip Hop Eh* (2012) by Vancouver DJ Joe Klymkiw are important mechanisms with which to raise awareness about hip hop in Canada. With the desire to continue to add to this archival and historical work, we made the concerted effort to interview several artists so that they could speak directly about their hip hop histories and herstories.[9] The interview material found throughout these chapters explores cultures in Vancouver, Montreal, Ottawa, and the Prairies, adding to some already excellent interview content from the Maritimes and Toronto by writers and scholars such as Michael McGuire (2011) and Remi Warner (2006). In the context of institutional power, academics focusing on first-person oral histories by members of the hip hop community is one crucial way to ensure that academics do not speak for hip hoppers. The archived interviews and oral histories captured on Northside Hip Hop Archive begin to increase the number of voices and perspectives to which the public can gain access in cities like Regina, Edmonton, Montreal, Ottawa, and Toronto.

One of the main goals of this collection is to provide a route to explore facets of Canadian identity and culture, such as bilingualism and multiculturalism, in ways that speak to a new generation of young people engaged in hip hop cultures. It has become apparent that, at an institutional level, hip hop speaks more eloquently to a new generation than did previous attempts on the part of museums, galleries, and school boards. Thus, *We Still Here* highlights some of the innovative ways in which racialized young people signify on existing dominant, and often static, relationships that involve race, gender, and class. For example, at the very moment that major galleries and museums struggle to grow audiences in youth "markets" and among racialized people and newcomers, hip hop festivals amplify visibility for those populations that institutions seek to develop as audiences. Even with hip hop exhibitions like *Beat Nation*,[10] the ongoing performances and festival events create more of a draw for young people than does the actual site. At its core, hip hop refuses the hegemonic invisibility placed upon racialized bodies, and it does so through its excessive stylistic engagements with, and significations on consumer culture. Spatially, as places like Hogan's Alley and Africville are systematically erased from our visual landscape, hip hop finds ways to resurrect the lives of historic black communities, speak truth to power, and make hyper-visible supposedly disposable other/ed non-white bodies. Halifax's Black Union is a great example of hip hop artists refusing the erasure of spaces of black inhabitance.

At one level, hip hop cultures work to decolonize the coloniality of their existence in Canada. Through subversive styling, a geopolitics of visibility, and aggressive attempts at constructing an ethical place to which to belong, hip hop can be, and at times does indeed become, a tool for reimagining our social world. Furthermore, as is illustrated in some of the following chapters, at the very same moment in which productively disruptive innovations in hip hop culture occur, there is a consumptive element – of records, equipment, and clothing – that limits these disruptive innovations. Hip hop cultures in Canada are also full of contradictions, which is yet another reason for us to engage in a deeper dialogue and to further understand the significance of hip hop north of the 49th parallel.

We Still Here is comprised of scholarly chapters, a number of which draw upon formal and informal discussions with artists, as well as one artist interview. It is our hope that, although this volume is not a complete representation of all hip hop cultures (past and present) that comprise hip hop in Canada, it does provide a solid foundation for, and perspective on, a culture that has been actively embraced and reimagined all over Canada – a culture that offers diverse, rich, and unique stories of hip hoppers and their communities living north of the 49th parallel.

For some, these narratives are demonstrations of the ways in which barriers are overcome. Politically, spatially, physically, and ideologically, the barriers erected around young people engaged in hip hop, sometimes installed by media misrepresentation, speak to ways in which hip hop cultures have demanded a different kind of future. From this perspective, hip hop is a lived strategy/politics/movement that deserves critical engagement and serious contemplation.

NOTES

1 Refer to Marsh (2009a) discussing the engagement of hip hop culture by Inuit youth living in some of the most northern communities in Nunavut.

2 For more discussion, see Jones (2004).

3 For a detailed description of Northside Hip Hop and its impacts on archiving hip hop histories in Canada, see Campbell (chap. 1, this volume).

4 For more specific local histories from all over Canada, visit Northside Hip Hop Archive, nshharchive.ca.

5 For more information, visit the DMC World DJ Championships website (n.d.).

6 For further discussion on DJ She and other female Canadian hip hop artists, see Marsh (chap. 11, this volume).

7 For a discussion of Northerns with Attitude's YouTube launch of "Don't Call Me Eskimo," see Marsh (2009a).

8 For further discussion on how media represents hip hop artists, particularly Indigenous men in Canada, see Marsh (2011).

9 To gain access to these interviews, visit Northside Hip Hop Archive (2018) and search under "oral histories."

10 For example, see Marsh (chap. 3, this volume).

PART ONE

Remembering, Narrating, and Archiving Hip Hop in Canada

1

DOING THE KNOWLEDGE

Digitally Archiving Hip Hop in Canada

Mark V. Campbell

... practice daily so that one day my children can look back at their mother and be proud of their descent ... so I try to contribute, ridiculous for anyone to dispute/my place in the musical coliseum/induct the name Chase in the hip hop museum, induct the name Chase in the hip hop museum.

Tara Chase, The Northside

There is no political power without control of the archive, if not memory. Effective democratization can always be measured by this essential criterion: the participation in and access to the archive, its constitution, and its interpretation.

Jacques Derrida, *Archive Fever*

Knowledge, hip hop's fifth element, does not lend itself well to the process of commodification hip hop has undergone since Sugarhill Gang's first record. Yet knowledge of self and a critical awareness of our social world are inextricably at the core of hip hop's ethos and the culture's ability to level serious social critiques. While some might dismiss the badly mislabelled "conscious rap" as part of a utopic past, knowledge, its excavation, and its dissemination, continue to be part of hip hop culture, more specifically with the rise of hip hop archives across a number of postsecondary educational institutions. These archives, designed not to entertain but to educate, nicely capture the ongoing tensions of the popularity of hip hop's commodification within the culture's attempts to seek knowledge of its history. Curiously, the critical discourse around digital archives and the politics of knowledge production circulate nowhere near hip hop studies or the existing hip hop archives in the United States. With excellent work on fan communities by Abigail De Kosnik and deep theoretical interventions by local Canadian scholars Brett Kashmere and Susan Lord, a great deal of digital archive theory has yet to be applied to Canadian hip hop cultures (De Kosnik 2016; Kashmere 2010; Chew, Lord, and Marchessault 2018).

Currently the only hip hop archive based in Canada, Northside Hip Hop Archive (NSHHA) emerged as an idea while I was researching Toronto hip hop history for a chapter on black Canada for a high school textbook. I found zero English language sources on the history of hip hop in Canada. I uncovered some articles from free zines, some interviews, but no academic sources focused on the country's historical development of hip hop cultures. After gathering some resources, I began to dig through both my own and my older brother's records and contacts (from a couple decades of djing on the radio) to learn more about the culture's earliest architects.

What one can say about hip hop Canada, with any kind of accuracy and authority, has historically been rightfully and importantly limited to those with lived experience of participating in hip hop culture. Historical accounts of "rap music" by dominant media in Canada, such as news broadcasts or local newspapers, have been limited, random, and reliant on the positionality of those outside of hip hop culture (Campbell and Stitski 2018).[1] The "sayability" of hip hop culture in Canada has traditionally hinged upon the media (as an ideological state apparatus), which means that the historical information one can gather from libraries and archives hardly produces a notion of hip hop that recognizes the culture as something more than rapping and entertainment (Foucault 1969; Althusser 2006). The rise of peer-to-peer sharing with the invention of Napster in 1998 not only dramatically changed how people shared music files but also transformed how people behave around digital content – as both producers and consumers (prosumers). Further, for those interested in doing historical work, the birth of digital archives made the formerly inaccessible available, and, as Cheryl Mason Bolick (2006, 122) reminds us, information can now be engaged in a non-linear fashion. The non-linearity of a digital archive presents an opportunity for users, audiences, and fans to engage hip hop culture, both beyond the dominant narratives inscribed in mainstream media outlets' coverage of hip hop and in a fashion that allows for new connections and ideas beyond the well-established and too familiar meritocracy or exotic "other" narrative.

Dozens of interviews, several unearthed collections, and numerous scanning sessions have produced the very beginnings of an archive of hip hop cultures in Canada. A digital archive works on a number of levels to enhance the general public's access to artefacts and information while simultaneously challenging some of the issues associated with a more traditional archive. Issues of access and accuracy come to the fore, but, as I argue in this chapter, archivization of hip hop culture holds the potential to: (1) resist the erasure of Canada's earliest hip hop architects, (2) increase access for new generations of hip hoppers in the digital era by democratizing the archival process, and, eventually, (3) increase recognition, value, and appreciation of a largely obscured racialized creative class of young people in the late 1980s and early 1990s. Finally, a digital hip hop archive can interrupt long-standing archival practices and discourses by developing counter-archives and "rogue" archival strategies (Kashmere 2010; De Kosnik 2016).

Ironically, at precisely the same time Northside Hip Hop Archive was emerging in 2009, influential curator Okwui Enwezor (2008) was organizing the hugely successful exhibition *Archive Fever*, a richly theoretical exploration of the archive that has responded to Derrida's book (of the same title) and has shaped contemporary discourses around digital archives.

Historically, archives have been manipulated to whitewash and straighten out histories and herstories. Erudite scholars like Laura Ann Stoler and Kate Eichhorn are but two of the many who have both revealed the nuances and biases in the Dutch West Indies archives and elucidated the importance of feminist digital archives, respectively (Eichhorn 2013; Stoler 2002). By recounting the origins of Northside Hip Hop Archive this chapter explores the following difficult questions: "How might the digital archive enhance inclusivity and belonging among racialized creative communities, especially hip hop communities?"; and "How do we harness the troubling power of archiving to produce a historical record of hip hop culture?" In what follows, I explore the digital archiving of Canadian hip hop, some of the methods of acquisition, and some of the benefits and outcomes of creating NSHHA.

Given that "the archive exists at the intersection of the visible and the invisible," it is an apt medium to tackle the continued erasures and absences of African Canadian and other racialized groups from the historical record, or the "official" record (Treanor 2009, 291). Historian Dominick LaCapra (1987, 92) has described the dangers of the "archive as fetish," of believing that the archive "is a literal substitute for the 'reality' of the past which is 'always already' lost for the historian." Whatever the archive contains is already a reconstruction, a recording of history from a particular perspective; it thus cannot provide transparent access to the events themselves. Dominick's insight is useful for thinking through why a digital archive might be important and the importance of the work of archiving Canadian hip hop, especially as the early pioneers were African Canadian young people.

Rather than following Dominick's lament, NSHHA is best understood as engaged in digital excavation work, in scanning, transcribing, and digitizing to fill the gaps of the "official records" with the use of multiple digital platforms in our algorithmic age.[2] By finding the gaps in the historical record in our case, the archive works not only to carve out what is sayable, or "the system of discursivity" as Foucault (1969, 61) would have it, but also, more precisely, to create the terms of social inclusion that policies, governments, and social activists have long struggled to make possible for racialized people in Canada. The rationale embedded in the work of NSHHA holds that, if we uncover the histories and herstories of the innovators and trendsetters of this now global billion-dollar industry, then we can make claims regarding the value of the racialized creative communities that have secured a certain sense of regional and national pride among many young Canadians. If the archive produces events as much as it records them, as Derrida (1995, 23) suggests in his term "archivization," then the goal for NSHHA is not only to achieve an increase in visibility and to provide young people with access to hip hop artefacts and performances but also to produce a new inclusive discourse and methods of knowledge production that centre the contributions of the racialized creative communities that made hip hop in Canada possible in its earliest years.

Methodologically, the archivization process for NSHHA is iterative and always evolving. Utilizing writing from Enwezor, Foucault, Eichhorn, Stoler, Mbembe, De Kosnik, and Derrida, I have designed methods that speak directly to many of the criticisms these archival scholars share. For example, the information architecture is designed in contrast to some of the ways traditional archives' physical structures impose powerful limits on access to historical documents. NSHHA's taxonomies and classificatory systems are laterally generous, refusing an isomorphic analysis and encouraging relational thinking. Additionally, as a digital archive it's in a centralized online location. While not universally accessible for those without high speed broadband, it is the beginning of a move in what many might consider a more accessible and more democratic direction. In terms of authorship and the power of the historian to erase or amplify specific historical actors, NSHHA's archived items are at times narrated by the key historical actors, the architects of hip hop culture in many cities across Canada, particularly in our "I Was There!" national project. The evolution of NSHHA includes shifting more narrative and curatorial power to Canadian hip hop architects, eventually not relying on an all-knowing single curatorial force to dominate the archive's narrative power. A third way in which the design and method of NSHHA incorporates and builds on academic critiques is through regular pop-up exhibitions and various community engaged events. Activities such as concerts, visual arts exhibitions, and panel discussions make the archive and its materials more accessible to the general public, helping to educate and excavate buried and obscured histories.

Access to historical information came largely through several interviews conducted with members of Toronto's hip hop communities active in the 1980s. Individuals were asked to recount their earliest moments of engagement with hip hop culture as well as distinct memories connected to the presence of American hip hoppers in Toronto. In addition to personal interviews, several individuals dug up and lent archive materials and artefacts to be digitized and shared with the general public. Interviewees were keen on sharing their stories and their collections, knowing that there had been little interest in documenting these stories and cataloguing hip hop artefacts in the past.

After several key interviews were conducted with seminal figures such as Rumble, formerly of the group Rumble & Strong; Johnbronski, former co-host of the *Masterplan* radio show on CIUT 89.5 FM; as well as Lady P, widely respected as Toronto's first female emcee from Killowatt Soundsystem, several narratives were partially reconstructed. Of several stories, two things were immediately clear: first, that women, in large numbers, participated in the emergence of hip hop in Toronto in the 1980s; second, that "jams" were all-ages affairs, sometimes with family members working the ticket booth and the doors.[3] Other notable stories highlighted the importance of tailor-made outfits, roller-skating rinks, and the centrality of family, particularly for women who sought to attend hip hop parties. Combined with uncovering several narratives, I also began reviewing newspaper articles and free street magazines as well as listening to community radio shows from the 1980s and early 1990s.

These elements were crucial to uncovering forgotten names, locations of former clubs, and radio shows. Listening to radio shows, in particular Toronto's *Fantastic Voyage*, *The Power Move*, and *Masterplan*, provided additional information on neighbourhoods and locales that held parties or hosted concerts. Similarly, Hamilton's *Live & Direct* show and Montreal's *Masters at Work* show provided similar historical references. Interestingly enough, it was the hip hop radio shows that became de facto community centres on Saturday nights in Winnipeg, Toronto, and Montreal, as community members would drop off new songs, promote their concert or event, or just hang out at the studio in informal networking opportunities or mentorships (O. Williams, personal interview, 2009).

To mitigate the traditional power dynamics of archiving, where the voices of the archived individuals get lost, a specific strategy was developed to launch the website – a participatory exhibition entitled *T-Dot Pioneers: An Exploration of Toronto's Hip Hop History and Culture* was launched in March 2010. This six-week exhibition put on display several of the items interviewees mentioned as central to their version of their earliest hip hop experiences. In this flattened power dynamic, as curator my job was not to narrate or interpret donated items but to coordinate and to facilitate them. This manifested itself in a timeline created to encourage individuals to tell their hip hop history and, using a thumb tack and a cue card, to add their voices to the exhibition. Over the course of the six weeks, two panel discussions, two concerts, and a keynote talk animated the *T-Dot Pioneers* exhibition at Toronto Free Gallery. Issues addressed at the panel discussions included gendered concerns around hyper-masculinity and the apparent absence of women in hip hop, with the two panels aptly entitled "When Rappers Used to Dance" and "Where the Ladies @?" In addition, a keynote address by the individual responsible for nicknaming Toronto the T-Dot-O, K4ce, highlighted the scene in Toronto's early years of hip hop cultural production.

By urging and encouraging hip hop community members to participate in reconstructing the narratives of Toronto's hip hop past, the explicit goal was to produce multiple voices and to reduce the kinds of singularized voices that always appear to speak for (and at times misrepresent) the majority of racialized artists, especially young people. All of the images from two subsequent exhibitions, *T-Dot Pioneers 2011: The Glenn Gould Remix* and *T-Dot Pioneers 3.0: The Future Must Be Replenished*, were compiled into a catalogue and given back to all donors and participants in the three exhibitions that spanned 2010 to 2013. The work of these exhibitions was to illuminate the successes in building the city's hip hop culture; to speak directly to the concept of the "Creative Class" that, unsurprisingly, downplayed racism; and, through the creation of a coffee-table book, to create tangible legacies so that future generations might have access to hip hop's past achievements in virtual and physical forms.

These exhibitions were ways to begin conversations and to collaboratively catalogue one city's hip hop his/herstories. The work of building NSHHA both in the Toronto context and the rest of Canada (an ongoing work) illuminated a number of important themes, all of which significantly contribute to how we might imagine hip hop in Canada and Canadian hip hop cultures. As opposed to simply seeing hip hop as a youth culture, or a culture of conspicuous consumption, what became clear was that hip hop cultures created institutions and long-lasting events that built the creative capacities of racialized young people and the city's culture. In addition, several transnational narratives illuminated the highly diasporic ways in which Toronto's hip hop cultures were engaged in a reciprocal creative cross pollination with other local cities and Afro-Caribbean youth cultures in places like New York City, Hamilton, Buffalo, Montreal, and Philadelphia. These insights come to complicate the hyper-local nature often associated with rap music today.

The stories of hip hop's early emergence spoke of deep ethnic and cultural diversity with several overlapping intersecting scenes and cultures, such as the new wave and dancehall scenes. The final theme illuminated by the work of NSHHA thus far is that of gender, with the early visibility of women being reduced by the mid- to late 1990s. Lady P, in her participation on the "Where the Ladies @?" panel, reminisced about how many of her female cousins would join her on stage as emcees and DJs. Similarly, in rare footage of Montreal's hip hop scene in the mid-1980s, artists like Blondie B and Baby Blue evidenced the early participation of a multi-racial cast of women hip hop artists.

INSTITUTIONS

Across the country there were and still are several ways in which members build soft infrastructure for their local hip hop communities. Today we have community radio shows in Montreal and Toronto – *Masters at Work* and *Masterplan*, respectively – that have been on-air continuously for more than three decades. They have provided both a home base for aspiring artists to promote their work, build their audiences, and receive critical feedback, and they have been a receiving ground for artists from around the world. It was not unusual to see KRS-1, OHNO, Dougie Fresh, or Crazy Legs at community radio stations in Toronto.

Former community radio stations, such as York University's CHRY 105.5 FM as well as Ryerson University's CKLN 88.1 FM, in addition to having several important radio shows also contributed to the creation of institutions such as the massively successful Monster Jam series of concerts. CHRY significantly contributed to the development of soft infrastructure to support the development of Turntablists by conceiving and organizing the Metro Mix Offs, an annual DJ competition whose competitors have gone on to win international accolades at the World DMC championships, and some of whom have also gone onto hugely successful careers as producers and club DJs.

Several former participants, such as Turntablist Lil' Jaz, shared their personal copies of flyers for the Monster Jam series and the Metro Mix Offs, demonstrating the importance of these events in their career development. Beyond the support and instigation of the radio stations, other institutions became clear through the retrieval of flyers, specifically the annual Honey Jam series that highlighted the massive numbers of talented women in the Toronto scene. These institutions – Monster Jam, the Metro Mix Offs, and Honey Jam – were all critical in the development of emerging artists, many of whom were racialized and were not supported artistically by funding councils or other funding institutions.

These flyers and posters form significant artefacts from CHRY's Metro Mix Off, Honey Jam, and Monster Jam, revealing very interesting partnerships and creative collaborations as well as capturing the exact dates when acts like the Ultramagnetic Emcees or Eric B & Rakim first came to Canada. These flyers also document many of the early visiting hip hop artists, the many female artists who are no longer publicly performing, such as Spesh K, Mischievous C, and many of the DJs and turntablists who have formed the backbone of the culture.

The flyers from various Monster Jams, an event organized by Ron Nelson, the host of the *Fantastic Voyage* radio show in Toronto, highlighted partnerships and sponsorship relationships with Pepsi and MuchMusic, two entities that would commercially benefit from their connections to hip hop culture. In the 1980s, during the embryonic phase of hip hop in Toronto, major corporations like Pepsi most likely gained a great deal by sponsoring or collaborating with the Monster Jam series. In terms of market research, exposure to emerging markets, and overall brand awareness, Pepsi had much to gain from having its logo on the Monster Jam flyer. Likewise, Honey Jam, an annual event since 1995, has increased the visibility of women in music exponentially and has worked with several partners and sponsors along the way, such as Toronto Dominion Bank, Universal Music Group, and Worldvision. Visibility has been and continues to be paramount in the lives of racialized people in Canada, who are often either hyper-fetishized or completely ignored by the mainstream media: both circumstances speak to the importance of events and festivals such as Honey Jam, particularly when we think of the polarized ways in which women are portrayed in the dominant media.

The shameful legacies of media misrepresentation for people of African descent, Asians, and Middle Eastern people are well documented and speak directly to the importance of visually representing hip hop culture in public spaces (Clarke 1997; James 2001; Yon 1995; Tettey and Puplampu 2005). Institutions such as Honey Jam have been vital to the career development of women both within hip hop music and beyond. For example, the careers of Nelly Furtado, Michie Mee, and Jully Black have all been enhanced by the exposure and the skills development opportunities provided by the annual showcase. Because Honey Jam has actively sought to document its events, NSHHA has been able to digitize and post their content, which highlights women speaking for and about other women, easily one of the failings of traditional archives. Founded by an Afro-Caribbean woman and governed by racialized women, Honey Jam has enhanced the positive visibility of women in the music industry, with hundreds of women having been involved in it since its inception in 1995. Canadian histories of erasure ensured that the lives of black women were hard to find in the historical record. With the exception of Maki Motapanyane's edited collection, *Mothering in Hip Hop Culture: Representation and Experience*, the voices of women in hip hop have not been well documented in Canada. The panel discussion held at the *T-Dot Pioneers* exhibition in 2010 brought to the fore many of the hidden and unknown herstories of women in Toronto's hip hop scene, and there are still many more narratives to be made digitally accessible.

Similarly, through annual battles, the Metro Mix Offs spent several years building the creative capacities of numerous young DJs and turntablists. The diversity of contestants was impressive, and, despite its lack of women, various ethnicities and people of various abilities competed for several years in the Metro Mix Offs. The formation of crews such as the Turntable Monks, the Turnstylez crew, Funky Technicians, and the Sick Kids demonstrated the ability of the Metro Mix Offs to stimulate communities of learning and mutual support. Cataloguing the posters associated with these events not only provides an opportunity for previous contestants to speak glowingly of their experiences but also captures the impact of one small fifty-watt community radio, an often overlooked fact that is nowhere overtly documented. Many of the DJs who have competed in Metro Mix Offs are now stationed throughout the world, engaged in successful DJ and producer careers, with even more DJs remaining in Toronto and significantly contributing to the cultural infrastructure of Toronto's music scene. Not only did Metro Mix Offs substantially stimulate the growth of DJ culture in Toronto, it also helped to place Canada atop the prestigious International Turntable Federation battles and the International Disco Mix Championships, with several competitors from Toronto's local scene being sent to the world finals.

Capturing footage, audio, and posters from the Metro Mix Off not only increases the visibility of Canada abroad but also provides local aspiring young DJs with access to the historical record and all of the creative elements that have made possible such unique digital DJ interface software as Serato and Tracktor (Campbell 2014). By archiving the foundational activities that helped to build Toronto's, and eventually the country's, DJ talent (through regional DMC battles), a digital archive can bridge regional boundaries and provide smaller Canadian cities like Saskatoon and Hamilton (which have robust local hip hop scenes) with greater access to recognition and a sense of historicity.

Likewise, in terms of visibility, festivals such as Montreal's Under Pressure Festival, Ottawa's House of PainT, Hamilton's Concrete Canvas, Toronto's 416 Graffiti Expo, and Winnipeg's PegCity Holla have been critical to the development of all local hip hop artists. These public festivals made all the elements of hip hop cultures highly visible to the mainstream, with cyphers, freestyle competitions, bombing, and DJ showcases, and, in doing so, both educated the public and provided artistic development opportunities for many young racialized individuals in the 1990s and beyond. These festivals concurrently allowed for the claiming of public space in the 1990s, when hip hop was still something that happened at night inside a jam and was not necessarily part of an organized nightclub scene or community organizations. Today, as hip hop stars frequent nightclubs and hip hop festivals take up major tourist spaces in Toronto, it should be remembered that it was the early festivals that laid the group work and developed the models that heightened visibility for those hip hop artists, often neglected by the mainstream, who were doing positive creative work.

Archiving events like the aforementioned festivals has been critical to increasing the visibility of both the racialized young artists bold enough to engage in outdoor performance and self-expression and the array of art forms encompassed within hip hop culture. These specific festivals have worked hard to demonstrate the artistic beauty of aerosol art and have worked to teach youth engaged in spray painting that there is an artistic side to using aerosol and that they can explore it. The interconnectedness of these festivals allows for populations to see hip hop culture in all of its elements, thus doing a specific kind of public education and allowing new generations to grasp all of hip hop's elements and their special place in the public sphere.

UNCOVERING HIDDEN DIASPORIC HISTORIES

A similar kind of interconnectedness was illuminated through the archival work of NSHHA with the uncovering of early record deals with German label LMR Records and Island Records, based in London, England, who signed Maestro Fresh Wes and Rumble, respectively.

Rumble, a talented Canadian emcee and a staple in the Toronto hip hop scene in the 1980s, signed to Island Records and regularly recorded in Kingston, Jamaica. Rumble exemplified the important ways in which hip hop's global circulation, even in the late 1980s, recapitulated the triangular trade route of colonial times. In his lyrics, delivery, and seamless mastery of slipping in and out of Jamaican patwa and localized Toronto vernacular, Rumble best exemplified hip hop's diasporic sensibilities. Following the works of both Paul Gilroy (1991a) and Rinaldo Walcott (2001), I am thinking here of diasporic sensibilities as ways in which individuals negotiate their positioning and self-fashioning in home/host locations (Burman 2002).

Rumble donated one of the first items to the archive, his seven-inch dubplate for his most successful commercial single, "Safe." Recorded with Prince Jammy in Kingston, Jamaica, Rumble's creative aesthetic followed the same trajectory as Jamaica's locally produced reggae records. The cutting of a dubplate (on acetate) as test material for clubs has been a long-standing method of music creation in Jamaica. Rumble's use of this model to cut and test what would become his first commercial single demonstrates the embeddedness of a diasporic sensibility in some of Toronto's early hip hop records. Rumble's bending and permeating of national boundaries in the former triangle of trade speaks volumes to the importance of archiving hip hop histories in Canada. The uncovering of Rumble's dubplate speaks to the ways in which Jamaican soundsystem cultures contributed to the expansion and success of hip hop in Toronto.

Almost two decades ago, Rumble's music hinted at more than hybrid roots and dynamic diasporic routes that work, on two levels, to destabilize the comfortable narrative of nation in Canada. The kinds of static renditions of multicultural others nurtured by Canada's multiculturalism policy are invalidated by the diasporic travels of Rumble and his art (Walcott 2001). Rumble's work demonstrates that the dynamic and diasporic nature of his hip hop music is insufficiently captured by the state's multiculturalism policy. Further, on another level, Rumble's early success highlights the ways in which marginalized immigrants and racialized young people employed diasporic resources (or a diasporic sensibility) to evade the strictures of their local circumstances. Rumble's record deal came years before Maestro Fresh Wes's deal with LMR and before Michie Mee was signed to First Priority Records. In fact, for these three hip hop pioneers, record deals would all come from outside the Canadian nation, pointing to the dearth of local opportunities for success in the recording industry. The flexibility and fluidity of diasporic identities expressed through hip hop in the 1980s suggests that the archiving of Canadian hip hop should be conceived as an active dialogue about national identity, creative cultures, and how to think more broadly about social inclusion for young racialized individuals.

CONCLUSION: THE INSUBORDINATE ARCHIVE

> Hip hop is about attitude: an attitude of insubordination. It is in fact insubordination to form, to content, and to respectability, that gives hip hop its most potent power of authority, desire and attraction.
>
> Rinaldo Walcott, "Towards a Methodology for Reading Hip Hop in Canada"

The work of archiving Canadian hip hop cultures is ongoing, its digital nature allowing for continuous updates, corrections, and narration. The archivization of hip hop in Canada presents an opening in the public discourse around black and racialized life in the Canadian context. Such an opening produces the possibility of a wider and interconnected discussion of hip hop beyond the perception of this youth "fad," as media outlets often articulated it early on (Campbell and Stitski 2018).

When Achille Mbembe (2002, 23) suggests the "very existence of the archive constitutes a constant threat to the state," he illuminates how we might understand the work of NSHHA on Canada's national imaginary as an egalitarian, multicultural country. While calling NSHHA "a threat" might be a stretch, I do want to illuminate how the process of archivization exposes Canada's multicultural histories not just as static performances of ethnicity but as dynamic processes entangled with racialization and marginalization embedded within the Eurocentric project of the devaluation of difference. Further, the archive uncovers and evidences models of co-habitation with race while moving beyond being overdetermined by race to create cultural modes that, diasporically and in an anti-colonial fashion, move beyond stale state-sponsored iterations of multiculturalism.

From Montreal's early breakdance battles in the 1980s to Vancouver's recent Raincity Rap events, the depth and diversity of Canada's hip hop cultures help to reshape Canada's national narrative as a more diverse rendering of voices from various geographic locations and social climates. By capturing the plethora of insubordinate stylings in hip hop cultures, a Canadian digital archive signals not just the addition of more diverse voices in the national narrative but also an attempt to refashion Canada into a more inclusive and dynamic heterogeneous nation.

NSHHA has thus far helped us examine the models of institution building within hip hop cultures over the last twenty years in Canada. As well, via this archival work we've learned of the centrality of diasporic sensibilities and frames of reference that foster highly creative and hybridized musical creations, such as the hugely successful Dream Warriors, who went on to sell more than 800,000 records in their sold-out twenty-seven-date European tour based largely on their jazzy Caribbean-influenced aesthetic.

Rather than reproducing colonial archives of hierarchically arranged knowledge production, NSHHA makes possible a discursive terrain in which racialized, creative young people are central to the creation of dynamic culture in Canada and are agents in the production of their own historical narratives. When we look closely at municipal culture plans and Toronto's recent desire to fashion itself as a music city, what becomes clear is that, over the last two decades, musical infrastructure has been built largely by racialized young people. These fledging sets of festival organizers, concert promoters, community programmers, and non-profit organizations are critical infrastructural scaffolding for the dynamic growth of Canadian cultures and are central to today's rise up the popular music charts by several Canadian artists.

In addition to collecting physical materials and artefacts, a digital archive also allows for access to film documentaries, videos, and personal interviews that help to fill some of the gaps in dominant accounts of the historical record. These forms of rich multimedia content challenge cultural institutions, such as the museum and the art gallery, to become more inclusive and willing to think more broadly about culture, cultural "preservation," and the centrality of arts in healthy communities. In a sense, Northside Hip Hop Archive, following Derrida's opening epigraph to this chapter, works to help democratize the access of marginalized communities to the kinds of social capital and value that archives, galleries, and museums foster. Archiving Canadian hip hop cultures is one way to begin thinking more broadly about how we might intentionally produce the kinds of knowledge that enable social inclusion, community development, and democracy and, thus, avoid reproducing the colonial residues of traditional archives.

NOTES

The original version of this chapter was presented in Regina as part of Dr Charity Marsh's the Flatland Scratch Seminar/Workshop Series and was originally titled "Doing the Knowledge: The Politics of Archiving Canadian Hip Hop," 26 March 2013. I would like to acknowledge the support of the Banting Postdoctoral Fellowship Program, which made this chapter possible.

1 See many of the earliest articles in the 1980s in the *Montreal Gazette*, *Ottawa Citizen*, and *Toronto Star* for negative, biased, or dismissive accounts of the phenomenon called "rap" music. See Campbell and Stitski (2018).

2 For example, there are several spaces online, on social media platforms like Instagram and Facebook, where hashtags like #Throwback Thursdays are utilized to share people's personal archives. I am thinking specifically of the Mixtape Museum out of the Schomberg library and the Instagram account called Flyer Vault. See Noble (2018) on racism and algorithms.

3 For further details, see Ron Nelson's keynote address at the Toronto edition of the "I Was There!" project on the Northside Hip Hop Archive website (Northside Hip Hop Archive 2018).

2

AND YOU RUN WHERE YOU CAN

Music and Memory in Three Canadian Hip Hop Videos

Jesse Stewart

In 2008, Toronto entrepreneurs, activists, and hip hop artists Neil Donaldson (aka Logikal Ethix) and Sourav Deb (Unknown Mizery) made a documentary film titled *Stolen from Africville: Broken Homes Broken Hearts* with the financial support of the Department of Canadian Heritage. Africville was a vibrant, predominantly African Canadian community in Halifax, Nova Scotia, that was destroyed in the 1960s after its residents were forced by Halifax City Council to disperse and relocate. The purpose of Africville was to house many of the Black Loyalists from the late 1780s who arrived in Nova Scotia as free subjects under the British Crown. In 1965, Africville was dismantled by municipal officials in the middle of the night citing several concerns around city ordinances. Today Africville is revered as sacred ground and is memorialized by today's black Nova Scotian community. Unlike previous films about Africville, such as the 1991 National Film Board documentary *Remember Africville*, the *Stolen from Africville* documentary uses hip hop culture as a lens to examine and memorialize the history of the community for members of the hip hop generation (Mackenzie 1991).

Singer-songwriter and activist Faith Nolan – who had previously paid tribute to the community and critiqued the unjust treatment of its residents on the title track of her 1986 LP *Africville* – is interviewed in *Stolen from Africville*.[1] Towards the end of the documentary, one of the filmmakers asks her:

> What do we do to ensure that the history of the land stays intact because unfortunately ... even where we're from in Toronto, a lot of people don't know that there are fifth- and sixth-generation blacks living in Nova Scotia. What do we do to educate those people?
>
> Nolan responds:
> I made a record. You're making a film. That's always been the way. We only get this kind of education when we take it upon ourselves to spread the word wherever we can as artists, as activists. It won't happen unless we go there and do it. So now you know too. So you run with it. And you run where you can.

As *Stolen from Africville* suggests, hip hop culture has become a trenchant vehicle for a new generation of Canadian musicians and cultural workers to "run where [they] can" with knowledge of African Canadian histories, which all too often are minimized, or erased altogether, by dominant narratives and institutional frameworks surrounding Canadian history and identity. An increasing number of Canadian hip hop recordings and videos explore African Canadian history, thereby serving as a powerful form of cultural memory that remembers the past as a means of critically examining social issues facing Canadians of African descent today.

Mieke Bal (1999, vi, emphasis in original) suggests that "the term *cultural memory* signifies that memory can be understood as a cultural phenomenon as well as an individual or social one ... Cultural memorialization [is] an activity occurring in the present, in which the past is continuously modified and redescribed even as it continues to shape the future." In *How Societies Remember*, Paul Connerton (1989, 3–4) suggests that cultural memory involves "images of the past and recollected knowledge of the past ... conveyed and sustained by (more or less ritual) performances." In many African diasporic communities, music has been an important avenue for ritualistic acts of memory transference. This is due, in part, to the history and legacy of slavery that characterizes New World African experience. Often isolated linguistically and denied access to literacy and formal education, communities of enslaved Africans in the Americas used music and dance to develop and solidify social bonds and to preserve and transmit cultural values, conceptual frameworks, ideologies, and memories rooted in the African diaspora. This shared cultural repertoire continues to affect processes of African diasporic identity formation and their expression in Afrological forms[2] – including hip hop – offering creative life strategies to communities that continue to deal with the effects of systemic racism, oppression, and the legacies of colonialism and slavery.

This chapter examines three hip hop representations of East Coast African Canadian history: the music video for Black Union's 2007 recording titled "Africville," the aforementioned documentary *Stolen from Africville*, and the video for Ghetto Child's 2010 recording "Welcome to Nova Scotia." Through a close reading and analysis of their lyrical, visual, and musical content, this chapter examines Canadian hip hop's potential to function as a powerful site for the cultural memorialization of African Canadian history.

THE ROOTS OF HALIFAX HIP HOP

Although a thorough discussion of the history of East Coast Canadian hip hop is well beyond the scope of this chapter,[3] a brief overview of the roots of hip hop in Halifax will provide some useful musical and cultural context. One of the main hubs of hip hop culture in Halifax in the 1980s and, indeed, in the present day, is Uniacke Square, a public housing project built in the mid-1960s that originally housed many of Africville's displaced residents. By 1984, several hip hop crews had formed in and around Uniacke Square and in other public housing areas, including Mulgrave Park and Dartmouth's Jellybean Square.[4]

One of the earliest east coast hip hop crews was JB and the Cosmic Crew, which began performing in Halifax around 1984 (McGuire 2011, 38). The group included James "MC J" McQuaid, who would go on to be an integral member of two other pioneering Halifax hip hop groups: New Beginning (formed circa 1985) and MCJ and Cool G (formed circa 1988), the latter being the first hip hop group from the East Coast to be signed to a major record label.

Despite several notable exceptions, including DJ Jorun (aka Witchdoc Jorun), who did a great deal to support Halifax hip hop in its early stages, the majority of the participants in the city's hip hop scene in the 1980s were African Canadian: groups such as the Care Crew (William Lopie, aka Beatmaster P, and Dino B), The Finesse Ladies (Nadine and Tanya Grey), US Posse (short for Uniacke Square Posse), LC Posse, and Down By Law helped lay the groundwork for hip hop in Halifax.

Many of these groups were supported in one way or another by an organization known as the Cultural Awareness Youth Group (CAYG).

Founded by artist, poet, and playwright David Woods in 1983, CAYG played an important role in providing opportunities for African Canadian youth in Halifax to learn about – and showcase – their cultural heritage. Music, including hip hop, figured prominently in CAYG's efforts to memorialize African Canadian – and African diasporic – history and identity. In addition to publishing newsletters and sponsoring black history quiz tournaments and debates (and, for a time, a cable television show called *Black Youth Today*), CAYG organized hip hop workshops and performance opportunities in and around Uniacke Square and in Halifax's inner-city schools. As McGuire (2011, 46) summarizes: "if you were a young, Black student in Halifax in the 1980s who had an interest in hip hop, the CAYG could help you pursue it."

With the support of CAYG, the pioneers of Halifax hip hop in the 1980s paved the way for the successes of subsequent generations of East Coast hip hop artists, including Mod'rn World Thang, Haltown Projex, Hip Club Groove, Sixtoo, Buck 65 (Rich Terfry, aka DJ Critical, aka Stinkin Rich), and Classified (Luke Boyd), to name only a few. Whereas the first generation of hip hop innovators in Halifax was predominantly African Canadian, the scene has become more culturally diverse in recent decades, with increased participation by white performers. As McGuire (2011, 25) notes, "in the 1990s, the local scene underwent a demographic shift that saw the production and performance of rap music move away from the Black community and into the hands of a predominantly White group of artists." This trend is in keeping with a wider pattern in Canadian hip hop that Roger Chamberland (2001, 309) describes as "a reverse 'integration' effect." Despite this process of reverse integration – or perhaps because of it – a growing number of East Coast hip hop artists of African descent are exploring African Canadian history through their music, focusing on the history of Africville in particular.

STATE OF THE BLACK UNION

In 2007, a group known as Black Union released a track titled "Africville" that features Kaleb Simmonds, along with Brail Optiks, P. Noompse, and pioneering Canadian hip hop artist Maestro (known formerly, and subsequently, as Maestro Fresh Wes). The video for

"Africville," which has received airplay on MuchMusic and continues to be available online through YouTube, where it has been viewed over sixty thousand times as of this writing, begins with the following on-screen text: "Dedicated to my home. In Loving Memory of all the Africville victims." The use of the possessive pronoun "my" in this context, as opposed to "our," suggests that the director of the music video, known professionally as Cazhhmere, made the dedication. Cazhhmere is an award-winning Toronto-based writer and director whose background as an African Canadian originally from Canada's East Coast uniquely situates her in relation to the subject matter of the "Africville" video and several others she has directed, including the video for Ghetto Child's "Welcome to Nova Scotia" discussed below.

This dedication is followed by a close-up shot of a stone monument in Seaview Memorial Park, located on the former site of Africville. The monument is inscribed with the following words:

SEAVIEW
MEMORIAL PARK

LAND DEEDED
1848 – 1969

DEDICATED IN LOVING MEMORY OF
THE FIRST BLACK SETTLERS AND ALL
FORMER RESIDENTS OF THE COMMUNITY
OF CAMPBELL ROAD, AFRICVILLE AND ALL
MEMBERS OF THE SEAVIEW UNITED
BAPTIST CHURCH.

FIRST BLACK SETTLERS
WILLIAM BROWN JOHN BROWN
THOMAS BROWN

'TO LOSE YOUR WEALTH IS MUCH
TO LOSE YOUR HEALTH IS MORE
TO LOSE YOUR LIFE IS SUCH A LOSS
THAT NOTHING CAN RESTORE'

ERECTED 1988

In *Razing Africville: A Geography of Racism*, Jennifer Jill Nelson (2009, 142) suggests that "Africville families have regarded this as their monument; it is understandably important as a rare acknowledgement of black space, community, and roots." But she goes on to note that "its message is perplexing. For instance, except in a few cases, Halifax never recognized the land as having been deeded to black settlers, and none received treatment in line with this assumption. It is unclear whose loving sentiment is represented here, as history obviously attests to quite a different view of blacks by whites" (ibid.).

In the "Africville" music video, the shot of the monument is cropped in such a way that the words "Seaview Memorial Park" – which are larger and bolder than the rest of the text on the monument itself – are omitted from view, thereby focusing the viewer's attention on the land's previous identity as Africville rather than on its status as a public park. This is reinforced by the fact that the subsequent shots are cropped in such a way that they focus the viewer's attention on specific words within the monument's inscription, notably "First Black Settlers," "1848," "Dedicated," "Settlers," and finally "Africville." Through judicious cropping and editing, the opening seconds of the video effectively remix the inscription in such a way that it emphasizes the history and identity of Africville and the contributions of its residents to the history of Halifax rather than the supposedly reconciliatory act of erecting a stone monument and renaming the site.

These opening shots are followed by archival photographs of Africville juxtaposed with shots of Black Union group members on the site, thereby situating the viewer in a liminal space between the history of the site and its legacy. Against this visual backdrop, we hear a recording of an archival interview with a former resident of Africville identified as Mr Steed. When asked by an unidentified interviewer about Africville, Mr Steed states: "The people who tore it down … that's the City of Halifax and the authorities of the City of Halifax." The interviewer interjects: "They said it was a bad place." "That's what they called it," Mr Steed replies. "But it was not to us. It was a heaven. It was a home, a real home." This sample emphasizes the impact of Africville's destruction on its residents, making the loss feel more personal to the listener. Underpinning this passage is a repeated vocal riff, sung in a doo-wop style, which mournfully intones a recurrent chromatic descent from D to C#. This sample reoccurs beneath each rhymed verse later in the piece, maintaining a plaintive sound throughout while gesturing towards earlier Afrological modes of music making that have informed, and continue to inform, hip hop music and culture. In combination, the visual and sonic samples in the first thirty seconds of the video create a powerful audio-visual montage that effectively memorializes Africville and the plight of its residents while setting a sombre tone for the remainder of the video.

After this introduction, the chorus enters, delivered in a soulful vocal style by singer, beatboxer, and season two *Canadian Idol* finalist Kaleb Simmonds, who sings: "You can't put a price on the lives that they've ruined / No reparations, no nothin', why would you do this? / Divide my people to fight / Out on the corners at night / Oh, Africville, look what they've done to me." Note that the lyric is not "Oh, Africville, look what they've done to *you*." Rather, it is "look what they've done to *me*," thereby suggesting that the effects of Africville's destruction continue to reverberate in East Coast African Canadian communities to the present day. Brail Optiks similarly posits a connection between the past and the present when he rhymes "See what happened to Africville, it happens still / They choose land over man to expand, extract and kill."

The contemporary social challenges that Simmonds and Optiks allude to can be traced, in part, to a larger pattern of institutional and economic racism in both Canada and the United States historically, of which the treatment of Africville residents is but one example. Well after the end of legalized slavery in Canada (in 1834) and in the United States (in 1865), persons of African descent continued to be prevented from owning property due to racially restrictive housing covenants in both countries that prevented minorities from purchasing homes in many residential neighbourhoods. Even though racially restrictive covenants have been illegal for more than a half-century, their effects continue to be felt in a variety of communities – including many of African descent – to the present day because of the extent to which land ownership is connected to the accrual of personal and familial wealth in North American society. By discouraging and/or preventing land ownership among several generations of African Americans and African Canadians, racially restrictive housing covenants contributed to the cycle of poverty that continues to disproportionately affect persons of African descent. This supports Black Union's suggestion that the forced dispersal of Africville residents – and their lack of adequate compensation – contributed to the socioeconomic problems facing some black Nova Scotians today. As in many other African diasporic communities and, indeed, in many aggrieved communities in general, hip hop has become both a powerful conduit to voice resistance to such systemic forms of oppression as well as a potential avenue of escape from those conditions.

The opening chorus is followed by a verse performed by Maestro, who brings considerable old school credentials to the recording: along with the Dream Warriors, Devon, and Michie Mee, Maestro was one of the pioneers of Canadian hip hop, so much so that he is often referred to as the "Godfather of Canadian Hip Hop." Unlike the other members of Black Union, who hail from Nova Scotia, Maestro is originally from Toronto and has spent much of his professional life in New York City. His inclusion in the "Africville" recording and video suggests that the group is advocating for a multi-generational and multi-regional "black union" within Canada that is united in its efforts to preserve and promote African Canadian history.

In his first verse, Maestro points to the erasure of African Canadian history in general and that of Africville in particular: "It's a part of our history they kept in the closet / Professors never taught the lessons; they neglected, forgot it / They kept it underneath the table, kept it under the surface / Nervous that we were reemergin,' they dispersed us and jerked us / Out in Africville, Halifax's ill / How can us blacks rebuild?" Similarly, Brail Optiks rhymes: "History don't like to tell of it / Discrete about its relevance / 'Cause the black community was a disease to their development." Both Maestro and Optiks highlight the fact that the history of Africville has been largely omitted from dominant histories and narratives surrounding Canadian identity. For example, there is no *Heritage Minute* television commercial devoted to the history of Africville.[5] In fact, the only two *Heritage Minutes* to focus on persons of African descent are one devoted to Canada's role as the terminus of the Underground Railroad and one devoted to baseball great Jackie Robinson, who played for one year on the Montreal Royals in 1946 before becoming the first African American athlete to play Major League Baseball in the United States for the Brooklyn Dodgers beginning the following year. In both cases, the heritage commercials present an image of Canada as a benevolent and racially tolerant nation. To date, the history of government-sponsored racism in Canada – such as the razing of Africville or the internment of Japanese Canadians during the Second World War – has not been featured in *Heritage Minute* commercials, although they too are very much "a part of our heritage" to quote the tagline from the historical advertisements. Likewise, the history of Africville was not widely taught in Nova Scotia public schools historically. Although there have been some positive changes in this regard in recent years, the history of Africville is still largely unknown outside of Nova Scotia. Thus, the "Africville" video offers an important corrective to the erasure of Africville and its legacy, memorializing and mobilizing its history in order to build community and to advocate for solidarity in response to the challenges that continue to face many Canadians of African descent today.

STOLEN FROM AFRICA / STOLEN FROM AFRICVILLE

Black Union's "Africville" is featured briefly in the 2008 documentary *Stolen from Africville.* The film is part of a larger project known as Stolen from Africa, which began in Toronto in 2004 as a T-shirt campaign. By printing the words "Stolen from Africa" on T-shirts, the organization aimed to draw attention to the history and legacy of slavery, and to "spark interest, ignite ideas and fuel discussion" (Stolen from Africa, "About," 2013, par. 2). Over the past decade, the Stolen from Africa organization has broadened to encompass four components: fashion, music production, community outreach (in the form of high school workshops and performances), and "alternative media," including interviews with hip hop artists and documentaries such as *Stolen from Africville.*

The film begins with a scene of Logikal Ethix and Unknown Mizery shot at night in Seaview Memorial Park. Addressing the audience, Unknown Mizery explains the preimise of the documentary by stating: "We're going to be speaking to everyone, embarking on a journey with you, with me. Let's learn together. Africville – Canadian Black History." After this introduction, the film shows archival photos of Africville as well as a variety of interviews, including some with former Africville residents and their descendants filmed at the 2007 Africville Picnic and Reunion Festival, which takes place on the former site of Africville each July.

At several points in the film, the soundtrack features a track titled "Africville PART 1" that was recorded by Logikal Ethix and Unknown Mizery, together with East Coast rappers Papa Grand and Mr. 902. The lyrics offer a pointed critique of the treatment of Africville residents, emphasizing pan-African solidarity and resistance to colonialism, while managing to work in a reference to the Stolen from Africa movement: "Fighting back against all the British tycoons / We're living the legacy of the Jamaican Maroons / I was stolen from Africa so I'm going back soon/ … / I'm standing fortified like Citadel Hill / 'Cause it's still trying to lie about Africville." The reference to Jamaican Maroons in this context refers to people of African descent in Jamaica who escaped from slavery in the seventeenth and eighteenth centuries and established free communities in Jamaica's interior. In 1796, over five hundred Jamaican Maroons were deported from Jamaica to Halifax for resisting British colonial rule. In Halifax, many Maroons worked on the city's fortifications, including Citadel Hill, thereby contributing to one of Halifax's most significant and enduring landmarks. However, less than four years later, almost all of the Maroons migrated once again, this time to Freetown in Sierra Leone, West Africa (Whitfield 2005, 23).

The migratory experience of the Maroons offers a particularly compelling example of what Paul Gilroy famously termed the "Black Atlantic" in reference to the widespread patterns of transnational cultural exchange between communities of African descent in Africa, the Caribbean, Great Britain, and the Americas. Given their resistance to colonial rule, the Maroons provide a resonant model for contemporary hip hop artists struggling to resist the legacies of colonialism in Canada. On "Africville PART 1," Mr. 902 claims to have Maroon ancestry, rapping "My Maroon blood rep[resent]s every African story." Even Logikal Ethix, who hails from Toronto, claims that he is "Startin' to prove / [his] bloodline came from Jamaican maroons / 416 to the 902."[6] Given the brevity of the Maroons' stay in Halifax, and the fact that virtually all the Maroons left Canada in 1800, it is unlikely that very many African Canadians are descended from the Jamaican Maroon community that lived in Halifax between 1796 and 1800. Whether or not these statements are accurate genealogically, they attest to Canadian hip hop's potential to remember and mobilize African diasporic – and African Canadian – history in the service of contemporary identity politics.

At one point in the film, Irvine Carvery, a former Africville resident and president of the Africville Genealogy Society, discusses the renaming of the site and the systematic attempts by city officials to eradicate the memory of Africville:

> When they were proposing building this park here, they did a survey of the people from Africville and asked them: "What would you like the park [to be] called?" Ninety-nine percent of the people said "call it Africville." What did it get named? Seaview. That goes back to the headlines in the newspaper after they moved my uncle Pa. They said "Africville gone, soon to be forgotten." So why would they name it Africville Park? They wanted to just completely eliminate Africville totally – name, memories, everything. You know what it is? It is memory genocide.

The tireless efforts of community activists such as Carvery, along with awareness-raising projects like Stolen from Africville and Black Union's "Africville," have played a crucial role in countering the "memory genocide" that has surrounded Africville for so many years. And those efforts have been rewarded. In 2010, Halifax mayor Peter Kelly issued an official apology to the former residents of Africville and pledged a $4.5 million compensation deal that includes $3 million to rebuild the Africville church. In addition, in July 2011, Seaview Memorial Park was officially renamed Africville Park, ensuring that future generations will know the history of the site.

WELCOME TO (BLACK) NOVA SCOTIA

Like the *Stolen from Africville* documentary and the video for Black Union's "Africville," Cazhhmere's music video for East Coast rapper Ghetto Child's 2010 recording "Welcome to Nova Scotia" memorializes black Nova Scotian history for the hip hop generation. The video begins with a shot of a series of *Chronicle Herald* newspapers strewn atop one another.[7] Beneath the headline "Welcome to Nova Scotia" a video plays within the frame of the newspaper's front cover photo. The video features Ghetto Child carrying a Canadian flag and standing in front of Peggy's Cove, one of Nova Scotia's most iconic landmarks. This gives way to a series of fast-paced camera movements from one newspaper to another, each of which features video vignettes of Ghetto Child rapping the lyrics of "Welcome to Nova Scotia" against a militaristic-sounding backing track. The moving images within each newspaper are flanked by headlines that highlight different facets of black Nova Scotian history, thereby constituting a parallel narrative to the one offered by the song itself. One headline reads "War of 1812 Brings 2000 Black Refugees to Nova Scotia." Additional headlines point to the history of slavery in Canada, the arrival of Free Black Loyalists in Nova Scotia, the immigration (and subsequent emigration) of Jamaican Maroons to and from Halifax, and the destruction of Africville as well as the achievements of notable black Nova Scotians, including Graham Downey, who was appointed deputy mayor of Halifax in 1979, and Delmore "Buddy" Daye, the Canadian Junior Lightweight Boxing Champion between 1964 and 1966. The shots of the newspapers are interspersed with full-frame shots of Ghetto Child rapping in front of a Nova Scotian flag or a stylized map of Nova Scotia.

The newspaper headlines in the video amplify and complement the narrative presented in the lyrics of "Welcome to Nova Scotia," which similarly highlight black Nova Scotian history. For example, Ghetto Child rhymes: "1775 / we arrive / to slavery days / Yes, our ancestors paved / the way for the streets." With these lines, he refers not only to the history of slavery on Canada's East Coast but also to the fact that previous generations of black Nova Scotians laid the foundations – both literally and metaphorically – for the streets of Halifax: in the late eighteenth and nineteenth centuries, many black Nova Scotians worked at construction jobs in Halifax, building roads and streets and other elements of the city's infrastructure (Vincer 2008, 23, 26). Furthermore, the idea of "the street" (and the related geocultural construction of "the 'hood") is an essential part of hip hop culture, wherein it is often conceived of as a marker of both musical and racial authenticity. As Murray Forman notes in *The 'Hood Comes First: Race, Space, and Place in Rap and Hip-Hop*, one of the defining features of hip hop culture is its intensely spatial nature. "A highly detailed and consciously defined spatial awareness" he writes, "is one of the key factors distinguishing rap music and hip-hop from the many other cultural and subcultural youth formations currently vying for popular attention. In hip-hop, space is a dominant concern, occupying a central role in the definition of value, meaning, and practice" (Forman 2002, 3). The importance of place is evident in the lyrics of "Welcome to Nova Scotia," which name-check several communities in and around Halifax, including North Preston, Porter's Lake, Beaver Bank, Sackville, and Beechville. In addition to the emphasis on place, Ghetto Child emphasizes the memory of place, drawing a parallel between places associated with the history of black Nova Scotian culture and their legacy today. This is particularly evident in his lyrics about Africville: "Black culture is here and it will never die / But they stole souls when they bulldozed homes; they took some pride / With no reparation, relocated to public housing – 800,000 vote expropriation / The next generation is here / coming from Mulgrave Park and Uniacke Square." Born and raised in Uniacke Square, Ghetto Child (Paul Smith) situates himself as a part of the "next generation" of black Nova Scotian culture, remembering and honouring the sacrifices of earlier generations. This idea is reinforced by the newspaper headlines that run parallel to the performative elements of the music video. Towards the end of the video, the headlines shift focus away from black Nova Scotian history to Ghetto Child himself: "2004: Ghetto Child Releases 1st Mixtape 'FAX OF LIFE'" reads one, "Ghetto Child Opens for Ludacris and Wu-Tang Clan" another. The final headline reads: "Ghetto Child Shoots Debut Music Video." This confluence of form and content suggests that Ghetto Child and, I would argue, Cazhhmere, who is shown briefly in the video at the very end, are active agents in the histories that they are memorializing through music and image.

CONCLUSION

At several points in the video for "Welcome to Nova Scotia," Ghetto Child is shown wearing a "Stolen from Africa" T-shirt, bringing us full circle to the Stolen from Africa movement discussed above. The inclusion of the Stolen from Africa T-shirt and slogan in Ghetto Child's video promotes solidarity among all Canadians of African descent and, indeed, among persons of African descent more generally given the widespread history of racial violence and oppression that characterizes a great deal of New World African diasporic experience. The implication is that African diasporic communities have a shared responsibility to preserve the histories of their ancestors for present and future generations. In Canada, hip hop has been an important site for the memorialization of African Canadian histories via inventive sampling traditions, video-editing techniques, and even linguistic innovations. It is my belief that educators and academics also have a role to play: we, too, ought to run where we can with knowledge of histories that have been marginalized by dominant discourses surrounding Canadian identity and history. This chapter is intended as a means to that end.

NOTES

1 A number of other Canadian musicians working in a variety of genres have paid tribute to Africville. In addition to Nolan's work, the Newfoundland screamo band Bucket Truck released "A Nourishment by Neglect" in 2007, which similarly chronicles and critiques the destruction of Africville. In 1997, jazz pianist and composer Joe Sealy, whose father was born in Africville, won the Juno for Best Contemporary Jazz Album for his twelve-part *Africville Suite*.

2 George Lewis (1996, 93) coined the term "Afrological" to refer to "historically emergent rather than ethnically essential" systems of musical logic that have developed in African diasporic communities historically.

3 For a detailed history of hip hop in Halifax, see McGuire (2011).

4 Jellybean Square/The Bean was a housing project in Dartmouth that was home to dance crews as early as 1984 (see McGuire 2011).

5 *Heritage Minutes* is a series of more than seventy television commercials that "portray exciting and important stories from Canada's past" that began airing on Canadian television in 1991 (Historica Canada n.d.). In 2009, East Coast Canadian rapper Classified parodied the *Heritage Minutes* commercials in the video for his piece "O Canada," also directed by Cazhhmere.

6 Note that 416 is the telephone area code for Toronto; 902 is the area code for Nova Scotia.

7 The *Chronicle Herald* is a Halifax newspaper, the largest in Atlantic Canada.

3

CELEBRATION, RESISTANCE, AND ACTION

Beat Nation: Hip Hop as Indigenous Culture

Charity **Marsh**

> From MCs to graff writers, video makers, painters and poets, Aboriginal rights and rhymes have inspired a new fusion of hip hop and diverse Indigenous cultures. Distilling these influences into contemporary art and experimental music was an extension of using these mediums to engage young people in their culture(s). Aboriginal cultural lyricscapes peppered N8V hip hop tracks and from Cree to Inuit to Haida to Mohawk and more, our realities and our dreams were reflected in the music, the art, and the culture of hip hop.[1]
>
> Tania Willard, *Beat Nation* co-curator

INTRODUCTION

From a simple online search of "hip hop" along with the keywords "community," "youth," and "empowerment," it quickly becomes apparent that hip hop artists, fans, activists, and researchers from across arts disciplines and regions around the world recognize the significance and potential of hip hop as a culture of storytelling, political activism, and resistance. Furthermore, as is evident from a number of chapters in this volume,[2] hip hop and its associated arts practices also offer possible strategies for understanding, withstanding, and reimagining contemporary Indigenous identities. Elsewhere I have made the claim that from such new imaginings Indigenous youth "mediate representations of themselves and their current lived experiences through mobile technologies and local networks, challenging common stereotypes and reified identities that continue to circulate in political, cultural, and national discourses" (Marsh 2009a, 112).

Turning to *Beat Nation: Hip Hop as Indigenous Culture*, it becomes even more evident that Indigenous youth living in Canada are embodying a global hip hop politics as they connect to other youth cultures around the world who have adapted hip hop culture and its arts practices as a means to organize young people, revolt against (neo)colonialism, and resist assimilation and extinction of "traditional" culture. In the essay "Rhyming Out the Future: Reclaiming Identity through Indigenous Hip Hop," Lindsay Knight (2015, par.1), a Cree hip hop artist and Indigenous studies scholar, makes the argument that "hip hop fills a cultural void within urban [Indigenous] people's identities, and assists in maintaining Indigenous worldview through resistance, revitalization, and connection to the spirit world." Contrary to criticisms that have been voiced by "older community members who see [hip hop's] influence as a break from tradition and the movement of the culture towards a pop-based mainstream assimilation," the curators and contributing artists, Knight being one of the artists, of *Beat Nation* highlight how hip hop is in fact "giving youth new tools to rediscover First Nations culture [and] embrace the traditional within its development" (*Beat Nation* n.d.).

Financed through Heritage Canada's Gateway Fund with support from the now cancelled Canadian Culture Online program, *Beat Nation* was initially developed as one production of Vancouver-based artist-run centre Grunt Gallery. *Beat Nation* began as an online project that "focuse[d] on the development of hip hop culture within Aboriginal youth communities and its influence on cultural production" (*Beat Nation* n.d.). Embracing the many hip hop arts disciplines (as well as other cultural practices that are at times tangentially related to hip hop, such as skateboarding, fashion, and dance), the interactive site and exhibitions of *Beat Nation* celebrate, promote, and help to define what is meant by an Indigenization of hip hop culture.

From its curatorial aesthetic, including the choice of contributing artists and their works, as well as its multiple exhibition styles (the online gallery site, exhibition for the Vancouver Art Gallery, and the touring exhibition), *Beat Nation* exemplifies how hip hop can be adapted to become a means to express, challenge, provoke, and make sense of Canada's ongoing legacies associated with colonialism. Drawing on an interview conducted with co-curator and artist Tania Willard, along with examples from the site, this chapter further proposes that *Beat Nation* also contributes to a meaningful process of reconciliation or, more usefully, what David Garneau (2016) articulates as "conciliation" through the telling of stories within multiple arts practices,[3] the celebration of diverse hip hop voices, and, as Knight (2015, par. 4) notes, a hip hop resistance "through Indigenous awareness of culture and identity, colonization and revolution."

BEAT NATION: STORYTELLING

> Just as in any massive form of communication, there are going to be sentimental statements made, broad sweeping fears expressed and lots of "documentation" to examine, but we should really consider ourselves lucky. Native youth, Native people, Indigenous people, hip hop people are presenting ideas making connections, drawing conclusions and asking important questions.[4]
>
> Skeena Reece, *Beat Nation* co-curator

On the homepage of the virtual *Beat Nation* exhibition, the viewer is offered multiple entry points into the world of hip hop through an Indigenous lens. Along with a statement from Glen Atleen (the producer of the exhibition) and some images of contributors' artworks, the gallery is divided into various sections through links to separate pages on the site, including: curatorial statements,[5] a music page,[6] an artists' page (visual, performance, and dance artists),[7] and a writer's page,[8] as well as a page highlighting credits, funders, and an online survey and blog. The audience can click on each link and move with ease through each virtual space, enlarging images, reading artist biographies, playing embedded videos, and listening to the *Beat Nation* soundtrack.[9]

For viewers familiar with hip hop history, politics, and aesthetics, the rationale for artists included in *Beat Nation* is clear. Each artist has drawn on hip hop aesthetics, styles, and performance practices, and yet has also included and/or created "elements that are distinctive, and generated from local vernacular, landscape, cultural practices, politics, and place" (Marsh 2012a, 356). In her curatorial statement, Tania Willard writes: "Aboriginal artists have taken hip hop influences and indigenized them to fit Aboriginal experiences: The roots of hip hop are there but they have been ghost-danced by young Native artists who use hip hop culture's artists' forms and combine them with Aboriginal story, experience, and aesthetics" (*Beat Nation* n.d.).

When I was speaking with co-curator Tania Willard in October 2014, she discussed how she and her co-curators made decisions concerning the various aspects of the gallery. Specifically, I asked how the curators found an overall vision for what culminated in such an amazing, huge, inter- and multidisciplinary project with multiple conversations and layers. Willard talked me through how the project took shape:

> We were co-curating together with Archer Pechawis, who is an Indigenous website designer. Originally we knew other artists in our community who were doing really great work. Corey Bulpitt being one, he was becoming a really great carver and doing totem poles and very traditional, beautiful work but also making some kind of blinged out rings and doing graffiti art. We focused in on that – artists who were both honouring and supporting and advocating and practicing their culture, as well as finding a way to do that through hip hop without it seeming like the two were at polarized ends of the spectrum. They were able to bring [hip hop and identity] together. For me, it was also about creating a picture, a non-stereotypical kind of picture, of Indigenous people as a people of many different diverse interests, cultures, practices and importantly, as contemporary peoples as well. In terms of the actual original site, there weren't a lot of parameters. This is my early work as a curator as well. I never trained as a curator. I came out of Fine Arts school and then came out of an activism culture and then started, working more and more in the Indigenous community and through art ... I wanted to have people who were doing great work and that I thought of as forwarding both political and cultural goals. I also wanted to make sure that people who were making the music themselves had a voice.

Recognizing the need for Indigenous musicians to have a platform from which to tell their stories is critical to understanding how projects like *Beat Nation* become so consequential for marginalized communities. Willard states: "On the original site there are musicians and writers like Kinnie Starr and Ronald Harris (aka Ostwelve) who talk about their own journey into hip hop. [I chose to have them tell their stories] because I felt like that wasn't my place; I wasn't a hip hop emcee. I was the curator and an artist and coming at it from a different perspective. I wanted to make sure those people's voices were heard – the ones who were really making hip hop their life."[10]

The following passage from Kinnie Starr is an excellent example of what Willard is talking about:

> Hip hop is a place where we share our stories eloquently at times, arrogantly or awkwardly at others. The beats and rhymes I have written showcase my background as a middle-class, white-red girl from Calgary, Alberta, raised on metal and old school rap, as well as an intellect, rocker and a seeker of truth. On top of my thick dub-rock sloppy hip hop beats, I throw words like they are stones in a river and make my way through life. Making hip hop gave (and gives) me a chance to slowly and articulately find my footing in the complicated landscape of Native and white Canadians. And though my feet sometimes stumble, I believe without hip hop I would still be hiding in the closet, afraid to take a step forward as the woman I am becoming. (*Beat Nation* n.d.)

Through such stories, the complex narratives of mixed ancestry, identity formation, and belonging within a settler colonial society are divulged. Genre blending, sampling, and the inclusion of various landscapes assist Starr in feeling at home within a genre like hip hop in spite of its contradictions, which, at times, result in empowerment for some and oppression for others.

As highlighted throughout the chapters of *We Still Here*, hip hop has multiple entry points and encompasses a range of arts disciplines, thus enabling a heterogeneous collection of voices to participate. "Young people from all around the world with diverse cultural, social, economic, and political backgrounds are drawn to hip hop because the culture allows for a confluence of a multitude of national, regional, and cultural sensibilities with its aesthetics, styles, and pleasures" (Marsh 2009a, 119). To tell one's story through hip hop presents the opportunity for both a shared language *and* uniqueness. Willard explains the importance of such stories included in *Beat Nation*:

> In terms of the project getting wider attention, it was when Kathleen Ritter had curated a small portion of the music part of *Beat Nation*, [she included] people like Christie Charles who [does her] rapping in Halkomelem, [and is of] Musqueam. I should also say that it was important for me, within the realm of different urban Indigenous people to also make sure that there was voice to the local Indigenous Nations which are the Squamish, Tsleil-Waututh, and Musqueam – Nations around Vancouver, BC. And so, Christie is this great, young hip hop artist mother and she does some rapping in her own language, which a number of other artists do as well. This has always been to me really inspiring. [On the site] there is that kind of hip hop, as well as Nicholas Galanin's early work with his videos.

Here Willard is describing the music of Miss Christie Lee Charles (aka Crunch),[11] as well as Nicholas Galanin, whose two works, "Tsu Heidei Shugaztutaan part 1" and "Tsu Heidei Shugaztutaan part 2," capture the combining of contemporary break dance with a traditional sound track and electro-beats with traditional dance.[12] Willard continues: "Those works really kind of framed for me what I was hoping to get at in the conversation around the project. I was really wary that people were going to see it and be like, 'Oh, you know, Native kids doing new things, it's all about new, new, new!' But it's not about that. It's about people seeing this continuum of their culture and incorporating a holistic idea of who they are as an Indigenous person that doesn't have to be divorced from [Indigenous] contemporary realities."[13] Willard's concerns around how *Beat Nation* is understood and read are significant. Too often, we are caught up in what Walter Benjamin (2002) refers to in his critique of culture as the "culture of the new." The shiny, new thing, whatever it is, becomes the object of discussion and promotion, rather than the larger systems and, in this case, the realities from which the new object, practice, art has evolved and/or from that which the stories and activism have manifested.

BEAT NATION: POLITICAL ACTIVISM

Through their raps, beats, graffiti, and dance, the students are telling stories – to each other, to their peers, to their families, and to their communities –

about how they understand their own politics, acts of resistance and compliance, fears, anxieties, dreams, celebrations, identity, and culture.

Charity Marsh, "Hip Hop as Methodology"

At one point, I asked Willard how she came to be interested in curating *Beat Nation*. In her response, she articulated the influence of grassroots activism and, more specifically, the impact of the zine *Redwire Magazine*, "a national [Indigenous] youth-run publication, that came out of Vancouver and started [in 1997] with two sisters, Nena and Billie Pierre."[14] From Willard's perspective, *Redwire Magazine* was ahead of the game: the zine was "tuned into the power and influence of hip hop in 2003 when they released their first Indigenous artist spoken-word CD, which they followed up in 2005 with another release of Indigenous hip hop" (*Beat Nation* n.d.). Speaking at length about how young Indigenous people living in British Columbia were mobilizing in order to stand up for their rights, Willard made a convincing connection between the utilization or engagement of hip hop as political activism and a youth-initiated strategy for resistance:

> After being abroad for a year I started working for *Redwire*. *Redwire* was an Indigenous youth publication. That project was really important because for the first time, it gave voice to an urban, Indigenous youth population that was at the time really politically active. Things were happening out at UBC, [with the Free Trade Summit] in 2000-ish, and that was overlapping at the same time with the province's push to have this new Treaty process where they wanted to consult bands and basically boil down the remaining Indigenous land claims, territorial claims – which is all of BC because that's still outstanding – over 99 percent claimed and unsettled by treaties – they wanted to settle those down to neat little packaged treaties that would create certainty for investors and municipal style governance for bands. Many Indigenous peoples stood up against that process ... In particular, Indigenous youth had a strong voice in standing against that process ... When I came back to Vancouver, what was really happening was Indigenous youth were using hip hop to talk about the BC treaty process and to talk about ideas of cultural pride and self-determination, as well as deeper political issues around capitalism and economies and how we understand these as Indigenous peoples.[15]

As a project, *Beat Nation* was initially connected to a particular community and regional activism. In British Columbia, there were a number of Indigenous emcees who were performing hip hop while simultaneously engaging in movements for social and political change. Willard explains:

> We all did all this kind of work and community activism for years with little recording studios popping up and women more and more getting into hip hop. It was actually at the tail end of when I'd stopped working with *Redwire* that Grunt Gallery approached [me. We'd] been doing a number of these curated online galleries which were kind of interesting spaces. *Redwire* had already endeavoured into doing online exhibitions. We were thinking ahead about where our magazine would actually make it to – rural communities and connectivity and all those kinds of issues in the early 2000s as well ... It became really important to me with *Beat Nation* that people who defined themselves through hip hop, who were my friends, and people I worked with, and activists I knew, that I had to honour that and that place and the activism that was happening as much as the works that were being created. That's the many threads that came together to form what became *Beat Nation* which originally, of course, was an online gallery site which still exists at beat nation.org.[16]

The necessity of honouring the connection between the artworks and the political activism of the artists, as well as her own activism, is very clear as one moves through the site. This led me to ask Willard a number of questions concerning her relationship to hip hop, as well as the impacts, if any, she has witnessed over the years of *Beat Nation's* existence. Specifically, I asked the following three questions: How were you drawn in to hip hop? What have you seen in the past number of years since *Beat Nation* has existed in terms of its activism through hip hop? What is your thinking on hip hop as a strategy, as an activism these days? Willard's answers take into account the complexities of one's own experience, the emancipatory possibilities associated with conscious hip hop, the realities of collaborating with a lot of artists, and the restrictions of actual physical and virtual spaces. She responds:

> I think [my understanding has] changed a bit. I think a lot of the people who are all working in that genre and that vein are still doing a lot of great work and still have conscious hip hop ideas. But it's also within that process that I've matured, had children, been through many life experiences. So whereas before I might have liked there to be "*the most amazing hip hop show*," every time the tour went to a new place, it wasn't possible for me, alone, to organize all that stuff. I had to coordinate with [institutions.]

After attending the exhibition of *Beat Nation* at the MacKenzie Art Gallery in Regina, Saskatchewan (MacKenzie Art Gallery n.d.), I found myself reflecting on the importance of community involvement with the show, and how challenging it would be to create a particular moment when grassroots activism through hip hop or other community arts programs could match the timing of a showcase like *Beat Nation*. Willard's discussion of how one is dependent upon others speaks volumes to the nature of collaboration. Although it may seem an excellent fit to run events, festivals, programming for youth, performances, and so on around such exhibitions, there is a spontaneity that is lacking. To create or facilitate a particular kind of experience during community arts-based projects or events can at times seem disingenuous, especially considering that continued funding for many projects is tied to achieving specific outcomes (Marsh 2012b).

From her perspective, however, Willard relishes the difference between performances and gallery exhibitions, highlighting the "quieter time for more of a conversation with the artwork … Something quite different than digesting a performer's spoken word or their ideas; you have this different entry point ... in individual art." *Beat Nation* originally started out from and promoted a grassroots kind of activism, but as the gallery evolved, took on different forms, and became embedded within other kinds of institutions, a new political lens was embraced. Willard explains the evolution process:

> I was happy with the way the show toured and everything, but at the same time, slightly mystified at the engines of how that all worked. I didn't have to do the logistics of organizing the tour, all that kind of thing, so in some ways it wasn't a – no, in a lot of ways it wasn't a grassroots project anymore. But I knew that going into the Vancouver Art Gallery that it wouldn't be ... And the

> weighing out of things was, well, as a curator I think it's my job to try and get the widest audience and criticality for artists' work. I couldn't deny an opportunity to do that in a more radical activist frame. That [activism] is happening anyway and you may hold up that work and some of it might get attention for a while, but the people who are committed to that work are doing that work and that activism is going to go on. It wasn't because of me that anyone was making hip hop or not making hip hop. Here was a chance to just talk about it a bit more, and hopefully, some people got, and will get, some more attention for their work and be able to continue it longer.

The creation of a formal exhibition and then a touring show in addition to the online gallery creates a variety of options for access and promotes the show to multiple audiences in Canada. As Willard notes, *Beat Nation* transitioned from a grassroots exhibition to something else. What I find interesting is Willard's take on this shift. Rather than viewing the shift from grassroots to a more mainstream exhibition as something less valuable or provocative, Willard understands this change as a positive one, suggesting the draw of different kinds of audiences and more exposure for the artists. And yet, for me, one of the key aspects of *Beat Nation* in its original, *virtual* form is its ability to reach international populations and for audiences around the world to identify with the artists and the stories featured on the site.

BEAT NATION: RESISTANCE - SHARING EXPERIENCES AND STRATEGIES AROUND THE WORLD

> Hip hop culture *is* a dialogue with the world – a dialogue between youth and the world in which they operate daily.
>
> Louie Rodriguez, "Dialoguing, Cultural Capital, and Student Engagement"

Education scholar Louie Rodriguez's statement draws particular attention to two key aspects of hip hop culture: (1) hip hop as a means through which young people communicate with more than just their own communities *and* (2) hip hop as a platform through which young people can articulate and share their own lived experiences in a meaningful way. As a virtual exhibition, accessible to anyone who is able to get online or gain access to shared recorded digital data like music, videos, interviews, poetry, and/or artworks, *Beat Nation* and its contributors enter into this global dialogue with potentially profound effects. For young Indigenous people to work through the complexities of every-day lived experiences, through the cultural practices of hip hop, especially during current social and political manifestations and uprisings, represents a profound form of communication and identification. Both a shared and unique politics of resistance is possible. In our discussion, Willard addresses the impact of *Beat Nation* and its role in global dialogues, stating:

> I think *Beat Nation* has opened up a conversation about many different things and not all of them are centred around hip hop. But definitely it has come to be known as a project that looked at Indigenous hip hop as tied to these many different art forms ... I wasn't coming from a trained curator's background. I was coming from [the place of] somebody who was part of a community who has lots to say, and who wanted to see change in the world. That was the emphasis and the motivation and passion behind what we were doing. But I do think it's had legs ... I have no idea what people in the wider hip hop community or international Indigenous community think about the project. It is out there and I think, I mean, there are lots of parallels I think. I've often talked with a Maori curator friend and we talked about different relationships with Aboriginal hip hop and Maori hip hop, that it would be something – and artists who are working in ways like that down there. You know, but the reality is we're often in smaller, less funded, isolated, marginalized communities and so large-scale projects, international Indigenous projects, are not something that happen all the time.

For Willard, the sharing of the artists' works in multiple formats had an impact. To move from only a digital platform to a full gallery exhibition (with co-curator Kathleen Ritter) and a touring exhibition enabled a wide range of audiences to interact and connect with the artworks. It also facilitated a lasting momentum for the project as a whole. But returning to her comments about international Indigenous projects, I asked Willard, as someone who has had some impact, how she views the rise of Indigenous hip hop cultures in Canada, whether it is associated more with community-based arts projects or with artists who are actually trying to make a living. She responded:

> I was thinking about [this. I] mean, before hip hop it was really metal on the reserves, heavy metal. I remember a lot more heavy metal stuff happening and then all of a sudden one summer, I used to work for my Aunty at the powwows, she used to have fruit stands, and we were at the Kamloopa Powwow and this crew came through who were doing break dance and blew everyone away and I was only about seventeen or something. So twenty-plus years on, I guess, I witnessed and had some kind of relationships with the growth of Indigenous hip hop. I mean, I think it's beautiful. It's a beautiful art form. In many ways I think Indigenous Peoples are drawn to it because, one, it has these multiple entry points; two, it has these strong relationships to not only the origin of hip hop coming from, you know, inner city marginalized, black youth communities. Indigenous peoples relate to that sense of poverty and social injustice I think. But there is also something really powerful about it in its storytelling form, and how important oral culture is to many of us, to many Indigenous cultures. And something about how it is more accessible. You didn't have to be ... it wasn't defined yet, what you had to "*be*" to be a hip hop emcee or to be into it. It was a subculture that was happening, so it wasn't already defined in some ways, so there were a lot of opportunities there.

I, along with others, have argued that hip hop as a culture of storytelling offers many opportunities, as Willard suggests (Marsh 2012a). Nevertheless, from a critical perspective, as an academic and a producer of community hip hop programming, I am often asked by various stakeholders to make a case for hip hop as an important community strategy. Certainly I can offer many examples from projects all around the world, and even from the projects I have had the privilege of facilitating in Saskatchewan, of how hip hop programming can assist in creating change, fostering productive activism, challenging colonial narratives, as well as promoting "good citizenship." At the same time, this research can also be drawn on for detrimental kinds of policy making and for policing youth. These are the kinds of ethical considerations I must not only watch out for but also engage head on. Willard and I spoke about how hip hop can also be exclusionary and hyper-masculine and heteronormative. And how in many cities across Canada, those of us involved in community hip hop programming or projects must also continue to be aware of how Indigenous youth, specifically Indigenous men, continue to be brought out on display. In one instance these men are celebrated – "Hey, look at these kids and these youth! They're doing this cool hip hop thing and including Indigenous cultural elements, and look at this neat stuff happening" – and in the next instance, the media and other authorities are reproducing discourse that suggests that these young Indigenous men who are connected with hip hop culture must also be participating in gang violence and drug culture.

Keeping these contradictions in mind as she worked on *Beat Nation*, Willard explains:

> I just basically came about it as I wasn't talking about wider, mainstream hip hop. I was talking about conscious hip hop. I was talking about artists who were using [conscious hip hop] as a way to express culture and not just mimic mainstream hip hop. I mean, you could say that about rock music, about country and western music. You can say that about any genre of music – that it's dominated by men and that representations of women are problematic. It's a wider issue of a patriarchal society. But with the work of *Beat Nation*, I always thought about gender, thought about sexuality, and made an effort to make sure that was part of the picture that I was bringing to people.

There are a number of examples of women-identified artists throughout the *Beat Nation* site and various hip hop art forms. Christie Charles, Jerilynn Webster, Kinnie Starr, and Eekwol are four of the women emcees who were included. "There are many different Indigenous women who are doing hip hop, emcee work, and were working in the visual arts in a way that was related to hip hop," Willard said. For me, the inclusion of so many women was synonymous with what I have found when researching hip hop in British Columbia. More specifically, if you look across the country, the number of Indigenous women thinking and talking about hip hop, different kinds of activism, and the kind of conscious hip hop that Willard is discussing, it seems that there is a strong and vital community of women in that province working on/through hip hop. As we talked this idea through, Willard reflected on why there is such an awesome and inspiring community of women from British Columbia who are involved in hip hop:

> I'm trying to think if I have any indication of why that is, or not why it is, but what it's related to as a picture. I mean, we have a lot of strong, distinct, different Indigenous cultures here in BC, right? We have many different languages throughout this area with many different cultures and, you know, some of the cultures are more matriarchal, matrilineally aligned. And those practices have been carried over in different kinds of ways. That's not to say there hasn't been dramatic impacts in terms of patriarchy and religious, Christianized systems. Even in terms of Secqwpemc culture or ethnographic records, women's and men's roles weren't drastically different or defined, certainly not in any way related to the strict Victorian types of definitions of gender. And then you have these other kinds of concepts of gender and sexuality and stuff which have been repressed through residential school and Christianization and dominance, abuse and colonial narratives. I don't know … maybe it's the wild west. You've got to be tough out here … And we have a radical history in terms of it not being Treaty, [BC] not being settled, people still stand up for their rights. They recognize their territory. They challenge governments. They challenge ideas that settler colonization should have more rights than original Indigenous governance systems. So, all that dialogue has been around for some time and so I think all that could have the effect of strengthening different communities and maybe those conversations are around more for women to be a part of. I don't know … And [it's] not just in the Indigenous community. I can think of a number of other female hip hop emcees. I mean, part of it is also mentoring, right? So somebody like Kinnie Starr, who is my ageish, she becomes a model for other Indigenous women who want to get into [hip hop], and they see somebody who's doing it and that gives them permission to explore [hip hop]. I think that certainly has something to do with it too. You have one or two women in hip hop, and then all of a sudden you have four, five, and six because they're watching those other women.

The rise of women-identified role models, networking opportunities, and supportive creative environments, as well as access to technologies and chances to perform, have been cited as key indicators for determining women's involvement and success within genres like hip hop.[17] *Beat Nation* offers examples of all of these, and it helps to challenge some of the conventional signifiers associated with hip hop culture as a whole.

At the conclusion of our discussion, Willard expressed her gratitude and respect for the artists who participated: "Curating is nothing if you don't have artists doing amazing work ... I'm ultimately very grateful to the artists who, in the end, are the people who have ... the courage to stand up and express themselves in ways that are not prescribed." For a project like *Beat Nation,* there are many players who have to be courageous, including the curators. It is through the curator's design that the exhibition comes to life, provokes dialogues, and, it is hoped, sees things that others have not seen. The role of the curator is indeed that of a storyteller as well.

Although the impacts of *Beat Nation* are not easily quantifiable, I can say with confidence that *Beat Nation* has helped to define what hip hop sounds/looks/feels like through an Indigenous lens. The conversations I had with co-curator Tania Willard offer a critical perspective in the imagining of such an incredibly diverse multi-platformed hip hop arts project. In its various forms, *Beat Nation* has contributed and continues to contribute to global hip hop dialogues – dialogues that offer both unique and shared identities, worldviews, and strategies for resistance to complex forms of colonialism and oppression among its youthful participants.

NOTES

This chapter evolved from hearing Tania Willard, co-curator of Beat Nation: Hip Hop as Indigenous Culture, speak at the MacKenzie Art Gallery as part of the curatorial events for the exhibition, from conversations we had in person and via phone, as well as multiple viewings of the online and gallery exhibitions. Her perspectives and insights are invaluable in understanding the significance of *Beat Nation* in all of its forms: an online gallery, a stand-alone gallery exhibition, and a touring exhibition. Each phase of the multi-year project invited different audiences into a discussion of hip hop as performed and understood through an Indigenous lens. Throughout this chapter, I use the term Indigenous as a political choice to refer to all Indigenous people living in Canada. At times throughout the chapter, the term Aboriginal is also used, in quotations from the online exhibition and in the conversations with Tania Willard, as this term was officially recognized in Canada to refer to First Nations, Inuit, and Métis people when Beat Nation was first created back in 2009. The research for this chapter was generously supported by the Social Sciences and Humanities Research Council.

1 See Curatorial Statements on the *Beat Nation* website (*Beat Nation* n.d.).

2 See Przybylski (chapter 4, this volume); and Robinson (chapter 9, this volume).

3 In his article, "Imaginary Spaces of Conciliation and Reconciliation: Art, Curation, and Healing," Garneau (2016) suggests that we look to acts of "conciliation" instead of reconciliation. However he also warns that Indigenous allies "must be cautious not to replace a Truth and Reconciliation model or models of quality framed by standards of colonialism and whiteness."

4 See Curatorial Statements on the *Beat Nation* website (*Beat Nation* n.d.).

5 Both Tania Willard and Skeena Reece have published curatorial statements.

6 The music page on the *Beat Nation* website includes features on Miss Christie Lee Charles (aka Crunch), Rapsure Risin, Kinnie Starr, Manik1derful, Eekwol, JB the First Lady, Daybi, Geoff Pranteau, and Ostwelve Ron Harris (*Beat Nation* n.d.).

7 The artists' page on the *Beat Nation* website includes features on Corey Bulpitt, Andrew Mark Dexel, Bracken Hanuse Corlett, Bunky Echo-Hawk, Cheryl L'Hirondelle, Doreen Manuel, Jackson 2bears, Jolene Nenibah Yazzie, Jordan Bennett, Kevin Lee Burton, Leena Minifie, Morgan Green, Nicholar Galanin, Rosc Simposon, Sonny Assu, and the Native Youth Artist Collective (*Beat Nation* n.d.).

8 The writers' page on the *Beat Nation* website includes features on Kinnie Starr, Ostwelve Ron Harris, and Peter Morin (*Beat Nation* n.d.).

9 The *Beat Nation Trax* includes eleven songs from nine different hip hop artists, including Eekwol, Miss Christie Lee Charles (aka Crunch), Rapture Risin, Ostwelve, and Kinnie Strarr.

10 Tania Willard Interview.

11 Hear Miss Christie Lee Charles's music on the Music section of the *Beat Nation* website (*Beat Nation* n.d.).

12 View both of these works on Nicholas Galanin's profile on the Artists section of the *Beat Nation* website (*Beat Nation* n.d.).

13 Tania Willard conversation.

14 Ibid.

15 Ibid.

16 As noted in the introduction, Grunt Gallery received funding for the

creation of *Beat Nation* as an online curated art gallery through a Heritage Canada grant. These grants focused on digital curation like *Beat Nation* and archival sites like Northside Hip Hop (see Campbell, chap. 1, this volume).

17 For more discussions on the impact of these indicators, see Marsh (chap. 11, this volume).

PART TWO

Representation and Belonging

4

RAPPING TO AND FOR A MULTIVOCAL CANADA

"Je M'y Oppose au Nom de Toute la Nation"

Liz Przybylski

INTRODUCTION

Samian, a Canadian rapper of Algonquin descent, released a controversial hip hop single entitled "Plan Nord" in March 2012. "Plan Nord" critiques the eponymous development plan to increase resource extraction in northern Quebec. In this song, Samian collaborates with Inuit throat singer Marie Belleau, in addition to a DJ and other instrumentalists.[1] The presence of throat singing brings into focus discourses about how Inuit musical practices are involved in compositions that represent national interests.[2] The rapper's lyrics, distilled in the line "Je m'y oppose au nom de toute la nation" ["I stand against it in the name of the entire nation"], echo statements he makes offstage: that he aims to speak for his nation.[3] This chapter aims to articulate how "Plan Nord" constructs a unique imaginary. It analyzes how Samian's merging of Indigenous musical material with representative speech departs from previous attempts by others to appropriate throat singing in musical soundscapes that often create a very different national narrative.[4] This comparison clarifies the message promoted by Samian's work, focusing on its cultural and political salience to Canada as a country and its internal nations, and to ethical issues of representation raised by musical citation.[5]

Although recognizably in the hip hop style of Samian's other songs, "Plan Nord" constructs a distinctive sonic environment. Created in response to the development policy for Northern Quebec, it uses multiple sources to evoke a sound of the North: Samian strategically orients the listener by presenting sounds of wind and Inuit throat singing before introducing the melodic and rhythmic content.[6] Ethereal flute melodies and lyrical violin lines, as well as a generous application of echo, create a distant and reflective sound world into which Samian's rapped verses and electronic drum beats enter. The track samples music from a variety of genres, including Northern Drum, performed by a soloist and chorus. Sung in the tight nasal tone typical of this genre, a phrase performed on vocables offers a narrow melodic range and small fluctuations around a central pitch.[7] A genre typical of peyote music is sampled at the end of the song; the voice uses different vocables and a slower tempo than the intertribal powwow singing.[8] Offering contrast to the earlier sample, this melody is sung with an open tone and covers a wide range of pitches.

This musical context underscores Samian's lyrics in several ways. As the sampling of nature sounds suggests, Samian's lyrics convey a concern for the environment.[9] His opening critique is both a disagreement with the former Quebec government's Plan Nord and a yearning for the natural world:

> Le gouvernement a décidé de perdre le Nord
> Pour des diamants, de l'argent et de l'or
> Il prétend vivre dans un pays libre
> Mais ils ignorent que la nature est notre parfait équilibre[10]

In addition to the land, the rapper asks of the government, "avez-vous pensé aux gens qui habitent ces forêts" [Have you thought about the people who live in these forests?], bridging his concern also to the residents of the land he wishes to protect. His song, literally multivocal through the inclusion of sampled musicians and featured artists, speaks for a larger group of people: "je représente mon peuple à travers l'art / Et je vous annonce de leur part que le peuple en a marre" [I represent my people through art / And I tell you on their behalf that they have had enough]. Among other things, he tells his listener that he has become their voice of opposition to the Northern development plan.[11]

Samian, aka Samuel Tremblay (See figure 4.1), is from the community of Pikogan in Abitibi-Témiscamingue, Quebec; his publicity materials (Samian n.d.) highlight that he learned Algonquin while retracing his roots, which come from his Algonquin grandmother.

4.1 Samian. Photo by Allan Mc Eachearn.

Samian reports in a 2012 interview that his specific goal for the music and lyrics of "Plan Nord" is for listeners "vraiment de prendre conscience de la gravité de la chose" [to really become aware of the gravity of the situation]. What meanings does this Indigenous rapper living in Canada encode by layering French-language rapped lyrics, hip hop beats, sounds of nature, echo effects, throat singing, rattles, bells, intertribal music, and ritual song?

At first pass, the subject matter of the rapped lyrics could be heard to overlap neatly with the samples and contributions of the rapper's featured collaborators. As Plan Nord increases energy harvesting in the province's Northern lands, sounds of nature and the now-iconic throat singing could place a listener solidly in Canada's imagined North. What happens, however, when we dig deeper? Citing throat singing, Northern Drum, and ritual music in the same song creates a multivocal musical tableau from which Samian speaks to and for the nation. As is discussed later, Marie Belleau represents the North through Inuit throat singing: intertribal powwow music expands the Indigenous genres represented in this song. Plan Nord affects the Cree territory; Northern Drum can be heard as an aural reference to this group as well. Peyote songs share the unaccompanied setting, open tone, and low pitch of the musical material sampled at the end of the song. This style evokes ritual, which may bring its sacred context to "Plan Nord." For some listeners, this association may present the land and people in the song as warranting protection. Protecting them thus constitutes a sacred action: the sampled music can be heard as extending its ritual context to the song "Plan Nord."

Given frequent collaborations between Inuit throat singers and musicians across a variety of musical genres, as well as lively debates around many of these musical endeavours, Samian's collaboration with a musician from this style enters a fraught area. "Plan Nord" offers an aural snapshot of Canada's Northern landscape (see figure 4.2), yet the vision is only a partial reflection of reality: the focus on vast space created through wind and Indigenous cultural references creates a soundscape that is also an imagined one. While the song's subject matter justifies the use of specific samples, effects, and choices in featured artists, it offers its own interpretation of a national narrative.

"PLAN NORD": REPRESENTING POLICY

The Plan Nord, advanced by the Parti Libéral du Québec (PLQ), provides strategies for mining, forestry, energy production, and harvesting other natural resources in the portion of Quebec north of the 49th parallel and the Gulf of St Lawrence.[12] The PLQ considers the plan sustainable development and defended it on both the national and international stages (Huijgh 2012). In the 2012 document *Building Northern Quebec Together: The Project of a Generation*, the minister of natural resources promised that the plan would deliver development "combined with environmental protection," yet the plan came under severe critique when Premier Jean Charest presented it at the United Nations Conference on Sustainable Development in Rio de Janeiro (*Le Devoir*, 18 June 2012). A major concern is that the PLQ focused extensively on the economic benefits of the plan while failing to put sufficient effort into environmental protection and consulting Northern communities. Many environmentalists and Indigenous rights activists oppose the plan's imposition, including Ellen Gabriel, Innu Power (2011), and Anti-Capitalist Convergence Montreal (2012; see also Aive 2012). However it is viewed, parties involved recognize that Plan Nord territory is currently inhabited and that there are differences among how the population is represented. The area concerned, 72 percent of the total area of Quebec, is home to only 2 percent of Quebec's population, of which 27 percent is Indigenous (Gouvernement du Québec 2012, 4, 6). Given the large percentage of Quebec's land covered by the plan, the small percentage of the total population that lives in the area, and the significant proportion of the population that is Indigenous, what narrative might Quebec's government choose to promote?

In response to a politically divisive issue, the government of Quebec answered with rhetoric that celebrates the land as a frontier and offers symbols of people rather than realistic images of individual lives. Government publications addressing an internal audience portray a romanticist vision of the North. They highlight the land's richness as well as the cultures of the Indigenous groups that live in the area covered by the plan.[13] In the 2011 promotional pamphlet *Faire le Nord Ensemble: Le Chantier d'une Génération* (Gouvernement de Québec 2011), Premier Jean Charest's message reads, "Voilà pourquoi le Plan Nord. Pour prendre position dans ce monde nouveau ... Pour développer notre potentiel économique dans un partenariat de développement durable, respectueux des Premières Nations, des Inuits et des communautés locales" [This is why we need the Plan Nord. To establish ourselves in this new world … To develop our economic potential in partnership with sustainable development that is respectful of the First Nations, the Inuit, and local communities]. He continues, "Le Nord du Québec fascine par l'immensité du territoire et par l'envergure de ses possibilités. Aujourd'hui, le contexte est propice à sa redécouverte. Le Plan Nord, c'est le projet d'une génération de Québécois" [Quebec's North fascinates us with the immensity of its territory and the scope of its possibilities. Today, the context lends itself to its rediscovery. The Plan Nord is the project of a generation of Québécois]. Charest paints the territory as vast, always fascinating, and even ready to be rediscovered. The choice of the words "monde nouveau" serves two functions. First, it points towards an emerging global marketplace that Quebec would like to enter. Second, the phrase "new world" recalls earlier colonialism and paints the North as a frontier. Taken together with the second part of Charest's statement, the frontier narrative comes into even sharper focus. He tells his reader that this is the moment for the "rediscovery" of Quebec's North. This new world, ready for discovery, acts as a frontier for southern Québecois. With a continuing colonialist narrative, government publications suggest that, like frontiers of the Americas in the past, this land invites "development."

Representation of Northern people by government publicity materials also presents an ideal rather than a reality. A 2012 Plan Nord promotional publication, *Building Northern Quebec Together: The Project of a Generation*, features an image of two children bundled in warm clothes looking down over a snowy village. The photo foregrounds the *inuksuk* next to them. Used as the logo of the 2010 Vancouver Olympics, the *inuksuk* is becoming a well-known symbol of Inuit peoples, Indigenous Canadians, and Canada more generally. The text references "collaboration" with First Nations and Inuit peoples and principles of "respect for the Aboriginal culture and identity." A tourism brochure tells readers that the North's "vibrant, authentic cultures" will "make it a destination that is both original and appealing" (Ministère du Tourisme 2011). Cultural tourism draws on the "authenticity" of the region's peoples as another natural resource; the *inuksuk* becomes an icon for the culture celebrated in Plan Nord publicity.

Public opinion studies reveal the centrality of Arctic peoples and lands to contemporary Canadian identity. As Payette and Roussel (2011, 940) report, "the vast majority of Canadians identify with this region, even if very few of them ever travel to the Arctic." Surveys indicate that most Canadians consider the Arctic to be of great national importance, and Québécois largely agree with this national trend (Ekos Research Associates Inc. 2011; Ipsos Reid 2008). Southern Canada borrows cultural symbols from the land and peoples of this rich North. Samian's "Plan Nord" offers an alternative image of both the plan and the peoples it involves. His song does, however, provide a similarly iconic image of the Inuit as he makes his argument. Rather than the visual image of the *inuksuk*, Samian offers the sound of *katajjaq*.

HIP HOP POETICS IN "PLAN NORD"

As Inuit throat singing is frequently used in "art music" compositions, with and without permission, Samian's referencing of this same material enters complex territory. Through direct collaboration with throat singer Marie Belleau, Samian's featuring of an Inuit throat singer has the potential to assuage some of the concerns levied against other kinds of citation of *katajjaq*. A significant critique of art music compositions that cite Indigenous music is that they alter the cited music in inappropriate ways. Contemporary hip hop composition, however, allows for recorded sounds to be digitally layered into new works. Instead of a composer needing to write in the style of a cited piece of music or having non-Indigenous performers recreate it, this technique allows the work of a sampled or featured artist to be directly replayed. A second criticism of art music citations is that composers maintain a concert genre, such as a symphony, and embellish it with a citation from Indigenous cultural practices. This can be characterized as derived from compositional styles in the late nineteenth and early twentieth centuries that evoke nationalism by means of primitivist quotations. Unlike concert works that transform musical elements into window dressing on an already established form, the throat singing in this song is integral to the larger tapestry of the work. As demonstrated in figures 4.2 and 4.3, respectively, the progressive adding and then subtracting of tracks comprised of environmental sounds, Indigenous musics, and spoken Inuktitut language comprise the intro and outro of this song. Beginning a hip hop composition by layering in tracks at the beginning and then taking them out one by one at the end is common. However, the piece does not sound like rap: the intro and outro lack the beat that marks that genre. In this way, the sampled material actually transforms the listening experience from one that is distinctly hip hop to one that is hip hop and something else.[14] The Indigenous music sampled is not subsumed into the work; it maintains a distinct presence alongside the hip hop elements. Other electronic genres can also directly replay Indigenous music, and composers in other genres have the option to cite segments of this music prominently. In addition to hip hop com-

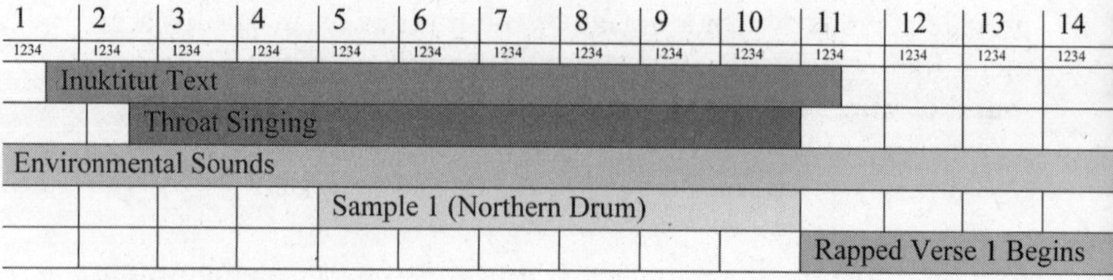

4.2 Groove Continuum (Intro).

position's layering style, the genre also has a popular history that makes its speaking on behalf of subaltern subjects unsurprising. From Samian's perspective in a 2012 interview, hip hop has a special role in political speech, as "le hip hop, c'est fait pour dénoncer des choses" [hip hop, it's made to denounce things]. He argues that from both its history and current use, the music is ideally suited to "parler au nom d'un peuple qui n'a pas de voix" [speak in the name of a people that does not have a voice]. This dual function of hip hop – to draw on a history of critique in order to denounce negative situations while also acting as representative speech on behalf of groups of people – makes the music both well situated to form political speech and poised to enter the fraught territory of taking over the right to speak for unheard others.[15]

After releasing two albums on the label 7ième ciel, *Face à soi-même* on 4 May 2010 and *Face à la musique* on 13 November 2007, Samian cut the single "Plan Nord." He recalls that he transitioned from being a poet to being an artist who collaborates in new ways. In a 2010 interview with Stefan Christoff, Samian offers, "I work with amazing musicians who are able to complement my verses with music. I think the relationship between my verses and the musicians that I collaborate with has become richer with time." The artist notes that, for his second album, "now that I work with musicians in developing my verses, the creative process has changed a lot" (ibid.). This collaborative process is audible on the single "Plan Nord" through how sounds are layered together.

Layering in existing sounds allows hip hop music to make references that are understandable to different groups of listeners. Some samples are hidden, requiring a breadth of background knowledge.[16] Others address a general audience, making their points via well-known sounds.[17] A clear example of the latter occurs between

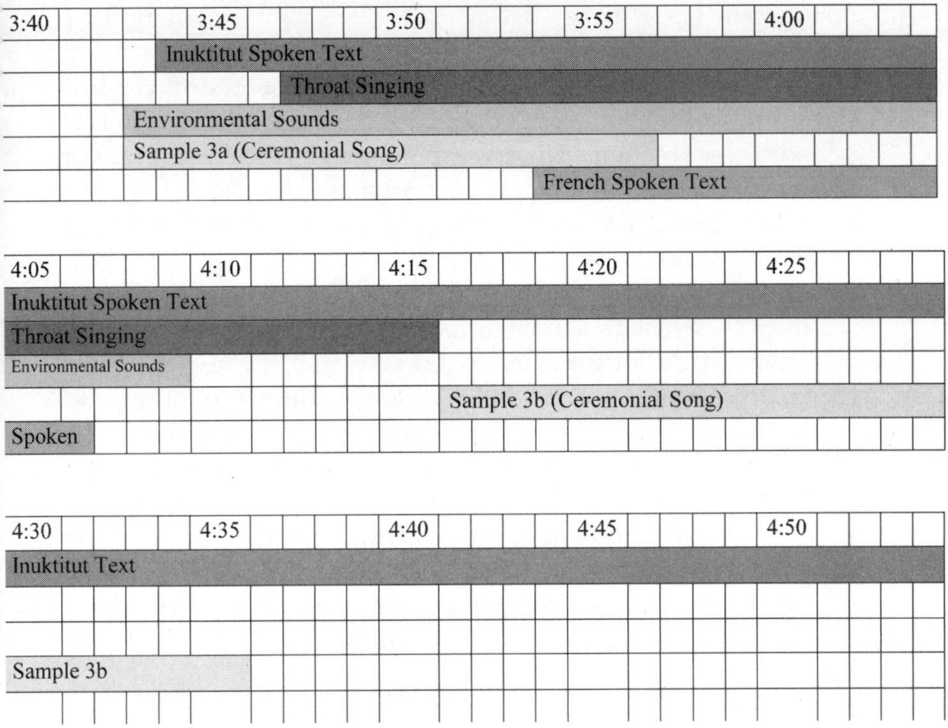

4.3 Groove Continuum (Outro).

verses three and four in "Plan Nord." After using a variety of nature sounds and music from other genres, the song incorporates the sound of a ticking clock. The timing of this citation allows the sound to convey the artist's message about the future. The rapped text has already used metaphor to portend effects of development. Verse one concludes with the lyrics, "Vous voulez profiter pour une seule generation / Mais ces terres nourrissent toute une population / Vous voulez déraciner tout le Nord québécois / Mais un jour vous comprendrez que l'argent ne se mange pas" [You want to profit for a single generation / But this earth feeds an entire population / You want to uproot the North of Quebec / But one day you will understand that money cannot be eaten]. Time appears in this verse as a contrast. Samian argues that those who support the Plan Nord are short-sighted and will later realize that they are no longer able to survive. This contrast in time continues in verses two and three, each of which ends with the warning that "un jour vous comprendrez que l'argent ne se mange pas" [one day you will understand that money cannot be eaten].

The directness of Samian's oppositional statement at the end of the fourth verse, "je m'y oppose au nom de toute la nation," is supported by his rhythmic delivery. After a speech-effusive flow at the beginning of the song, offering, for example, the text "chaîne alimentaire" [food chain] and "colline parlementaire" [Parliament Hill] on two short beats each, his rhythmic patterns change. Because of a pause in his delivery before each highlighted word, the emphasis on the lines "Les rivières sèchent, les arbres tombent. / Les avares se réjouissent, car le dollar monte" [the rivers dry up, the trees fall. / The cheapskates rejoice and the dollar climbs] is shifted to fall on the verbs "dry," "fall," "rejoice," and "rise." The natural world is subjected to the former pair of words, which indicates active decline, while the businesses claim the latter pair, which indicates ongoing ascent. These parallel actions demonstrate what will continue to happen if the plan goes ahead unchecked. Just after he makes this point through parallelism and rhythmic delivery, the sound of the ticking clock is incorporated. This sound is loud enough to be heard over other musical layers and clear enough to be easily distinguishable. The ticking here recalls a watch or a countdown clock, timing the parallel degradation of nature and amassing of private wealth, the moments until the business interests will be left with only their money to eat, the time it will take Québécois to realize they are making a mistake, or perhaps all three.

When I asked Samian in a 2012 interview why he chose to record "Plan Nord," he replied, "c'est simple. Pour moi c'est un cri du coeur" [It's simple. For me it's a cry from the heart]. A quotation is the seed of this composition: "l'inspiration vient de Sitting Bull" [the inspiration comes from Sitting Bull] he explains, whom Samian credits as saying, "quand vous avez coupés tous les arbres, quand vous avez pollués tous les rivières, quand vous avez tués tous les animaux, peut-être comprendrez-vous que l'argent se mange pas" [When you have cut down all the trees, when you have polluted all the rivers, when you have killed all the animals, maybe you will understand that money cannot be eaten].[18] The final line of this quotation forms the end of each of the first three verses; it informs the entire song.

This French quotation is layered with spoken Inuktitut words at the end of the song (see figure 4.3). The outro is not organized by the drums that were heard up to this point; instead, sounds of wind and waves accompany the Inuktitut text. Bells, violin, and throat singing are added over the flow of words. Marie Belleau, who grew up learning Inuktitut, also speaks French and English. She put the words together for this portion of the song in collaboration with her mother to make sure the significance was captured appropriately. In a 2013 interview, she describes crafting the words as an experience of looking for "a message that goes with song." The whispered words enumerate land, rivers, and flowers, and indicate that all of these are extremely important. The lyrics contrast this with the impermanence of money. In this way, both French and Inuktitut words lead listeners to the same conclusion: outside incursion into the North will have negative consequences for the land and its peoples. These ideas, which overlap in content, are sonically concomitant, literally weaving over each other in time as both Inuktitut and French languages are simultaneously uttered (see figure 4.3). At the close of the song, the Inuktitut text is once again foregrounded, and flute, violin, rattles, and group singing support the spoken words. The melancholy violin line rises in pitch slowly; echo makes the sound appear increasingly distant and murky.

Samian's move to speak for a people draws from the way he projects his message from a specific location. Wind and echoes conjure a Northern sound world. Throat singing, Northern Drum, and ritual musics further recall Inuit, Métis, and First Nations traditions of North America. Lyrically, Samian also harnesses the space of this land. He mentions "les plus belles rivières" [the most beautiful rivers] with their fishes. When he reminds listeners that "ces terres nourrissent toute une population" [this earth feeds an entire population], he calls attention to a life-giving force between earth and people. Layering techniques reinforce this link: the sounds of wind and culturally specific singing practices intermix. "Plan Nord" samples the "gens remplis de sagesse" [people full of wisdom] who inhabit this "territoire rempli de richesses" [land overflowing with riches]. In this light, Samian's concern for the uprooting of the forest takes on two meanings. The government wants to "déraciner tout le Nord québécois" [uproot the North of Quebec]. Understood literally and highlighted through sounds of nature, this refers to the uprooting of trees. Taken figuratively and supported by featuring Indigenous artists and sampling Indigenous musics, this uprooting also references a separation of people from culture. In his final verse, Samian's narrative voice speaks as one who has lived here for generations: "on habite ces terres depuis plus de dix mille ans" [we have lived here for more than ten thousand years]. It is both the land and its peoples that form the identity of the North.

Rappers often use markers of location and assert themselves as leaders, often using lyrics and musical signifiers of place to indicate that they speak for a larger group of people. As Tricia Rose (1994, 2) explains, "rappers speak with the voice of personal experience, taking on the identity of the observer or narrator." Some locations, often specific neighbourhoods or cities like the South Bronx or Compton, become locations imbued with larger meanings of realness for rappers who speak for groups via these places, while others never attain the ability to stand in for larger concepts.[19] The gendered nature of this representative speech is significant. It is male rappers who most often take on a universalizing tone, while female rappers far less frequently promise to become the voice of a diverse constituency (Marsh 2011). In "Plan Nord," Samian's lyrics explicitly state that he speaks for a larger group, notably with the phrases "Je représente mon peuple" and "je vous annonce de leur part" cited earlier. He goes so far as to announce that he speaks against the Plan Nord "au nom de toute la nation" [in the name of the entire nation]. Who is the nation for which Samian speaks? When Samian uses the word "nation," he creates an ambiguous reference. Speaking from Quebec, in which pockets of separatist enthusiasm continue to thrive, "nation" may refer to the larger country of Canada, to Quebec as a distinct entity within Canada, or to a potential future independent francophone nation. Musical references to multiple kinds of Inuit and First Nations musical practices complicate the idea of "nation" further. Through cited sound, "Plan Nord" pulls from not one nation but, rather, from multiple First Nations.

That the word "nation" is imprecise is instructive. Listeners bring their own ideas of "nation" to the song "Plan Nord"; indeed, Samian's own description of the word is complex. When I asked him about his use of the word "nation," Samian reported, "je pense a ce qui vivent au Québec, en fait … les Premiers Nations, et les Québecois" [I think of everyone who lives in Quebec, actually … First Nations peoples and Québécois]. By referring to the two groups distinctly, Samian draws a separation between First Nations and Québécois. Though he may refer to the groups separately, he reassured me that he is not just speaking for Indigenous peoples or for Northern peoples but that "quand je dis 'toute la nation,' c'est vraiment tout le monde au

Québec" [when I say the entire nation, it's really everyone in Quebec]. These internal divisions – between north and south, between Indigenous and non- Indigenous – demonstrate a lack of uniformity within the "nation" for whom Samian aims to speak even as he professes to portray a uniform position.

His claim that he is able to speak for such a large and diverse group of people has precedent in hip hop as Rose (1994) and Forman (2008) have noted; it may yet cause anxiety among listeners. Using this song as an attempt to speak from multiple communities, Samian offers an opportunity for voices to be heard at rallies and debates that might otherwise be silenced. Some critics of the Plan Nord suggest that Northern groups most affected by it were not adequately consulted during the planning process, so the song can be heard as an attempt to give voice back to First Nations, and particularly Inuit, communities. As Samian explains, "on ne peut pas ignorer les Inuits" [we cannot ignore the Inuit]. Yet by extending voice to certain people and ideas within the schema of his musical work, Samian takes on representative speech on behalf of those same groups. As he explains, with this song, "on est leur voix, simplement" [simply put, we are their voice]. Despite Samian's desire to speak for a certain group of people, not everyone who is Québécois, or First Nations, or Inuit, or Canadian, or who falls under any of the other possible interpretations of the "nation" represented will agree with his message.

Layering sounds from multiple genres further complicates the qualms raised by this kind of representative speech. Debates continue on how representations of Indigenous, particularly Inuit, peoples are sometimes used unethically: no use of an *inuksuk* or *katajjaq* occurs outside of this context. The re-presentation of a culturally specific sound in a new composition may come off as what Tara Rodgers (2003, 318) terms "a sort of sonic colonialism, whereby aural fragments are used for perceived 'exotic' effect, without investment in, or engagement with, the music culture from which the sample was gathered." While much energy has been dedicated in scholarship to working through concerns of the ethics of citation and musical appropriation, no consensus yet exists.[20] It is not the prerogative of this chapter to deem some compositional practices ethical and others unethical;[21] rather, it is to consider how hip hop collaboration invokes questions of ethics and aesthetics differently than do other genres.

In "Plan Nord," Samian collaborates with a featured Inuit artist. This strategy of working together may lessen the kinds of exoticist concerns to which Rodgers gestures, yet certain listeners will no doubt prickle upon hearing the ubiquitous timbre of vocal games recontextualized. Given throat singing's central location in the construction of Canadian multicultural identities, its citation inspires both increased attention to ethics and problematization of the way it evokes "nation." Despite collaborative compositional style, this kind of musical fusion faces problems that are yet unsolved: there is no agreement about who can sanction using *katajjaq*; there is no defined structure for investment in the musical culture. For some listeners, Samian creates a feeling of solidarity by drawing on his background as Québécois, as Indigenous, and as an environmentalist when he claims to speak for the "nation." Describing his own motivations, Samian reports, "je parle de ma communauté, je parle des réserves, je parle de ce que, de ce que les gens ignore un peu au Québec … C'est un génocide extrêmement silencieux ce qui se passe avec nous au Canada. So voila, je fais du rap pour parler de qui on est." [I speak about my community, I speak about reserves, I talk about, about what people ignore a little in Quebec. It's an extremely silent genocide that is happening to us in Canada. So there, I rap to talk about who we are] ("On se met au point avec Samian" 2012).

SINGING AND COLLABORATION

Marie Belleau's performance of Inuit throat singing in "Plan Nord" is consistent in sound with other instantiations of this genre, though her use of digital recording technology demonstrates one of the ways in which the practice has changed over time. This music differs based on location and function, yet Jean-Jacques Nattiez (1999, 403) notes that *katajjaq* of Northern Quebec share "rhythmic and morpheme patterns, intonation contours, voiced/voiceless and inhaled/exhaled sound patterns."[22] A solo vocalist occasionally performs the music, but two or more people frequently participate in songs. Singers inhale and exhale in rhythmic patterns, creating sounds both on and off the voice. Throat singing is alternately a game of skill, an activity to pass time, a way to tell stories, and, according to some participants, a strategy to encourage the return of geese or bring men back from hunting.[23] As an extended technique, throat singing requires control of the voice that is beyond what many singers possess. Marie Belleau explains in a 2013 interview that, for the practice, "it's as if you have a watch mechanism that's all rusty, that's a regular person's throat. In order to throat sing, you have to slowly move it, slowly oil it, start getting the rust off to start producing all the sounds."

Belleau's vocals on "Plan Nord" offer only some of the numerous expressions of which the genre is capable. In other songs, Belleau sings mimetically, mimicking animals on tracks including "Nirliq/Canada Geese." For this collaboration, however, she provides solo vocalizations that convey repeated rhythmic patterns and a strong sense of breath rather than melody, mimesis, or improvisation. In another song of hers, "Bloom," she layers flute and throat singing with a beat; she is the only singer on the track. While there is some variation, throat singing is often practised by two singers who face each other and sing together. It is an important departure, then, that, like on this solo track, Belleau does not have a singing partner for "Plan Nord"; rather, she uses studio technology to sing both parts with herself. Belleau explains in the same interview, "we recorded one track, they would play it in my headset and I would respond to it ... It was a bit tricky in the beginning because usually you are face to face and we are holding each other's arms, you usually have the visual. I had none of that. It was hard to get into that." While she describes the studio process as "trickier than in real life," the singer says she got the hang of recording in this way and it ended up sounding good. Belleau notes the difference in the embodied practice of singing alone, a shift that digital audio recording allows. Charity Marsh (2009a, 119) has observed, "for young people living in Nunavut, hip hop has become a medium (space/place) to connect practices read and understood as both 'traditional' and 'contemporary' Inuit culture with recognized global cultures." This example of studio-mediated throat singing worked into a hip hop song demonstrates such an encounter. The "traditional" and "contemporary" no longer exist in separate spheres as musical practices meet and mutually transform. This digitally recorded duet is layered with environmental sounds, as shown on the Groove Continuum (see figure 4.3); wind situates the song outdoors. Delay effects are applied to the instrumental tracks layered with her vocals, creating a sense of cavernous open space.

Vocal games are not the most commonly practised traditional Inuit music, yet they have come to represent both Inuit culture and Canada.[24] Numerous composers have used the identifiable and rich music as recorded sound, imitated sound, or via collaboration with throat singers.[25] This phenomenon is most notable in art music compositions.[26] While *katajjaq* is geographically centred in the Arctic, composer Christos Hatzis (1999, para. 10) believes that it stands for the larger nation of Canada: "Nunavut ('our land' or 'homeland' in Inuktitut, the language of the Inuit) is to me an appellation for the whole of Canada, not just the newly founded territory of Nunavut." Using Nunavut as metonym for Canada, the composer contributes to a narrative that foregrounds Canada's ownership of a Northern frontier. *Katajjaq* also serves an identity-forming function in the North beyond individual community practice. Within Nunavut, current efforts endeavour to reflect Inuit cultural knowledge within the workings of the territory's government. The *Qaujimajatuqangit* (Traditional Inuit knowledge) task force argues for the use of the Inuktitut language and insists that cultural symbols like singing should have a central role in quotidian government activities (Mancini and Mancini 2007). These inclusion efforts may be seen as symbolic, adding customs to a pre-existing structure without profoundly altering it. At the same time, they offer a less overtly exclusionary rhetoric.[27] These inclusions can be seen as examples of lived and official multiculturalism, and are together part of the hegemonic narrative of Canadian identity against which syncretic songs like "Plan Nord" are counterposed.

SYNCRETISM IN CANADIAN MULTICULTURALIST NARRATIVES

Scholarly and popular commentary often cite mixture or fusion as contributing to the Canadian sound (Diamond and Witmer 1994). Elaine Keillor (2008) calls "rababou," or musical mixture, constitutive of sound particular to Quebec. This mixture draws from French, British, and German influences as well as Indigenous musics for its timbres, rhythms, and textures. Keillor posits that the 1858 work *Stadaconé* is the first iteration of this in art music as it draws from the composer's idea of Iroquois elements – repetition and use of accents. This typifies later fusions as well: Indigenous elements are subsumed into European forms rather than, for example, French musical gestures being added into an Iroquois song.[28] Ralston Saul offers a similar narrative of syncretism, arguing that, as Canadians, "we are a Métis civilization" (in Robinson 2012, 226). While Dylan Robinson (2012) argues that uncritical acceptance of this métissage poses risks, he echoes the many instances in which Canadian music includes fusion.[29] Recent compositions bear out these assertions; iterations of

Indigenous musics as focal point for Québécois and Canadian identity are frequent.[30]

Just as many composers and critics cite musical syncretism as constitutive of Canadian music, many national narratives, especially those put forth in some government publications, cite multiculturalism as constitutive of Canadianness.[31] Samian's featuring of *katajjaq* portrays a particular Canadian narrative that stretches the definition of Canada as multicultural. His dynamic effort can in some ways be heard as avoiding the cultural reification that government rhetoric depicts. The multiculturalist narrative put forward in government documents is one of unproblematized celebration. According to Citizenship and Immigration Canada's (2012) *Annual Report on the Operation of the Canadian Multiculturalism Act, 2010-2011*: "Canadian multiculturalism is fundamental to our belief that all citizens are equal. Multiculturalism ensures that all citizens can keep their identities, can take pride in their ancestry and have a sense of belonging." Furthermore, it underlines the need for acceptance and integration: "Acceptance gives Canadians a feeling of security and self-confidence, making them more open to, and accepting of, diverse cultures… [and] encourag[es] them to integrate into their society and take an active part in its social, cultural, economic and political affairs" (ibid.). Through multiculturalism, this neoliberal viewpoint suggests, all citizens are invited to fully participate in established systems.

Multiculturalism is interpreted differently in Quebec than in the rest of Canada.[32] A narrative that establishes all cultures as equal, some Québécois fear, could weaken the special status of francophone Canadians (Erfurt 2010). The Québécois policy of interculturalism, thus, highlights that Quebec is a pluralistic society and encourages all to participate democratically while still underlining that the province is thoroughly francophone.[33] Interculturalism as policy contributes to an understanding of acceptance of other cultures without "implying any intrinsic equality among them. Diversity is tolerated and encouraged, but only from within a framework that establishes the unquestioned supremacy of French in the language and culture of Québec" (Leman 1999, 13). The local policy of interculturalism and the national policy of multiculturalism are reflected in decisions that affect residents of Quebec as well as in narratives that describe their identities.

Criticism of multiculturalist and interculturalist policy attacks both the degree to which it provides all citizens with access and whether full participation in established systems is beneficial for all parties.[34] While critics have requested and foretold its demise, multiculturalism continues to play an active role in public policy (Christensen 2012). Indigenous populations are increasingly acknowledged as a founding people of Canada, yet their role in contemporary multicultural society is debated.[35] The particular legal and historical position of Indigenous peoples in Canada establishes these groups as different from other subgroups; critiques arguing that Indigenous peoples are not justly treated under Canadian diversity policy abound (Blackburn 2009; Srikanth 2012; Maaka and Fleras 2005; and Alfred 2001). Contrary to the stated ambitions of the Canadian Multiculturalism Act, critics assert that it has had negative effects (Ahmad Ali 2010). These critiques focus both on lived and official multiculturalisms, or the quotidian experiences of Canadians facing racism and inequality and the ideological implications of the policy. Ethnographies reveal the difference between narratives of multiculturalism as celebratory and the lived experience of racism that non-white Canadians encounter. Mehrunnisa Ahmad Ali (2010, 100) traces second-generation youth who live in ethnically diverse neighbourhoods, noting that leaving the neighbourhood for the larger city reveals to them the "boundaries of their naïve faith in the promise of Canadian multiculturalism." The ideology of equality is revealed as empty when these "visible minority" Canadians leave a protected sphere.

Multiculturalism has also been critiqued as a substitute for reform. Himani Bannerji (2000, 89) reflects, "we demanded some genuine reforms, some changes – some among us even demanded the end of racist capitalism – and instead we got 'multiculturalism.'" Multiculturalism did not coincide with substantive changes in how policy was applied; as in the case of *Qaujimajatuqangit*, demonstrated earlier, cultural visibility does not necessarily coincide with responsible policy. A further concern with multiculturalist policy is how it instantiates "communities." As Bannerji describes it, because of the policy, "'communities' and their leaders or representatives were created by and through the state, and they called for funding and promised 'essential services' for their 'communities,' such as the preservation of their identities" (ibid.). The communities in question are created entities. How they are defined, which voices are seen as worth promoting through funding, how leadership is acknowledged, and the messages of a preserved identity are all controlled by the same structures that create them.

Finally, multiculturalism as policy has been critiqued for creating a situation in which unmarked (white, European-descended) Canadians are at the centre and those who qualify as diverse (including Indigenous peoples and certain recent immigrants) are on the periphery. Eva Mackey (1999, 85, emphasis in original) describes "official multiculturalism" as "a discourse in which minority groups are valued for their *contributions* to the Canadian nation." In this conceptualization, the Canadian nation already exists before the "contributions" of minority groups. This is problematic for two reasons. First, it indicates that the Canadian nation exists as an entity without these groups. This marks minority groups as capable of augmenting a pre-existing nation and thus as not fundamentally constitutive of it. Second, the power dynamic of official multiculturalism is such that the unmarked nation can take the contributions that it desires from minority groups, placing a (unmarked) nation at the centre and (marked) minorities at the margins. The power structure imposed during colonialism remains unchecked as "the people of other cultures, their artefacts and customs, their *difference* from the unmarked national culture are defined always so that Canada, and the construction of a unified Canadian identity along Western principles of progress, are *first* (ibid., 89, emphasis in original). Emphasizing this centre-periphery problem, Richard Day (2000, 5) insists: "the problem of Canadian diversity … has always involved state sponsored attempts to define, know, and structure the actions of a field of problematic Others (Savages, Québécois, Half-breeds, Immigrants,) who have been distinguished from the unproblematic Selves (French, British, British-Canadian, European) through a variety of means (civilization, humanity, race, culture, ethnicity, ethnocultural origin)."

This list of Other-Self pairings demonstrates a historical lineage of subgroups created within Canada, reflecting a notion that diversity is both a long-standing situation and often-reproduced problem. Trenchantly, Day names Indigenous and Québécois figures as Others; the rapper Samian may be included in both of these subgroups.

The effects of official multiculturalism are felt through a process in which, as Bannerji (2000, 100) explains, "non-European 'others' are made to lend support to the enterprise by their existence as a tolerated, managed difference." Official discourses and government policies involved in constructing these "others" have changed over time; the role of Indigenous peoples has recently become more central to this official multiculturalism. Celebrations of Inuit, Métis, and First

Nations culture within Canada can be interpreted as propping up an image of settler Canadians as tolerant. Further, the inclusion of Indigenous cultural markers within narratives that celebrate provincial and national governments may be seen as legitimizing those governments and minimizing past and ongoing colonial practices (Wolfe 2006). Despite concrete efforts on the part of First Nations, including land claims and sovereignty projects, Bannerji (2000, 92) explains, "there is a remarkable and a determined marginalization of First Nations. And yet their presence is as the absent signifiers within Canadian national politics works at all times as a bedrock of its national definitional project, giving it a very peculiar contour through the same absences, silences, exclusions, and marginalizations." At the same time that Indigenous residents of Canada experience racism and structural inequalities, cultural symbols are proposed as identifiers of provincial and national identity. Citing *katajjaq* music, then, can be heard as advancing a narrative of diversity, adding colour to a national identity, and continuing to locate Indigenous peoples outside of the power centre of Canadian political and social structures. Analyzing the inclusion of tepees at the Canadian Museum of Civilization, Mackey (1999, 78) asserts that "the tepees send the signal that Canada recognizes its Aboriginal peoples … But although Native people are highlighted as Canada's heritage, they are at the same time frozen in the glorious past of tepees and headdresses." This freezing of culture, particularly a freezing of culture in the past, is a risk posed by citation of "traditional" musical forms. Taken uncritically, this can play into the larger problem of reifying cultures that multiculturalism poses.

The mosaic is frequently offered as a symbol of Canadian multiculturalism (Bannerji 2000, 16). In this image, discrete pieces come together to form a larger picture without losing their particularity. This narrative of unity encounters problems when faced with lived realities. As Day (2000, 12, emphasis in original) argues, "only by *abandoning* the dream of unity" could Canada "lead the way towards a future that will be shared by many other nation-states." If equality is indeed a goal, "it may, in its failure to achieve a universal mass identity, or even a universal mass of identities, inadvertently come closer to its goal of mutual and equal recognition amongst all who have chanced to find themselves within its borders" (ibid.). Not only will the yearning for a single unified identity ultimately remain unfulfilled, but the individual pieces of identities that a national multicultural narrative includes are themselves specious. It is practical to have discrete segments to make a mosaic. In order to create a nation from individual communities, these must be represented as static. Communities lack the static quality that this representation requires of them. As described earlier, symbols of the North are deployed in a larger demonstration of Canadian multiculturalism. The *inuksuk* and *katajjaq* promote an idea of the North that becomes subsumed within a larger idea of Canada. In this way, this move constructs Inuit culture as a static piece of the mosaic, a conceptualization that is limiting. "Plan Nord" can in some ways be seen as attempting to avoid this problem as the use of a studio sound and hip hop aesthetic bring this piece into the contemporary realm.

National narratives often rely on many sets of people with fixed identities – Immigrants, Indigenous Canadians, and others – as discrete groups, while the actual experience of Canadians is more likely to include fluid and mixed identities. The Canadian national narrative that is advanced by citing *katajjaq* or depicting the *inuksuk* shows Canada as possessing something unusual – the North. This becomes part of a national narrative as Canada presents itself to the international community. In contrast, Stuart Hall points out that identity is most productively understood as becoming, not being. Indeed, he recalls the difficulty of representing a "diverse people" with a "single, hegemonic 'identity,'" though government agencies and figures often attempt to do so (Hall 1996, 119). In the "Plan Nord" collaboration, artists who are both francophone and Indigenous inhabit this mutable space. They navigate a sort of "in-betweenness" that spans multiple conceptions of home in physical, linguistic, and musical senses (Diamond, Crowdy, and Downes 2008, 6). Belleau notes the need for locations in Nunavut where Inuit people can speak French, recognizing the small but relevant minority of francophone Inuit (George 2009). Narratives that cite the Canadian mosaic require a myriad of distinct pieces, a compilation of static identities to make the larger picture of the whole. "Plan Nord" demonstrates that this vision is not sufficient for many individuals as inhabiting both traditional and modern, urban and rural, north and south, with a language basis in French and Inuktitut or Algonquin, presents a lived reality that does not fit the mosaic narrative.

As Samian wishes to speak for a variety of people, his citation of multiple musical styles is significant. The act of throat singing itself restores past traditions. As Frantz Fanon (1963, 210) argues, "the claim to a national culture in the past" is able to "rehabilitate the nation and serve as a justification for the hope of the future national culture." This action is necessary as "colonialism is not satisfied merely with holding a people in its grip and emptying the native's brain of all form and content. By a kind of perverted logic, it turns to the past of the oppressed people, and distorts, disfigures, and destroys it" (ibid.). Samian's recuperation of his ancestors' Algonquin language, Belleau's relearning of Inuktitut, and Belleau's and other Inuit people's learning throat singing, demonstrate the recovery and reformation of culture that has been uprooted and altered by colonialism. Here, through music that reclaims Indigenous cultural expression, the artists work together to present a political statement about how land is being changed by policy.

Samian offers his own take on how national narratives are constructed. He recalls in a 2010 interview:

> In Quebec, we have a national slogan: Je me souviens. But really, what do we remember in Quebec? In Quebec we forget some of the biggest parts of our own history. How was Quebec and Canada founded? What ever happened to the people who originally lived here? Why does the world forget that there are over five hundred languages spoken across Canada, and not just English and French? So much about our history has been hidden or erased, and so young people never learn about the First Peoples. These are all questions that – incredibly – aren't well answered in our schoolbooks. The government is also directly responsible for the lack of knowledge about our history, because Indigenous culture and history is not a priority, and not taught seriously within the public school curriculum.

Samian references one kind of memory that makes up the nation. Here, he references an official discourse that government agencies convey through school curricula and textbooks. Another kind of memory that creates nation here is the living history conveyed in and by Indigenous languages. As Samian reminds his listeners, these continue to be spoken throughout Canada. The English/French dichotomy that plays out in many narratives of multiculturalism does not include attention to the lived and living history of Indigenous peoples the way Samian understands it. From this vantage point, Samian's music is able to further reinforce his alternative national narrative.

CONCLUSION

Many narratives cite multiculturalism as an intrinsic component of a Canadian identity, just as scholars frequently define musical syncretism as intrinsic to a Canadian sound. There is a useful parallelism here. First, it demonstrates the creation of a national narrative in which the stitching together of distinct cultural sources, be they communities of people or musical motifs, creates a syncretic whole. Like a mosaic, it takes on a distinct identity only when pieced together. A musical or national whole by this logic preserves the stable identity of each constituent piece; it is the fusion of these pieces that consists in a transformational action. Furthermore, highlighting this parallelism allows for counter-narratives applied to one situation to question the other. In other words, as Richard Day (2000, 12) suggests, giving up on a single national identity or a "universal mass of identities" will allow individuals to find a place for themselves within the nation. This is equally applicable to musical composition. The creation of a national musical narrative often relies on specific sounds. For Canada, this is increasingly the use of environmental sounds and Inuit throat singing; selecting these elements necessarily means not selecting others. It also moves elements of living cultural practice into a sphere of official recognition. This runs the risk of making these living practices into static symbols, and it may also create a situation in which voices that stand for the nation musically are not heard when the conversation moves to policy issues. As narratives of nation interact with policies that affect majority and minority populations, the crafting of rhetoric profoundly affects the daily lives of individuals. In Canada in particular, the ideology of multiculturalism first helps to create and then differently affects discrete segments of the country's citizenry. Conceptualizing identity as fixed, as malleable, or as community-based has differing impacts on creating both national identity and policy. In this context, contemporary hip hop responses have the ability to challenge the notion of a national mosaic of static pieces by presenting a dynamic representation of cultures.

"Plan Nord" invites the listener to consider how musico-national narratives are emerging in a twenty-first-century context and demonstrates a contested instance of Indigenous culture being used to represent Canada as a whole. As Indigenous peoples are being increasingly included in multiculturalist narratives, Indigenous culture is being used as a symbol of nation. This is problematic as symbolic inclusion does not change structural policies that continue to have disadvantageous effects on many Indigenous people living in Canada. Second, the very structure of multiculturalism both requires static identities and assumes an unmarked centre to which, as Mackey describes, "multicultural" Canadians contribute. Urban Indigenous people living in Canada, like other Canadians, have fluid and complex identities and thus are not well represented as static pieces from which a larger culture can be depicted. Further, multiculturalism depicts Indigenous peoples, like other people in Canada racialized as non-white Others, as continually on the periphery.

As the analysis of different responses to the Plan Nord has shown, this process of representation is complex. While government messaging depicts the North through reified stereotypes of Inuit culture, Samian and his collaborators attempt to provide a dynamic vision of the North, one that includes the voices of those it aims to represent. Even in this collaborative context, however, recordings of throat singing can present reified culture. The specific selection of featured and sampled sounds invites a familiar debate on ethics of representation: the use of *katajjaq* is charged, even when grounded in a concrete location. Samian is not unusual among (male) MCs in that he speaks from a location and aims to speak for a larger group of people. Speaking for larger groups is complicated in this situation, as it is for other rappers, as it silences and elides some voices as it coheres around a message. While far from a utopic solution to a complex problem, hip hop collaborations do offer possibilities for representational strategies. The structure of this composition affects the power dynamics between participants as hip hop offers a formally distinct way to combine sounds that provoke standing debates on ethics of representation. "Plan Nord" offers a crucial perspective that is under-heard in the political realm – that of young, urban Indigenous individuals. Further, the layered compositional style of hip hop and the use of recorded sound means that contributors' voices are literally replayed and that their contributions are on the same scale as other elements of the piece. In its social context, hip hop draws from a history of critique and has an origin story in the subaltern, making this a well-suited musical format for resistance. Unlike compositions that fuse Indigenous music into European forms, Samian's use of the layering structure in hip hop composition allows for the incorporation of many kinds of music in a way that allows them to change the overall aesthetic of "Plan Nord."

In the context of government-deployed narratives of nation, the collaborators in "Plan Nord" offer an alternative strategy that has multiple implications. This could indicate a way to go forward, as future compositions that include Indigenous musics could consider factors that Samian and his collaborators faced: What is the nature of the collaboration between the primary named author and the collaborators? Does the compositional style allow for collaborators' voices to come through? How can multivocality resist the reification of cultural stereotypes? How aware are artists of the ways their song can become representative speech? It could demonstrate yet another situation in which a musical voice from the North becomes part of a national narrative without the full participation of a community that it represents. Or perhaps, the layering of voices that comes through in this song can be heard as the cacophony of opinions, individuals, and groups that are part of any aesthetic response to a debated political situation.

APPENDIX I: "PLAN NORD" LYRICS

These lyrics appear as published on Samian's website, www.samian.ca/plannord.

Translation by the author.

Le gouvernement a décidé de perdre le Nord
Pour des diamants, de l'argent et de l'or
Il prétend vivre dans un pays libre
Mais ils ignorent que la nature est notre parfait équilibre
Trop de consommation pour des biens matériels
On est en train de perdre le Nord et les enjeux sont réels
Vous profitez de la terre pour vos propres envies
Sans même réaliser qu'elle nous maintient en vie
Vous voulez profiter pour une seule génération
Mais ces terres nourrissent toute une population
Vous voulez déraciner tout le Nord québécois
Mais un jour vous comprendrez que l'argent ne se mange pas…
T'inquiète j'ai compris, c'est une question de business
Vous gouvernez un territoire rempli de richesses
Ne venez surtout pas me faire croire que cette terre vous appartient
C'est plutôt grâce à elle qu'on respire chaque matin
Je représente mon peuple à travers l'art

Et je vous annonce de leur part que le peuple en a marre
Mais on connait vos politiques, des êtres obsédés
Là où y reste un peu d'air frais, vous devez le posséder
Vous faites même basculer notre chaîne alimentaire
Assis bien au chaud sur la colline parlementaire
Vous pensez refaire le monde avec votre projet de loi
Mais un jour vous comprendrez que l'argent ne se mange pas…
J'ai vu sur ces terres les plus belles rivières
Mais à cause de vos mines, les poissons ont le cancer
Nos ressources naturelles s'épuisent rapidement
Tout ça pour aller vivre près des tours de ciment
Les rivières sèchent, les arbres tombent
Les avares se réjouissent, car le dollar monte
Les esclaves de l'argent n'auront rien dans leur tombe
On fait tous des erreurs, mais à leur place j'aurais honte
On sera tous concernés quand la terre sonnera son heure
Je veux juste vous rappeler que vous commettez une grave erreur
Je suis honnête avec vous, votre politique me déçoit
Mais un jour vous comprendrez que l'argent ne se mange pas…
Sur ces terres, il y a des gens remplis de sagesse
Enfermés dans vos réserves prisonniers de vos gestes
Qui protège ce territoire depuis la nuit des temps
Parce qu'on habite ces terres depuis plus de dix mille ans
Avez-vous pensé aux gens qui habitent ces forêts?
Vous avez mal calculé l'impact de votre projet
Cette terre est fragile, sauvage et indemne
Aussi riche et fertile qu'une terre africaine
On ne peut la posséder cette terre nous a élevé
On doit la protéger elle est mère de l'humanité
Le plan nord repose sur une génération
Je m'y oppose au nom de toute la nation!

The government has decided to lose the North
For diamonds, silver, and gold.
It pretends to live in a free country
But they never knew that nature is our perfect balance
Too much consumption for the material goods
We are on track to lose the North and the stakes are real.
You profit from the earth for your personal desires
Without even realizing that she keeps us alive

You want to profit for a single generation
But this land feeds an entire population
You want to uproot all of Northern Quebec
But one day you will understand that money cannot be eaten …

I get it, I understand, it's a question of business
You govern a territory full of riches
Don't try to make me believe that this land is yours
Rather it is thanks to her that one can breathe every morning
I represent my people through art,
And I tell you on their behalf that they have had enough
But we know your politics, you obsessed beings
Wherever there is a little fresh air – you must possess it
You even break the food chain
Comfortably seated up there on Parliament Hill
You plan to remake the world with your law project
But one day you will understand that money cannot be eaten…

I've seen on this earth the most beautiful rivers
But because of your mines, the fish have cancer.
Our natural resources are quickly being depleted
All that in order to go live near cement towers
The rivers dry up, the trees fall
The cheapskates rejoice because the dollar climbs
Slaves of money have nothing in their tomb
We all make mistakes, but in their place, I'd be ashamed
We will all be implicated when the earth marks its hour
I just want to remind you that you are making a fatal mistake
I'm honest with you, your politics deceive me
But one day you will understand that money cannot be eaten …

On this earth, there are people full of wisdom
Shut away in your reserves, prisoners of your actions
Who protect this land from the beginning of time
Because we have lived on these lands for more than ten thousand years
Have you thought about the people who live in these forests?
You have poorly estimated the impact of your project.
This land is fragile, wild and unscathed
As rich and fertile as African land

One cannot own the land that has raised us
We need to protect her, she is the mother of humanity
The Northern Plan will impact a generation
I stand against it in the name of the entire nation.

NOTES

In this chapter I use the terms "Indigenous," "Aboriginal," "First Nations," and "Inuit," depending on the specific context of each statement. Currently within Canada the term "Aboriginal" is inclusive of First Nations, Métis, and Inuit people. However, from a social justice perspective, and in agreement with current scholarly conventions, the term "Indigenous" may be a preferred choice. Additionally, all interviews are by the author unless otherwise noted.

1 "Plan Nord" was produced by Félix-Antoine Leroux and features the throat singing of Marie Belleau as well as François Lalonde on drums and Jonathan Tobin on guitar and keyboard.

2 Also referred to as *katajjaq* or *les jeux vocaux.*

3 All translations by the author unless otherwise noted.

4 The term "imaginary" here derives from Anderson's (2006, 6) notion of imagined community, in which "communities are … distinguished not by their falsity/genuineness, but by the way in which they are imagined."

5 First Nations in Canada can be understood as distinct nations contained within the country of Canada (see Flanagan 2000). Specifics on the construction of the province of Quebec and the Québécois people as another interpretation of nation are detailed in Carment, Harvey, and Stack (2001) and Warren (2003).

6 Robinson (2012, 222) refers to the use of loon calls and Inuit throat songs to evoke Canadianness. The myth of the North and its myriad representations in film, music, literature, and visual arts are described in detail in Morissonneau (1978) and Grace (2001).

7 Useful resources from a vast powwow literature include Goertzen (2001), Scales (2007), and Ellis, Lassiter, and Dunham (2005).

8 Peyote songs refer to a category of ritual music now often associated with the Native American Church. This genre, which includes influence from Apache and Navajo music, varies widely, but its sonic and ritual elements are clearly distinct from powwow music. The singing style is less nasal, though, like powwow, non-lexical text is often employed. Refer to McAllester (1949) and Lassiter (2001).

9 Connections between sound, culture, and environment are taken up in the emerging discipline of ecomusicology, which "considers musical and sonic issues, both textual and performative, related to ecology and the natural environment" (Allen 2012, 375).

10 "The government has decided to lose the North / For diamonds, silver and gold / It pretends to live in a free country / But they forget that nature is our perfect balance."

11 The complete lyrics appear in Appendix 1.

12 When Samian released "Plan Nord," the PLQ was in power. The Parti Québécois (PQ) has since been elected with a minority government. It promotes altering but not destroying the Plan Nord. The history and fallout of the Plan Nord is summarized in Chalifoux et al. (2011), Cousineau (2012), and Lévis (2011).

13 Government materials cite four groups (Inuit, Cree, Innu, and Naksapi), while it could be argued that the Attikamek and Algonquin are also affected.

14 "Plan Nord" differs from the songs of many other Indigenous hip hop artists who cite Indigenous music of other genres. Rather than citing small segments of music, the cited sounds change the aesthetic of the piece's entire intro and outro.

15 Rose (1994) describes a history of critique in detail. For analysis of examples, refer to Demers (2003).

16 When artists engage in parody or make response records, listeners who are able to identify the source sounds can engage with the references, while those who cannot do not have access to this level of meaning. The use of extremely short or obscure clips can also create exclusivity in listenership. For a description of this kind of sampling, in which a hip hop listener's ability to find and identify samples can be not just a source of pleasure but a way to establish credibility and garner respect, see Schloss (2004).

17 Goodwin calls attention to types of sampling that are easily understood as using sounds from other sources. DJs play with samples to show off their skill in manipulation of sounds; the manipulation itself is obvious (see Goodwin 1990). The way samples are harmonized can also make them more seamless or more noticeable, if the harmonization is jarring (see Krims 2007).

18 This citation has not been conclusively attributed to a single author. Various sources attribute it to Chief Seattle, to Sitting Bull, or to Alanis Obomsawin; or they name it as a Cree proverb or Native American saying. The phrase has also been taken up by Greenpeace and, more recently, by some participants in the Idle No More movement. In my other writings, I consider this

ambiguous authorship and Samian's focus on Sitting Bull as a figure of resistance.

19 Initially, the South Bronx served both as a literal point of genesis for rap music and as a signifier of urban blight to a larger audience. Later, other areas developed as markers of particular kinds of rap authenticity. Compton became a location from which rappers have drawn markers of authentic street life; particular artists such as N.W.A. assert a special right to speak due to their ability to represent this particular location. For more on the function of speaking for and from place, see Forman (2008).

20 Musicology and ethnomusicology scholars frequently engage in debates on cultural ownership, copyright, and the ethical uses of sound. Zemp's (1996) frequently cited article demonstrates how French musicians Eric Moquet and Michel Sanchez profited financially from sampling Afunakwa, a singer from the Solomon Islands, without her knowledge or permission. He contends that this kind of sampling is ethically dubious. For an examination of ethical questions in popular music citation, consult Feld (2000).

21 Debates on copyright and intellectual property, particularly as they relate to the technology of audio sampling, are addressed in DiCola and McLeod (2011), Porcello (1991), and Horowitz (2012). For analysis of contemporary copyright law, particularly as it relates to "traditional" musics, consult Hill (2007), Mills (1996), Rees (2003), and Seeger (1996).

22 The musical style or cultural practice is alternately termed throat singing, throat games, vocal games, or *katajjaq*. Individual games or performances show a great deal of variation. They may include words with lexical meanings, use vocables, and imitate sounds of nature or the home. Singers sometimes incorporate melodies from other sources. Some vocal games are narrative, while others may be tongue-twisters, juggling games, or games that show contrast. Women typically sing *katajjaq*.

23 For further detail, see Keillor (2006).

24 Inuit drum song music is more frequent. See Nattiez (1999).

25 Popular genres involve the easily distinguishable sound of throat singing, though hip hop collaborations are uncommon. Pop examples include Lucie Idlout's collaboration with throat singer Madeleine Allakariallak on her 2002 CD *E5-770, My Mother's Name.* Known for her particular style of solo performative throat singing, Tanya Tagaq collaborated with Bjork on the 2004 album *Medúlla*. Working with a string quartet, she was involved in the composition process for "Nunavut" with the Kronos Quartet and also performed the commissioned work "Tundra Songs" with them. At the Aboriginal People's Choice Music Awards in 2010, Tagaq's performance with rapper and singer Kinnie Starr was well received.

26 Hatzis (1999) describes throat singing as visceral and fascinating. He incorporated recordings of *katajjaq* in a 1994 string quartet titled *Nunavut,* the digitally sampled piece *Hunter's Dream* in 1995, the radio documentary *Footprints in New Snow in 1996,* and a 1999 composition *Viderunt Onmes.*

27 For a discussion on how the image of Indigenous peoples in Canada in the popular press has – and has not – changed since 1869, consult Anderson and Robertson (2011).

28 Composers achieve this kind of métissage in a variety of ways. Some listen to source material and then write in the same style, as in the case of John Weinzeweig. Others, such as Sylvaine Martin-Kostajnsek, write for Indigenous instruments, obtaining the timbre and referential qualities these bring. Portraying an Indigenous history is a third strategy: John Metcalf's "Tornrak" tells the story of an Inuit woman. Composers also create reference through language or melody, both of which occur in Harry Somers's *Louis Riel.* The opera engages in multiple strategies to reference Indigenous cultures: using Cree text, directly quoting a Tsimshian melody, and also writing new songs after the same model. Throughout, the piece uses melodic markers that composers frequently associate with the idea of Nativeness, such as microtones and repeated iterations of fourths and fifths, the timbral marker of handclapping, and an evocative solo flute line.

29 If we uncritically identify Aboriginal music as part of Canada's multiculturalism, he argues, we risk making it part of a nationalist project its creators did not agree to and may not agree with.

30 Keillor published representative lists of concert repertoire influenced by Native sources in her 1995 chapter "Indigenous Music as a Compositional Source." More recent examples include *Canadian*: Melissa Hui, "The Journey (Pimooteewin)" (2008); Derek Charke, "22 Inuit Throat Song Games (Katajak)" (2005); Patrick Carrabré, "Inuit Games" (2003); Christos Hatzis, "Light (Arctic Dreams 2)" (2002) and "Arctic Dreams 1" (2001); Sadie Buck, "Bones: An Aboriginal Dance Opera" (2001); and *American*: Linda Tutas Haugen, "Pocahontas" (2007); Anthony Davis, "Wakonda's Dream" (2007); Henry Mollicone, "Coyote Tales" (1998); David Carlson, "Dreamkeepers" (1996); Stephen Paulus, "The Woman at Otowi Crossing" (1995); John Luther Adams, "Earth and the Great Weather" (1994); and Ross Lee Finney, "Weep Torn Land" (1984).

31 Multiculturalism in Canada encompasses legal policy that defines and acts upon diversity, ethnic identity, visible minorities, immigration, and cultural difference. State publications define it as intrinsic to the nation: it became official national policy in the 1970s, and the Multiculturalism Act, 1988, established it as fundamental to Canadian society. For a fuller description of

Canadian multiculturalism, consult Garcea, Kirova, and Wong (2008), Howard-Hassmann (1999), Esses and Gardner (1996), Cairns and Williams (1986), Berry and Laponce (1994), and Berdichewsky (1994).

32 It should be noted that francophone Canada does not just consist of Quebec and that multiple languages are spoken within that province. It is relevant, however, that Canada's only francophone majority province has some differences in its attitude towards diversity policy.

33 For additional specifics on interculturalism, refer to Bouchard (2011) and Labelle (2008).

34 For more on the intended and unintended consequences of group formation through multiculturalism, refer to Hesse (2000) and Okin (1999).

35 Earlier narratives cite British and French founding peoples of Canada, now Indigenous peoples are often added as a third. For more on this shift and ongoing debates, see Darnell (2000).

5

FOLLOWING THE THREAD

Toronto's Place in Hip Hop Dance Histories

Mary Fogarty

INTRODUCTION: THE "LEG THING NO ONE CAN DO"

In February 2014, Jimmy Fallon and Will Smith performed a version of dance history on the *Tonight Show* that they called the "evolution of hip hop dances." Starting with dances such as the Cabbage Patch and the Running Man, they catalogued various hip hop dance steps that were listed on the bottom of the screen.[1] As a comic sketch, accuracy seemed to be of little consequence, as movements, terminologies, and the order of dance moves were jumbled or loosely presented. Most of the dances were readily recognizable moves although a few included embellishments. They concluded their encyclopaedic comedy duet with the twerk, which was being mainstreamed at that moment. For the twerk, Jimmy Fallon started to booty shake without much skill, much to the dismay of Will Smith, who refused to join in, perhaps highlighting the one hip hop dance that, at least for Smith, simply does not make the cut. At one point in the performance, they each grab a foot with the opposite hand and make a failed attempt to thread their other leg through the opening they've made with their bodies, while jumping off said leg. The move they attempted to perform was listed at the bottom of the screen as the "Leg Thing No One Can Do." This move, popularized in hip hop dances of the 1990s, is often referred to as "threading the needle." Despite the *Tonight Show*'s vaguely dismissive nomenclature, "threading the needle," I argue, is an important aspect of Toronto's contributions to a global b-boy/b-girl dance culture.

While the Cabbage Patch and the Running Man are considered hip hop dances (although they are more accurately described as "moves"), they are considered to be distinct from breaking as a dance style with its own codes and conventions. Breaking may have been the original hip hop dance, but this is then complicated by dances, distinct from breaking, that came later and are often referred to as "hip hop dances." In other words, the categories of "breaking" and "hip hop dance" overlap but are not identical, and this tends to complicate historical accounts, be they vernacular or scholarly. This chapter offers, in many ways, a serious counterpart to that comedic performance. First, I want to suggest that the aesthetics of breaking are best understood within the contexts of other hip hop dances. Examining hip hop dances within the context of a case study of a local dance tradition shows the value of this type of approach, which allows me to address broader aesthetic trajectories, tying local histories to questions of how styles circulate globally. Second, through discussions of local developments in Toronto, I suggest some of the formal contributions that b-boys in Toronto have made to the global aesthetics of breaking as a dance style. In particular, I highlight how dancers developed a localized style through their incorporation of hip hop dances such as threading the needle. In the case study of Toronto's hip hop dance scenes offered here, I also address the significance of local forms of arts funding (such as Toronto's Fresh Arts program) and other cultural policy around diversifying arts practitioners, all of which are shown to play a particular role in the evolution of Toronto's hip hop histories.

Finally, the evidence provided by this case study of a local hip hop culture allows me to raise more theoretical questions about the threading of local histories with a larger global history of related dance styles. In particular, I am interested in how a local culture that focused its attention on "originality" in the hip hop dance performances of individual practitioners also established one of the most internationally recognizable Canadian styles.[2] In other words, a scene that focused on each dancer's having his, her, or their own distinct or original flavour ultimately became known for a particular, shared style, a common "Toronto" version of threading that manifested itself across competing crews. Here creativity, as a collaborative act, is examined to elaborate on the paradox of individual contributions (and attributions) and communal creativity. I argue that even signature dance movements, accredited to particular individuals, are the result of collective creativity and competition and that local histories can be woven together to create a larger narrative of meanings.

BREAKING IN TORONTO

Toronto breakers are known in the international breaking scene for creating a complex, localized style of threading. Threading involves delineating a space with your body parts, and sometimes the floor, and moving another part of your body through that space to create a dynamic illusion. "Threading the needle" is a key part of the American hip hop dance vocabulary of moves and is commonly used around the world. Toronto hip hop dancers adapted this concept and began to bring it to the floor and into their breaking. That is not to say they are the only dancers that were adapting threading to the floor as European b-boys can also be seen "threading the needle" in their footwork in footage from events of the late 1980s and early 1990s. Also, Mr. Wiggles from New York City began to experiment with bringing boogie moves to the floor, and this also involved moves involving grabbing his foot and threading the other one through in his breaking (Toprockcity 2011). Later on, Mr. Wiggles would feature b-boys from Toronto on one of his underground video magazines to showcase the style of threading that the Boogie Brats crew developed called "origami style" (Mr. Wiggles n.d.).

This aesthetic development can be traced to a particular historical point in the mid- to late 1990s when Toronto b-boys practised, and then emerged on the international map of breaking competitions with a distinctive, localized style and aesthetic – one that would later be codified and taught around the world. The style, already known as "threading," was developed into a subfield that was named by Toronto members of the Boogie Brats as "origami style." I expand further on the origami style later in this chapter, when I cover some features of the most recognizable crews to date that have represented Toronto internationally – namely, Bag of Trix (and its arch rivals locally Intrik-it), Boogie Brats, and Supernaturalz.

Breakers from Toronto became widely known for the intricate footwork that they developed as crews such as Bag of Trix, Boogie Brats, and Supernaturalz began to compete, win, and place at international competitions. New generations of dancers, having learned the latest social dance steps in the hip hop dance genre, honed moves such as "threading the needle," appreciating the slower beats popularized by the 1990s hip hop sound that allowed for more elaborate and intricate downrock. In other words, developments in musical tempo, articulated with new dance moves, contributed to a historical shift.

Significantly, the dancers under discussion built crew affiliations that often involved DJs and rappers. Many of the dancers who would become key to developing the threading style that Toronto is known for internationally cut their teeth as backup dancers for hip hop rappers. Although the resurgence and popularization of breaking in Toronto did not take off until after GhettOriginal performed there in 1994 on the first stop of its international theatrical tour,[3] we have to trace the histories back even further in order to understand the Toronto scene's own contributions to the global aesthetics of the footwork form.

BACKDROP: TORONTO BREAKING PRE-THREADING

Although most children of the early 1980s likely tried their hardest to master breaking moves such as the "worm" or the "backspin," the origins of the dance in New York City in the 1970s were clearly laid out against a backdrop of rough living conditions, exacerbated by local social policies (Hager 1984; Banes 1985). However, by the early 1980s, "breakdancers" were mingling with members of the art world's elite. In places like New York City, graffiti artists and breakers were being filmed and placed in art galleries, alongside club performances and international world tours of hip hop music. The word "art" was frequently tossed around in relation to this new dance. Some of those early tours involved crews such as the Rock Steady Crew, featuring iconic b-boys such as Crazy Legs and Frosty Freeze performing alongside pioneering musical acts such as Afrika Bambaataa.

One of the unique features of hip hop dance, as an artistic movement, is that it was an art form created initially by racialized youth who competed with other b-boys and b-girls from different neighbourhoods. As the histories of the earliest days of the dance get collected, recorded, and passed along, we tend to rely mainly on the memories of middle-aged men, recalling their experiences from when they were around fourteen years old, recollecting who came up with which moves, and remembering which values they held. These stories necessarily involve competing voices.

The early history of the dance in Toronto was of course influenced by the emergence of breaking in New York City, but the local context was different and did not involve the art world contexts with which New York City b-boys such as the Rock Steady Crew were associated. In the first half of the 1980s, before breakers in Toronto were defining themselves as "artists" or "professionals," they were often experiencing their position as "outcasts" and "misfits" who faced racism as new immigrants to Canada. Dale Sammy of Cold Crush recounts: "Take the place where we're from, the time we're from ... We were misfits in this place. Racism was rampant, you got skinheads everywhere, [then] you got people trying to come together and figure out what their culture is about compared to our culture. We were strangers, all of us, ... we were the next set of immigrants ... But we met up with the other set of immigrants like the Guyanese and the Eastern Europeans ... and our crews were an amalgamation of all of these people and so was the [hip hop] culture" (Fat Laces TV 2012). This experience of alienation, ostracism, and racism is crucial to acknowledge in a city that defines itself by its diasporic population and in a country with a nationwide government policy devoted to multiculturalism.

Toronto is a "quintessential diaspora city." According to Walcott (2005, 438): "Toronto lives an everyday or popular multiculturalism (Bannerji, 2000) that is vastly different from the nation's description of it and what it should do. In Toronto people criss-cross cultural spheres continually, and thus produce moments of cultural translation, creative cultural confusion, and culture recombination – in short, making the city a genuine creole space." Toronto also experienced rapid expansion into boroughs such as Scarborough, North York, and Etobicoke with the Metro (Sewell 1993). The Metro is Toronto's subway system. Breaking in Toronto became one way of creating multicultural alliances and mingling among young dancers in one of the most multicultural cities in the world. Yet, as one early b-boy participant points out, the 1980s experience of racism was perhaps more explicit than the implicit racism that would govern the 1990s.

Many of the early participants of the dance experienced their outsider status at their school dances. For example, Dizzy of Magnetic Rockers recalls: "I remember when we used to go to school dances back then hip-hop itself was ... even though with breakdancing the media sort of exposed a lot of people to hip-hop but you go to a school dance and when they played hip-hop I remember kids sitting down on the floor, almost in protest, 'what is this music? This sucks.' Everyone was into Duran Duran and that sort of thing so you were almost a bit of an outcast" (Fat Laces TV 2012). As one dancer of this period suggested, breaking died out as a dance style because females began to enjoy different styles of dance, and the young males accommodated by learning new moves and steps to impress.[4] These new moves didn't "cause" breaking to die out; it's just that the interests of many of the participants were changing, from showing off spectacular moves to the achievement of social status in (heterosexual) dating. Some of the new moves that became popular included the Cabbage Patch. New sources of inspiration came from hip hop dancers contributing new moves to the social, club dance atmosphere presented in the media, exemplified by performers such as Kid 'n Play. Kid 'n Play were a well-known American rap/dance act that became successful in the late 1980s. In a feature film series, *House Party*, and in their music videos, Kid 'n Play showcased their hip hop dance styles, which became popular in Toronto at that time.

Threading the needle was a move often seen in the performances of backup dancers for hip hop acts or in clubs, known as an upright move whereby a dancer grabs their foot and hops or jumps the other leg through the loop created by their body. This was a move that could be seen clearly on stages when done in the upright position. "Threading," the shortened term, describes a footwork style developed from this move in breaking and designed to create illusions of a flexible and bendable body, as in the "origami style" that Toronto members of the Boogie Brats created. Rather than being a singular move, threading as a style grew to have as many variations as there are dancers doing that style. The complexity of the styles that Toronto developed were in many ways a result of the one-upmanship mentality that grew out of the different crews battling each other and comparing their styles locally.

I am interested here in asserting the fluidity of Toronto's histories of hip hop dance and in challenging the notion of breaking as a bounded practice, distinct from other dance styles and practices. The hip hop dance move of threading the needle, which influenced a whole style of moves within breaking and popping, is an example of this.

Although I am providing a simplified historical narrative of the early days of breaking in the 1980s and the development of a localized tradition in Toronto in the 1990s, I also want to make clear the sheer number of different hip hop dance communities and practices extant in Toronto. Even within one city, the research about this could take another decade. Even then, I still would not be satisfied that I had covered all of the practitioners in different neighbourhoods whose experiences might not align or provide any consistent historical narrative, not to mention all of the neighbouring cities that affected the development of the dance as practised here. This fluidity results in a complex set of relationships not only with narratives of hip hop histories but also with institutional infrastructures in Toronto. I am focusing on formal contributions as they are so rarely examined in hip hop dance scholarship to date.[5]

What appears to be the death of "breakdancing" in Toronto between the mid-1980s and early 1990s actually created the social milieu and context that would later prove to be central to the innovations in the style that emerged as it was reincarnated in the 1990s.

TORONTO CONTEXTS: FUNDING, MEDIA AND INSTITUTIONAL OBSTACLES[6]

> Something as successful as Fresh Arts should've become as successful as the Toronto Symphony, National Ballet, the Rom or Theatre Passe Muraille … All levels of government should have institutionalized it.
>
> Allen, quoted in "The Youth Program That Worked," *Eye Weekly*

Developments within a dance practice can be followed not only through the narratives about individual histories provided by its participants but also through the various institutions that inform the practice, whether from above or beyond. The influence of educational and arts institutions is not always felt directly by participants in local "subcultures," but ultimately these shape the ways in which their practices are framed, not only by those outside the practice but also by those within it. One example arises in my interviews with Karl "Dyzee" Alba.[7] He pointed out, when thinking about his own history, the important role played by community programming at his local mall. The programming developed to keep youth out of trouble in the mall led to his substantial progress with the dance as it gave him a place to practice.

Funding also invokes different framings. Sometimes funding for hip hop dance is located within initiatives around "high-risk" youth and marginal communities or diversity projects. These funding sources have certainly had some of the biggest impacts on hip hop culture and the specifics of its localized aesthetics in Toronto. For example, Fresh Arts was an initiative that has been cited by many dancers turned rappers or musical artists as being instrumental in their development. The Fresh Arts program was a Jobs Ontario youth initiative created in 1993 and facilitated by the Toronto Arts Council (More or Les and Murray 2006). The program focused on youth in "priority neighbourhoods," including those with a high proportion of new immigrants to Canada (Black 2011).

A few initiatives, such as Fresh Arts, involved individuals working within the frameworks of local city arts funding around diversity issues. These funded projects were able to open up spaces for rappers, musical artists, and radio DJs in a way that demonstrates the distinctions between arenas. In situations where the arts of youth (especially those coming from the Caribbean) were supported through mentorship programs there was far more successful than in situations where young people did not experience the same sorts of initiatives. For whatever reason, dancers did not receive the same level of support as musicians; however, given their interest in breaking prior to their emergence as musical artists, many of these youth supported the dancers through bringing them onstage with musical acts. In this way, hip hop dancers in Toronto were tied more to these commercial and musical arts funded-programs than they were to any dance initiatives at this time.

In this respect, radio host and promoter Ron Nelson, who provided opportunities for many young hip hop artists from the Toronto area, heavily influenced hip hop in Canada. He is clear in interviews that he was part of a longer lineage of hip hop participants, and his significant place in the history of hip hop in Canada comes from the opportunities provided by his local radio station – opportunities those who came before him (whom he valued and whom he considered to have made significant contributions) – did not have (Koganometry 2011). He names the Sunshine Crew as an earlier group that had made contributions but that hadn't had the institutional support that he had had to promote new hip hop artists coming up. This humility and sharing of opportunity reflects the ethos of the emerging hip hop community that spanned art forms and platforms, even as the funding situations created silos dividing music and dance opportunities. Importantly, events that Nelson organized, such as Monster Jam, provided a space for practitioners of all hip hop elements in Toronto to be showcased and legitimized as particular crews, dancers, DJs, and rappers became household names. This connection is crucial in contributing to some of the innovations in the form.

It is thus no surprise that part of what gives the particular style of threading its specificities, aside from the complex, intricate, and dynamic dance moves and bodily acts, is a certain musical appreciation. As mentioned previously, the communities breaking at this time were often dancing to slower breaks than those of sped up breakbeats by British hip hop artists that b-boys in Germany and Italy were listening/practising to (see Fogarty 2011). These sounds were the breaks (and beats) found in the early 1990s hip hop music of North America. And what had once been in a hip hop dance style known as threading the needle was now embodied in a unique balance of social dances and breaking in the Toronto style of threading, which highlighted an apparent act of magic (the incomprehensible speed and shifting directions of the footwork, both of which rendered it illegible) and accessibility (the ability to communicate movements to crowds that didn't dance in ways that would render those movements legible). The one quality (illegibility) was intended to create styles so incomprehensible that other dancers couldn't figure out, let alone emulate, what they had just seen, while the other quality (accessibility) was honed through performances with hip hop acts in stage performances intended for the public.[8]

Before threading became a recognizable attribute of the "Toronto style," particular individual b-boys emphasized "originality" as the essence of a good breaking performance. For example, when Bag of Trix crew appeared on the syndicated television show *Rap City*, on the Canadian music video channel MuchMusic, each member of the crew had a style distinctly his own. Here, b-boying is presented next to popping and hip hop social dances and routines, and the crew members become the onlookers for each other's performances. In this performance, it is evident that part of the pleasure of the dance involves impressing and surprising your own crew as much as the television audience. In other words, Bag of Trix found an aesthetic balance between complex, intricate footwork that was difficult to decipher and a performance quality that considered the art of pleasing spectators and the general public.

Threading

Threading is a complex footwork style designed to create illusions of a flexible and bendable body. In Toronto, the speed at which one executed threads was accelerated, and this contributed part of its distinctiveness. The aim was to thread so quickly that other dancers and audience members could not figure out how it was done. When hip hop dancer and b-boy Leg-o, from Supernaturalz Crew, came to give a workshop in one of my breaking classes at York University (in Autumn 2015), the students described his style as "magic." Leg-o was influential in Toronto as he taught many of the teen-age b-boys at a community centre while in his twenties, some of whom became known internationally for their breaking.

One of his early students was Karl "Dyzee" Alba, who recalls being influenced by both Leg-o and Leg-o's hip hop dance partner Stripes. Footwork patterns that became influential for him were "blender clocks" (a variation of a move created by Gizmo from Toronto's Bag of Trix Crew), "wraps" (involving legs wrapping around arms in threads), "leg-o legs" (named after Leg-o and involving catching one leg with the other leg behind the knee), and "dead legs" (leg-o legs in reverse).[9] Deanna Zubrickas describes Dyzee's movement qualities as follows:

> After watching a few montages of Dyzee, it was extremely easy to see that he is very flexible ... In one of many sets, Dyzee folds his leg in half, backwards so his foot is up by his hip, and is tucked there until he's finished doing a worm like movement. The intricate little details that set him apart from other b-boys, especially his flexibility ... At points he will move at lightening speed as if he's rushing through the movements, and proceeds to slow right down like he's dancing through molasses ... Another highlight of Dyzee's style is his lower and upper body integration, simultaneously looking integrated yet separated. In a complicated six step like movement, his upper body is stable on the ground supporting his weight while his legs almost flail around in a 360 degree space. Looking exactly like his upper and lower body are somehow detached yet working together at the same time. Watching him throw down in a cypher or competition is extremely mesmerizing, in a few videos online he does a freeze where his entire body weight is balanced on his elbow, not his whole forearm but

> solely his elbow joint. It is completely mind boggling and confusing to watch.[10]

While describing the qualities of movement that she felt made Dyzee unique, she also registers the magical quality of threading created by speed, flexibility, and illusions. These qualities were also present in the hip hop dance routines performed by Leg-o and his partner Stripes.[11] Similarly, Megas ("Vengeance") from the Boogie Brats Crew also developed intricate freezes on his elbows that flowed straight from his threading "origami" footwork.

In an interview (19 February 2013) for the BBOY NORTH website, Leg-o describes how a manager for Canadian rap acts influenced the direction of his dancing. Farley Flex, who managed Maestro Fresh Wes, encouraged Leg-o to blend hip hop dancing with breaking in the 1990s. Likewise, Leg-O cites Big Daddy Kane's dancers, Scoob and Scrap Lover, for being major influences on the style that he developed and that has become associated internationally with Canadian b-boys: the art of threading (BBoy North n.d.). In other words, Toronto crews modified a standard hip hop move and made it an entire style, in turn contributing to the global vocabulary of breaking as practised today.

Crews

As I suggested at the start of this chapter, a number of hip hop dance styles have been influential in the development of breaking as practised locally in Toronto. Many of the b-boys performed theatrical showcases in clubs, on stage, and touring with rap acts as backup dancers. For those who are part of the hip hop scene, the best of these dancers are typically referred to as "hip hop dancers" rather than as "backup dancers," even though they would often inhabit the "background" for live musical acts. Hip hop dancers played an important part in the development of breaking movement vocabularies. They thus had a significant influence both on the history of breaking in Toronto, and, through this, on the international scene that often credits Toronto dancers for their contributions to this dance art form through, but not limited to, threading. In fact, many of the international backup hip hop dancers for rap artists are considered stars in their own right, hence the reluctance to relegate them to the background of a performance or to reduce their status with the label "backup dancers."

Crews in Toronto were not limited to breakers. Most hip hop crews had emcees, DJs, writers, and dancers. Crews were like a family.[12] In breaking cultural practice, crews are not necessarily limited to a particular neighbourhood or place as members from other cities or countries can also be put down in a crew. For example, the well-known American b-boy K-Mel joined the Boogie Brats crew and spent time training with the majority of the members who, at that time, resided in Canada. Also, female breakers also contributed to the dance, alongside women who did hip hop, house, and dancehall in clubs, in hip hop crews, and professionally[13].

Arnold "Gizmo" Vidad, a member of Bag of Trix Crew, was put down with Rock Steady Crew and flown to different parts of the world.[14] He was the first b-boy from Toronto to gain an international reputation. Bag of Trix also began to compete in international competitions and make a name for itself. In fact, Bag of Trix shared the stage with Rock Steady Crew at one of its anniversary events in New York City (Fogarty 2011). Bag of Trix's aesthetic style references other hip hop dance styles, especially in the memorable tandem routines that Bag of Trix created at that time (Fogarty 2014b). There are also examples of individual b-boys playing with a mix of dance styles. Corrie "Benzo" Daniel of Bag of Trix still does a version of threading the needle upright (reversing the direction) as part of his breaking vocabulary. Rather than the "pop and lock" mixing with "breakdancing" that those media misconceptions often produced in various locations,[15] Toronto breakers developed complex, hybridized routines that mixed styles fluidly and convincingly. For example, Mariano "Glizzi" Abarca developed a style that took conceptual elements from popping, breaking, and other hip hop dances to create a style uniquely his own.

Bag of Trix Crew had a main competitor locally, Intrikit Crew, who also took its dancing to a professional level at that time and attempted to make money as dancers. In doing so, it helped to put Toronto b-boys on the map locally in various cultural spaces. As Michael "Mad Money Mike" Joseph recently pointed out, his crew Intrikit aspired to professionalism: "What we were doing in Toronto with the hip-hop scene was unique and the challenges we had in the hip-hop scene were unique to our city. Bag of Trix and Intrikit [crews] were very fortunate to have each other to play off ... From the grassroots level hip-hop, breakdancing, b-boying, b-girling, or whatever you want to call it, wasn't accepted. The club scene didn't accept it; promoters had a hard time to understand it, DJs ... people didn't want you in the circle because it took up space. So we had to force it into the scene and really cool things happened."[16]

Having worked hard at their practice, dancers from crews such as Intrikit began to apply for funding to the Toronto Arts Council and the Canada Arts Council. Their manager remembers receiving a letter in the mail that denied them funding, explaining that their dance was not an "art" like ballet. Although dismayed, they refused to quit and turned to the "commercial" sector so that they could continue their work as professional dancers. Their involvement in dance showcases and as backup hip hop dancers gave them a credibility and status within hip hop culture and local club scenes. As I have suggested, the dancers considered themselves "artists" even when rejected by art-world funders. Most of their accolades are related more to the music industry than to the art world. For example, Benzo from Bag of Trix performed in music videos for Timbaland, Missy Elliot, K-OS, Naughty by Nature, Kardinal Offishall, and more, and he has opened for Grandmaster Flash, De La Soul, Jazzy Jeff, and Maestro Fresh Wes.[17]

Two dancers from the Boogie Brats Crew – Megas "Vengeance" and Nathan "Gadget" – put out an underground video (ichkuro 2012), and in it Megas explains their "origami" style, which they developed conceptually out of threading.[18] Origami style involves using a series of threads and folding the body to create sculptured footwork with a flow evolved from the threading foundation. Inspired by the Japanese art of folding paper, their footwork style was developed for complexity of pattern making. Before their video was created, Megas, through word of mouth, was already considered an underground legend across Canada.[19] Their American crew member K-Mel would go on to become the bigger household name, and his style of threading became one of the closest to manifesting the energy and clarity of the original threading-the-needle move, in large part due to the fact that he would actually incorporate the standing version of the move into his vocabulary without flipping it.

Dyzee from Supernaturalz Crew was one of the first b-boys to blow up on the internet when a video he made went viral. This ushered in a new era of breaking reputations, enabled by the World Wide Web. If Gizmo, from Bag of Trix, could be said to be one of the first Asian b-boys to become well-known internationally, as has been reported widely, then Dyzee, a fellow Filipino Canadian, certainly followed this lead by becoming at one time the most recognizable b-boy from

Canada. Today, Illz from Ground Illusionz Crew gets more name recognition abroad, demonstrating the speed with which new histories get made and the stories of older generations fade away. Now, b-boy Dyzee is more likely to be known for his contributions to a controversial international judging system. He developed this in Toronto but found support in South Korea at R16, the international b-boy event held there. Dyzee opted to do what b-boys and b-girls before him had done: he moved countries to follow the support of the dance rather than staying in a local context where his ambitions would not receive institutional support.

Recently, the tables seem to have turned here in Toronto. Local arts agencies, educators, and institutions are increasingly enthusiastic and excited to work with "street dancers" now that they have begun to see their aesthetic and educational values. Organizers of youth programming outside of hip hop and marginalized communities appear dismayed that "street dancers" ask for so much money for educational workshops.[20] This is often read as a sign of the commercialized roots and values of street dance. Ironically, it is precisely the rejection of b-boys by arts funding bodies that initially drove them into the industry and increased the income they were able to earn as demand grew for their skills in the commercial world of music videos and live tours. It was the initial rejection from the club and school scenes, and much later success in finally breaking into these worlds, despite the obstacles, that gave them a sense of how much their efforts were worth financially. The confidence to call themselves artists according to their own definitions of the term also means that they often provide different financial scales, depending on the client and the request. Most b-boys and b-girls still teach marginalized or underprivileged youth for free in informal educational settings, only asking for money and support from those communities that not only can afford more but that are also part of the institutional structure that historically created obstacles to the inclusion of hip hop dancers.[21]

CONCLUDING REMARKS

In this chapter, I examine some of the formal contributions that Toronto b-boys and b-girls have made to breaking as an art form that is practised internationally. Although they were not the first dancers to develop threading, Toronto dancers created a complex, dynamic version of threading that became recognizable and associated with

Canada internationally. The backdrop to the emergence of this contribution lay in the temporary fading out of breaking, a style that was seen locally in the mid- to late 1980s and early 1990s as unpopular, and the hybridization of breaking with other hip hop dance moves and dance styles such as popping. The emergence of rave culture informed appreciation by some hip hop dancers for house music and also infused the dancing at this time. Also, the fusing of cultures and traditions reflected what was happening musically at the time, with emcees such as Michie Mee mixing reggae, dancehall, and hip hop, and touring with Public Enemy.

Hip hop culture in the 1990s received some institutional support centred around the development of musical talent, including funded projects such as Fresh Arts. This program helped the launch of rappers such as Kardinal Offishall and Saukrates, alongside singers such as Jully Black, who was born to Jamaican immigrants and grew up in the Jane and Finch area of Toronto, where b-boys from the Supernaturalz Crew live. B-boys and b-girls benefitted only indirectly from this support since it was not directed at dancers. At the same time, they found support through community programming at malls for "high-risk" youth. American influences were certainly prevalent during this time, with the influence of hip hop acts such as Kid 'n Play, the American touring acts that Ron Nelson helped to bring to Toronto, and the circulation of videos by American dancers that featured b-boys from other cities, including Aktuel Force from Paris, France (Fogarty 2006). However, distinct formal contributions and a localized Toronto b-boy style were clearly developing. So, while receiving visits from touring artists and mediated examples of the dance as it was developing in other locales, Toronto was simultaneously contributing to the development and circulation of styles internationally.

Local crews competed against one another and, through doing so, developed their own codes and conventions, values, and judgments. That is not to say there were any sort of officially agreed upon codes and conventions but, rather, that through the competition among opposing crews, *disagreements* also produced new aesthetic understandings. The local styles got established not only through collaborative creativity, found within crews, but also through the aesthetic experiences that dancers created while battling each other.

Although the focus on originality continues to be a predominantly North American concern within the dance form of breaking, Toronto breakers credit their development to the upholding of this integration of aesthetics and ethics, in which judgments of "dope or freshness" are informed by a proud refusal to copy (Fogarty 2014a). The "Leg Thing No One Can Do" thus became, in Toronto, the "Leg Thing Everybody Can Do," only each dancer's version of this local tradition is uniquely her, his, or their own (a dancer is called out by other dancers if not following this moral rule). As Megas from the Boogie Brats Crew explains in his underground video, "Don't bite it ... flip it," meaning copying is bad, signifying (i.e., modifying) is good.

Through this narration of Toronto's breaking history, I am suggesting that there is value to understanding hip hop dances, such as breaking, as part of a trajectory of styles of dance that influence each other. This is not the singular tradition of a specific people but, rather, a social history that makes the formal contributions of specific individuals visible. This involves sociological factors, such as the ways in which groups of people develop sets of codes and conventions aesthetically through their practice, as well as through their dialogues, which include *disagreements* about what makes a good performance.

I highlight the significance not only of individual dancers but, just as important, of crews. Crews create agreed-upon aesthetic codes and conventions through their practices, which are then held up against those of their rivals. Dancers collaborate not only in the making of moves but also in the legitimation of codes and conventions, and in placing localized emphasis on particular values. Here competition is not pejorative, a negative type of expression rooted in winning and losing, but, rather, is credited by dancers as fuelling the creative development of the form. As Mariano "Glizzi" Abarca has stated over and over, if it weren't for their local rivals, Intrikit, his own crew, Bag of Trix, would never have become so good. Here competition is about elevation and about responses that matter. This parallels the spirit of jazz music's collective improvisation. In other words, dancers define themselves through who they are *not* as much as through who they are, and this is significant for identity and the act of becoming involved in performance practices.

Through performances, aesthetic practices are both created and codified. It's less that aesthetic codes and conventions are agreed upon by a community and more that disagreements create and shape aesthetic tastes, and these come to fruition in performance. The local style of Toronto can only be understood aesthetically through the disagreements and tensions between social groups, whether this stems from the support (or lack thereof) from cultural institutions, as seen in the 1990s and early 2000s, or from the tensions between crews themselves. In other words, comparison is at the heart of aesthetic judgments here, and practices give rise to, activate, indeed stage, these comparisons. This explains why "Biting" (i.e., stealing someone else's moves) is such a moral offence in hip hop culture.

My task here is not to raise a "low" form to a "high status" by thinking seriously about the aesthetic contributions of hip hop dancers but, rather, to address the formal contributions that Toronto made to breaking history. Even contributions attributed to individuals were made by groups of dancers, often in opposing crews, who were fuelled (and inspired) by their rival crews. For breaking, pleasure is pronounced both in the experience of peers watching the performance and in the act of competition that enables the performance itself to occur. When it comes to deciphering Toronto's impact on the art of threading in breaking and the collaborative creative processes involved, Gadget from the Boogie Brats explains it best (on an online forum thread no less): "Megas and I never invented threads and nor did we ever claim that we did like some people said ... that is a misunderstanding ... Kid 'n Play were dropping and threading the needle long before us, but to the best of our knowledge we were the first to build an entire style on that and we called that style origami. Threading became the entire bboy style and footwork that we centered on for a while. Don't make it too scientific – It's simply rolling your ass around the floor and threading whatever your part of the body is blady well closest to you" (BBoy World n.d.).

NOTES

I would like to thank Kwende Kefentse, Laura Wiebe, Mark Campbell, Serouj Aprahamian, and the anonymous readers for their helpful comments about my chapter in progress.

1 Their performance alludes to one of the most viral YouTube videos of all times, Judson Laipply's comedic performance in "The Evolution of Dance." The video was uploaded on 6 April 2006 and to date has just under 300 million views. At one point it was the most watched and talked about video ever posted to YouTube (Laipply 2006).

2 See About bboy (2012) for evidence of b-boys crediting Canada for the development of styles that were local to the city of Toronto.

3 See my chapter about the development of hip-hop dance theatre in Fogarty

(2011) for a more extended survey. See also footage here of GhettOriginals in Toronto, Canada (Bricks69 2006).

4 Personal correspondence, 2011.

5 Banes (1985) and Schloss (2009) are notable exceptions. Schloss addresses the exaggerated aesthetics of the dance, and Banes covers the early stylistic influences on the moves b-boys created.

6 There isn't room to discuss the outdoor hip hop festivals and the impact they had on hip hop culture in Toronto in this chapter, but this would be an interesting topic for further research.

7 Personal correspondence 2008, Toronto, Canada. This interview was conducted when b-boy Dyzee was still living in a high-rise building near the Jane and Finch intersection in Toronto before he moved to South Korea. See Fogarty (2012b) for more details about this specific case study of teaching practices and aging in breaking culture.

8 Interview with Gizmo and Flex of Bag of Trix, 2007. Their intentions were often to make their style legible to audiences through repeating a movement pattern three times and modifying the final repetition for effect once the audience was able to comprehend the original pattern.

9 Karl "Dyzee" Alba presents the various threading moves that Toronto became known for in a video clip for Strife TV (2012).

10 Deanna Zubrickas wrote about Dyzee's style for a university assignment on Toronto b-boy/b-girl histories at York University; FA/DANC 3510D: North American Dance Practice. This was a winter 2013 course I taught with both a studies and studio component about breaking. Quote used with permission.

11 Some early footage of Supernaturalz Crew members can be seen via Snc1Generation (2012).

12 See Fogarty (2011, chap. 5) for an extended discussion of crews and the analogy to a family.

13 See more about female involvement in my article on influential Canadian b-girls (Fogarty 2015).

14 Interview I did with Arnold in August 2007 for my PhD dissertation (Fogarty 2011).

15 See Imani Kai Johnson's extended work about hip hop dance vocabulary in Johnson (2015).

16 Quote is from a public talk at York University's Department of Dance, 14 October 2011, to which I invited members of Intrikit Crew. Here Money Mike is recalling Toronto b-boy history in the early to mid-1990s.

17 See *Benzo: Bag of Trix* (n.d.).

18 See part of "Boogie Brats Just to Prove a Point! Vol. 1" (ichkuro 2012). See

also "Megas aka Vengeance (Boogie Brats) Trailer" (Jeanaro 2010), where Megas describes his origami style.

19 See Fogarty (2012a) for an extended historical account of the videomaking practices of b-boys and b-girls in the 1990s before the rise of the World Wide Web.

20 In large part, street dancers are actually paid less per hour than their peers in the contemporary world for performances in art world venues.

21 Personal correspondence with b-boys, b-girls, and house dancers on their pay scales in Toronto, 2012 and 2013. Also see Fogarty (2012b) for more about informal education structures.

6

EXPLORING THE HIP HOP AURAL IMAGINARIES OF NEW IMMIGRANT AND INDIGENOUS YOUTH IN WINNIPEG

Charlotte Fillmore-Handlon

INTRODUCTION

This chapter introduces the concept of the "aural imaginary" as a tool for understanding the transformative potential of hip hop and its use as an everyday social practice by disenfranchised youth from diverse cultural groups. In developing this concept, I draw on Arjun Appadurai's (1996) expansion of Benedict Anderson's (2006) concept of imagined communities from a global perspective and Inés Dussel's (2009) notion of the global visual imaginary. To explore the concept of the aural imaginary, I situate this notion in the context of a Winnipeg hip hop project spearheaded by Crossing Communities Art Project (CCAP), a non-profit arts organization dedicated to working with women and youth who experience marginalization.[1] With the support of funders, CCAP launched its innovative Hip Hop Project in the summer of 2007.[2] The project evolved over three main stages: (1) between August 2007 and November 2008, CCAP offered introductory workshops throughout Winnipeg and on a Northern reserve, and established community partners, including the Immigrant and Refugee Community Organization of Manitoba (IRCOM), Ndinawe Youth Resource Centre, the University of Winnipeg, and Winnipeg's Contemporary Dancers; (2) between November 2008 and April 2009, fourteen youth participated in an intensive twenty-week, multi-media arts training program; and (3) between April and August 2009, CCAP provided training and employment opportunities for the youth to work as art mentors in local community centres and schools.

This chapter consists of three main sections and focuses on the second stage of the project, which culminated in two public performances entitled *Winnipeg Child*. The methods for my analysis include in-depth interviews with the youth (which took place during the middle and end of the twenty-week training program), observations of their public performances, and a textual analysis of the hip hop songs and spoken word poetry they wrote and performed.[3] In the first section I build an interdisciplinary framework, drawing on concepts from globalization studies, ethnomusicology, cultural studies, and sociology, and advance the concept of the aural imaginary. In doing so, I underline the importance of both hip hop and the aural imaginary as everyday social practice. The second section introduces the project participants and outlines the main components of the CCAP Hip Hop Project. Using interview narratives, this section explores how the project mobilized the youth to express feelings of marginalization and to (per)form resistance identities. The third section grounds my analysis of the aural imaginary in the context of the CCAP Hip Hop Project and public performances. I argue that, through the music and poetics of performing hip hop, the aural imaginary creates a space for dispersed and marginalized youth to voice their lived realities, mobilize resistant identities, and cultivate new imaginings of community. Finally, I close the chapter by reflecting on the hip hop aural imaginary, its positive transformative possibilities for youth, and its potential as an agent of social change. Through this study, I aim to provide a sense of how the experiences of creating and performing hip hop mobilize youth and allow them to envision their place in the world, evoking new imaginings of communities along both local and global lines.

UNDERSTANDING THE WORK OF THE AURAL IMAGINARY

In *Imagined Communities*, Anderson (2006, 4) attempts to make sense of the phenomenon of nationalism, questioning why it continues to elicit such strong "emotional legitimacy." Introducing the idea that the nation is "an imagined political community," he explains that, despite our inability to encounter each and every member of our nation we can conjure an image of our connection with one another through our imaginations (6). The dominant style or mode in which a nation imagines itself distinguishes it from other nations. Anderson broadens the concept of imagined communities beyond the nation, suggesting every community is imagined (ibid.). Moving from a national to a global scale, Appadurai (1996, 33) transforms Anderson's imagined communities into *imagined worlds*, "the multiple worlds that are constituted by the historically situated imaginations of persons and groups spread around the globe." The value of Appadurai's notion of imagined worlds lies both in its extension of community on a global scale and in its ability to capture alternative (transnational) imagined worlds that have the potential to subvert official (national) discourses.

In *Modernity at Large*, Appadurai's (1996, 3, emphasis in original) analysis hinges on two key interconnected social forces – mass mediation and mass migration – which he argues affect the "*work of the imagination* as a constitutive feature of modern subjectivity." For Appadurai, the imagination in the context of new global flows of images, sensations, and persons plays a new and critical role. He identifies three significant impacts of mass mediation, which open up possibilities for global imaginaries. First, electronic media offer ordinary people greater opportunities to use their imaginations in their everyday lives; second, the consumption of mass media has the potential to provoke agency, not merely escapism, through the work of the imagination; and, third, mass mediation brings individual imagining to the collective or group level (3–5). Significantly, it is this shift to a collective imaginary that provides the foundation for "the plurality of imagined worlds" (5). Appadurai's observations on the role of the imagination in the transnational electronic world form the backdrop for my exploration of the notion of the aural imaginary.

Dussel's (2009) view of the global visual imaginary in "Education and the Production of Global Imaginaries: A Reflection on Teachers' Visual Culture" also informs my conceptualization of the aural imaginary. Building on Appadurai and accentuating the role of the visual in the production of global imaginaries, Dussel positions globalization as "a visual discourse that allows people to make sense of the world, to attribute actions, and configure sentiments and emotions" (107). As Dussel's article indicates, research on global imaginaries largely concerns the visual aspects of social imaginaries (90). The idea of the aural imaginary represents another path to explore the work of the imagination as it recognizes the limitations of visual perceptions alone in reading a text or viewing an image (Kalyan 2006, 238). In "Hip-hop Imaginations: A Genealogy of the Present," Rohan Kalyan proclaims: "So many times the politics of what is seen masks what can only be revealed through sounds. People resist not only by making their struggles visible, but by making their voices heard, by being loud. The trick is to hear what is being said" (ibid.). Shifting the focus from the visual, I conceptualize the aural imaginary as a process through which the production and/or consumption of music becomes a framework for imagining and making sense of our place in the world, for mobilizing action, and for arousing sentiment.

My attention to music in conceptualizing the aural imaginary is vital in a number of respects. In *Ethnicity, Identity and Music*, Martin Stokes (1994, 3) regards music as an integral part of our understanding of modern life as it articulates "our knowledge of other peoples, places, [and] times ... and ourselves in relation to them." Moreover, he claims that, without music, "the social and cultural worlds that have been shaped by modernity" would be difficult to imagine (ibid.). Exploring the aural imaginary in relation to hip hop music is particularly illuminating. Recent research corroborates the growing importance of hip hop in the lives of youth, including many Indigenous (urban and reserve) youth in Canada. It documents hip hop's capacity to open up a space for telling stories and allowing expression of the experiences and impacts of cultural dislocation and colonization (see Lashua 2006; Lashua and Fox 2006; Low 2001; Marsh 2009a, 2011, 2012a, 2012b; Proulx 2010). Kalyan (2006, 239), for example, argues that hip hop offers a form of resistance to groups who experience marginalization and abjection from the dominant society. He contends that, through the performance and poetics of rap music, hip hop provides a means for cultural expression that holds the potential to transform "marginalized existences into creative sites [of] cultural resistance" (249). In *Global Englishes and Transcultural Flows*, Alastair Pennycook (2007) accentuates the socio-political and cultural aspects of hip hop as a creative response to oppression. Furthermore, in "Bits and Pieces of Truth: Storytelling, Identity, and Hip Hop in Saskatchewan," Charity Marsh (2012a, 348) demonstrates how Indigenous youth in Saskatchewan utilize hip hop culture to "convey the contradictions, struggles, resistances, and celebrations of their current lived experiences while simultaneously attempting to acknowledge and respect the (hi)stories of their ancestors." All these writers in varying degrees underscore the transformative possibilities of hip hop. Examining the aural imaginaries of youth involved in hip hop, especially those who have been marginalized or silenced as a result of poverty, racism, and migration, is critical in understanding how music and hip hop in particular allow youth to imagine resistant identities and social change.

Appadurai (1996, 4) asserts that electronic media equip individuals and groups with the resources for self-imagining "as an everyday social project." Recognizing the everyday aspect of the aural imaginary as a framework and social practice is integral to my analysis. It underlines the pivotal role of both music and the imagination in the day-to-day lives of ordinary people and maintains a populist perspective that sees "all people, not just the talented elect, the educated, and the powerful" as having the capacity for such activity (Berger and Del Negro 2004, 19). Appadurai (1996, 53) points out that, until recently, we tended to view fantasy and imagination as "residual practices, confined to special persons or domains, restricted to special moments or places." He observes that today the connection between the imagination and social life is progressively more a "global and deterritorialized one" (55). Mass media play a crucial part, offering a "store of possible lives" that cross the threshold into the "lived imaginations of ordinary people" (53). Similar to Appadurai's statement that ordinary people use their imaginations "in the practice of their everyday lives" (5), the production and consumption of music is likewise no longer limited to dominant social groups or restricted to special times, events, and places. The new participatory media landscape provides widespread access to a diversity of music as well as recording, producing, and mastering software. The music industry has experienced massive changes with the proliferation of websites and software that allow musicians to self-produce, promote, and distribute their own music, without relying on music industry professionals and major record labels. Stokes (2004, 54–5) contends that, despite the efforts of major transnational recording companies to manage the global circulation of music recordings, they exert little control over illegal downloads and have virtually "no control over the meanings, practices, and pleasures of listening … at the site of consumption" or over the production of local music, including rap and hip hop. In "Aboriginal Hip Hoppers: Representin' Aboriginality in Cosmopolitan Worlds," Craig Proulx (2010, 48) observes the internet's capacity to "in-reach" an internal Aboriginal public and "out-reach" an external non-Aboriginal public and how, in turn, this process contributes to the "decolonization of both Aboriginal and non-Aboriginal minds." Increased access to social media and new technologies clearly expands the work of the aural imaginary as an everyday social practice.

It is imperative to consider Appadurai's (1996) distinction between imagination and fantasy. Rejecting the contention that "electronic media are the opium of the masses," Appadurai argues that the consumption of mass media has the potential to "provoke resistance, irony, selectivity, and, in general, *agency*" (7, emphasis in original). He reasons that, while fantasy carries the "inescapable connotation" of thought removed from action, the imagination "has a projective sense about it," evoking action rather than escapism (ibid.). Highlighting the imagination as a social practice, Appadurai affirms:

> No longer mere fantasy … no longer simple escape … no longer elite pastime … and no longer mere contemplation … the imagination has become an organized field of social practices, a form of work (in the sense of both labor and culturally organized practice), and a form of negotiation between sites of agency (individuals) and globally defined fields of possibility … The imagination is now central to all forms of agency, is itself a social fact, and is the key component of the new global order. (31)

This definition of the imagination, with its emphasis on agency, is fundamental in exploring the work of the aural imaginary.

The construction of music as inherently national obfuscates the import of local and global influences. Stressing the global significance of hip hop, in "Another Root – Hip-Hop Outside the USA," Tony Mitchell contemplates the reach of hip hop beyond its origins in African American culture. For Mitchell (2001b, 1), hip hop culture has become a "vehicle for global youth affiliations and a tool for reworking local identity" across the globe. While hip hop developed more slowly in Canada, largely within black communities of Caribbean descent in Toronto, Halifax, and Montreal (Chamberland 2001), current research supports Mitchell's observations. In "Hybrid Identities in Quebec Hip-Hop: Language, Territory, and Ethnicity in the Mix," Mela Sarkar and Dawn Allen (2007, 117) argue that Quebec hip hop, with its many ethno-linguistic origins, has produced a local form of hip hop culture, providing a "dynamic site for the development of an oppositional community" and "new, hybrid identities for youth."

Bonar Buffam's research also points to the engagement of racially marginalized youth in hip hop globally. In "Can't Hold Us Back! Hip-hop and the Racial Motility of Aboriginal Bodies in Urban Spaces," Buffam (2011, 341) documents how Indigenous youth in Canada use hip hop to "contest and disrupt" racism and how the practices of hip hop offer the creative potential for self-transformation. In "Globalization, Identity, and Youth Resistance: Kenya's Hip Hop Parliament," Charity Marsh and Sheila Petty (2011, 133, emphasis in original) show how youth globally have turned towards hip hop culture, refashioning it for their particular locality and engaging in a "global *hip hop politics*" to "initiate dialogue, express lived experiences, tell collective stories, and enact youth agency." More specifically, Marsh and Petty examine the Hip Hop Parliament in Kenya (a youth collective of more than sixty underground hip hop artists established in Nairobi in 2007) and its engagement with hip hop as a mode of political expression, action, and resistance (133). Marsh has also studied the emergence, forms, and impacts of hip hop culture among Indigenous youth in Saskatchewan and on Baffin Island (see Marsh 2009a, 2009b, 2011, 2012a). This link between the local and the global evokes the concept "glocal." In *Globalization: The Key Concepts*, Annabelle Mooney and Betsy Evans (2007, 118) elucidate glocalization as another example of the way in which globalization involves "an interplay between micro (individual, localities) and the macro (global forces and players) that often bypasses the meso (states and other forms of collective representation)." Correspondingly, the imagined communities and imagined worlds of the youth of *Winnipeg Child*, which emerge through the work of the aural imaginary, surpass the nation, encompassing local and global settings.

THE CCAP HIP HOP PROJECT: PARTICIPATION, DESIGN, AND YOUTH MOBILIZATION

Youth Participants

While CCAP sought youth participation through informational campaigns, workshops, and music concerts during the first phase of the project, the recruitment process for the second phase of intensive training evolved over a one-month period between November and December 2008. During this time, many youth informally dropped by the studio to take part in the evening workshops. By January 2009, a group of ten youth was attending the studio workshops five evenings a week. Four other youth also participated in the training and public performances but were unable to attend on a consistent basis. The fourteen participants were Indigenous and new immigrant youth from Afghanistan, Kyrgyzstan, Ethiopia, and Sudan. The eight male and six female youth were between the ages of fourteen and twenty, mostly from lower-income neighbourhoods in the North and West Ends of Winnipeg. Six of the ten youth who regularly participated in the workshops were not attending school, and none of the youth had completed their high school education.

Project Design

There were a number of key components in the design of the CCAP Hip Hop Project. These included: establishing a safe, trusting, and comfortable environment for the youth; providing multi-media arts training; offering a high school credit course in Global Issues; and working with community partners towards the goal of staging the public performances of *Winnipeg Child*. In creating a nurturing and relaxed environment for the youth, the studio workshops (held each evening from Monday to Friday) began with a shared meal, giving the youth time to catch up with one another, talk about their day, and discuss music as well as to reflect upon their progress in the project with staff and artists. The youth often spoke of the family-like atmosphere at CCAP's art studio, and their interview narratives reflected strong bonds among participants and project mentors. One youth observed that CCAP was "a place where you can feel comfortable with yourself and hang out and laugh and not worry about … anybody starting a problem" (Youth End Interview #6). He emphasized: "They show that they want to understand where you're coming from and the hip hop. They *want* to understand" (Youth Mid-Interview #6). Over time, the youth developed close friendships, referring to each other as "a bunch of brothers and little sisters" (Youth Mid-Interview #7), which reinforced the feeling of the art studio as a second home.

CCAP staff and contracted artists formed mentorship relationships with the youth,[4] and they organized workshops in music, dance, film, photography, painting, mixed media, and computer animation. The artists worked individually and collectively with the youth to gain an understanding of what they wanted to express and how they might want to communicate their ideas through performance. The group had regular formal and informal meetings to share their ideas and to collaborate on designing the final performances. The youth spoke with excitement about working with the art mentors. One youth exclaimed, "When I first met the rap artist I was happy 'cause I've heard a lot of … like things about him, 'cause he's so good, and I hear that he got nominated for like the best rapper in Winnipeg, or whatever, so that was cool" (Youth End Interview #5). Referring to the dance instructor, another youth remarked: "She was so talented, man. She does these dances, like they're so crazy when she does it, but when she shows you, they're so easy, like you could do it" (Youth End Interview #10).

CCAP partnered with the University of Winnipeg Collegiate to provide a Grade 12 Global Issues course for the youth in the Hip Hop Project. Of the six students who took the Global Issues course, only one was attending school on a full-time basis. The instructor taught the course at the art studio twice a week throughout the twenty-week training period (later with the support of a student tutor); for the lab component of the course, instruction took place at the Collegiate campus. The instructor designed the course, which was highly participatory and interactive, with the aim of providing a curriculum that the youth saw as relevant to their daily lives. This was key as many youth spoke about their boredom and dislike of school as well as their experiences of conflict with teachers; several of them were on suspension from their schools. Although initially reluctant, one youth commented: "[The course] will help me get somewhere for sure. Go somewhere … plus, you're learning. Yeah, we learn about the world, you know " (Youth Mid-Interview #1). Another youth similarly commented: "Then, I was like, whatever, but then you know, I got the hang of it, got used to it, and … it's a good thing 'cause I've learned a lot … I just didn't know there's that much out there … This course makes me well … wanna go to school" (Youth Mid-Interview #6).[5]

Working together towards the goal of a final public performance entailed over five hundred hours of training in dance, audio recording, visual art, videography, photography, set design, and painting. With guidance from the CCAP staff and art mentors, the youth were involved in developing the entire production from stage preparation to props to performance. Over time, the youth grew in confidence and self-esteem and began to experiment with writing hip hop songs. One youth remarked, "Making the track and actually having it turn out to be good, it makes me feel good" (Youth Mid-Interview #2).

Another explained how his success inspired confidence in writing rap songs:

> Well, before I would just rap whatever comes to my head, whether it's bad or good, or whatever, just say anything, and now I write about a topic, you know. A topic that … something that means something to me … yeah, like my neighbourhood, for sure, my friends, too. And like … you'd be surprised, I think … like now I write about something they would be thinking about too. And they would be like, "holy shit" because they were thinking about the thing that I write too. (Youth Mid-Interview #1)

Guided by the art mentors in developing their ideas for the final performance, the youth drew upon their everyday lives and experiences, their feelings and responses to marginalization and cultural isolation, and their hopes and dreams for the future.

MOBILIZATION AND RESISTANCE THROUGH HIP HOP

The predominant feeling the youth shared about their neighbourhoods was one of isolation and estrangement. They reported little involvement in activities at their schools, community clubs, and other organizations. One youth commented that she does "nothing" in her neighbourhood because "really, I don't like my neighbourhood" (Youth Preliminary Survey #7).[6] According to another youth: "I don't really do nothing really with anyone in the area 'cause everyone is just really fucked up around here … like it makes me just want to stick to my own stuff … make my own music, you know?" (Youth Mid-Interview #1). Moreover, the youth spoke of the difficulties living in the inner city and their concern that the media negatively distorts their real lives. For these youth, performing hip hop in front of a public audience was a crucial way of communicating their views. One participant reflected:

> Yeah, I want people to realize how the real world is and how real children and the youth and the inner city are. I want them to realize how real it is. It's not something you just see on TV or something. It's real life that goes on around here. And when the media portrays kids, you know, why don't you go into the families and see

> what's going on? See where the kids are being raised, then you'll understand, you know. So that's what I wanted to bring across. Finally, get it across people's minds that, you know, we're here, and they're finally going to listen to me, now that I finally have the chance to say what I want to say. (Youth End Interview #6)

In another narrative, one youth addressed the issue of racism confronting new immigrants, relating her own feelings of being mistreated and dehumanized. This was the message she wanted to impart in her performance:

> I had like real problems with them because most of the time, not all of them, but most of the time, I've been treated like … not the way I should have been. I kind of feel bad, but to show them that we could do it. Even though we're immigrants, we came here to have a better life. We're still human beings! So, yeah I want to get that across. (Youth End-Interview #10)

Other youth talked about the demeaning stereotypes of inner-city youth and how they wanted to change these perceptions. For example, one youth said that he wanted to perform for adults to show them another side of youth:

> Because it's like, you know, they don't know … what they think is that we're just, you know, we're running around like hoodlums, but … until they actually, you know, like see the show and know what we're doing and how we're doing it and why we're doing it, then they won't know. They'll just think we're just running around being bad. (Youth Interview #5)

Through the public performance, this youth felt that "people got to know who we are and not just, you know, what we do."

The youth's narratives suggest that involvement in hip hop transformed their sense of self, serving as a vehicle for expressing hopes and dreams for the future. One youth felt his talent for hip hop gave him a more positive outlook on life and that having a voice made him feel like he had a future:

> It's changed a lot of things for myself. I'm more positive, um, I got to know a lot more people and I feel like I've a new start. A new,

> you know, new start. And seeing my future, and what I want to do right now in life. I have a talent and I shouldn't let it go to waste. Oh, the poetry and the spoken words … and I have a voice … [I'm] seeing, seeing what I want to do in life, being strong in my vision and looking more on the positive sides of life. (Youth End-Interview #6)

Another youth spoke of his dream of going to the United States and performing his unique style of rap for youth, especially for those who had experienced living in a war zone. He recognized the importance of rap as storytelling, stressing that "it's not just you talking about some money or something; you're telling a story, you know" (Youth End-Interview #4). He wanted to tell his story in a positive way and to connect with youth in an international community.

THE GENDERING OF HIP HOP CULTURE

While hip hop offers the potential for alternative and resistant forms of identity, its persistence as a male-dominated arena and its perpetuation of patriarchal gender norms remains problematic (see Marsh 2011). In this context, the gendering of various hip hop practices in the CCAP Hip Hop Project requires comment. In the project, it was predominately the male youth who wrote the rap songs, produced the beats, recorded the tracks, and performed the hip hop songs, whereas the female youth were more involved with dance. The prior experience of the male youth with writing and performing rap music seemed to give them more confidence, and their enthusiasm in working with a well-known Winnipeg Indigenous rap artist reinforced this self-assurance. The male youth were initially opposed, however, to participating in the hip hop dance workshops. One male youth informed the dance mentor, "We don't dance, we rap. The girls dance" (Art Mentor #1). Over time their attitude towards dance changed significantly, and they learned dance movements alongside the female youth. Similarly, as the female youth became more exposed to the writing and recording process, their interest grew in developing and performing their own songs. While this excitement did not materialize in the final public performances, I believe the female youth might have engaged in a more active role in writing and performing music had the project been offered a second time. (Unfortunately, funding could not be secured for additional hip hop projects.)

In "Hip Hop as Methodology: Ways of Knowing," Marsh (2012b) relates her experiences with the Scott Collegiate/IMP Labs Hip Hop Project, a curriculum-based program for high school course credit offered five times between 2008 and 2012. Reflecting on the predominance of male students in the project, she discusses her initial concern that the project may reinforce the perception of hip hop as a male-only domain and may not benefit both young men and women (196). Before long, it became clear to Marsh that the Hip Hop Project was advantageous to both male and female youth alike. The male students, who had lower graduation rates than the young women at Scott Collegiate, began to find the curriculum more meaningful and the participation rates of the female students started to rise (196–7). Apart from designing a unique hip hop curriculum, this may be attributed to Marsh's attempt to address the gender imbalance in the project by employing female research assistants, who were "experts on the technologies used and were able to demonstrate, teach, and perform in at least one or more of the primary elements of hip hop" (197). Such an initiative challenges the traditional gendering of hip hop and works towards ensuring a more active and participatory role for young women in hip hop culture.

In the CCAP Hip Hop Project, the art mentors were primarily female. While there were both male and female dance mentors, there was only one rap mentor, who was male. This might help to explain why the male youth transitioned more easily to dance, while the female youth hesitated to fully participate in the rap elements. Assuring greater gender diversity among the art mentors could be seen as a future step in breaking down barriers to access and supporting the participation of both male and female youth in all areas of hip hop. Unfortunately, the view persists that dance is the only gender-appropriate form of hip hop culture in which girls and young women can participate (see Marsh 2012a, 351). As Marsh points out, for female hip hop artists such as emcee Eekwol (Lindsay Knight) "access, opportunity, networking, and collaborative partnerships" remain the issue (359). The CCAP Hip Hop Project illustrates to some extent how gender binaries can begin to break down once youth have the opportunity to share a common goal and collaborate with both male and female mentors. Male and female youth equally articulated how working towards the final performance drew them closer together. For example, one youth explained: "It really meant something … the shows and everybody rehearsing and being on stage and everyone bringing out positive energy, and everyone being happy ... being close to everybody, being cool with everybody, like that means a lot to me. That *really* means a lot" (Youth Interview #6).

THE HIP HOP AURAL IMAGINARIES OF WINNIPEG CHILD

The youth's public performances of *Winnipeg Child* took place on 3 and 4 April 2009 at the Rachel Browne Theatre in Winnipeg, Manitoba. While the multi-media performances combine music, dance, and visual art, I turn to the hip hop songs and spoken word poetry as a means of understanding the aural imaginary.[7] As a guide for this analysis, I pose the following questions: What kinds of imagined communities and imagined worlds do the youth articulate in their lyrics? How does an aural imaginary cultivate these imagined communities and worlds? That is, how does music, and hip hop in particular, contribute to the work of the imagination? Further, how do the youth translate and communicate these imagined communities and worlds through performance? And, finally, what imagined communities and worlds are these youth speaking for and addressing, and how do they envision their place within these communities and worlds, now and in the future? Tackling these questions, I argue that, through the music and poetics of performing hip hop, the aural imaginary creates a spacc for dispersed and marginalized youth to voice their lived realities of marginalization and disenfranchisement, to mobilize resistant identities, and to cultivate new imaginings of community.

Through an analysis of seven hip hop songs written and performed by the male youth, I identify a number of imagined communities and worlds. The overarching imagined community expressed by the youth of *Winnipeg Child* is a global hip hop community, or what Samy Alim (2009, 3) refers to as the "'Global Hip Hop Nation (GHHN),' a multilingual, multiethnic 'nation' with an international reach, a fluid capacity to cross borders, and a reluctance to adhere to the geopolitical givens of the present."[8] This imagined global community represents a diversity of local hip hop scenes found across the world. The awareness of belonging to a global hip hop community is essential as it connects the youth of *Winnipeg Child* to other musicians locally and globally and fosters the imagining of community on a global scale. As Russell Potter (1995) argues, hip hop is a "transnational, global art form" whose locus is "simultaneously local and global" (quoted in Kalyan 2006, 249). While the youth of *Winnipeg Child* convey a sense of inclusion within a global hip hop community, they also evoke locality in their lyrics. The youth vocalize their imaginings of Winnipeg, which they refer to as W-P-G and Peg city, as a city where "racism wins again" (*Winnipeg Child* Program 2009, 8). In "The Truth," AMR expresses the racism, social problems, and repressive state regulation of Indigenous peoples in Winnipeg, depicting Winnipeg as a city where racist stereotypes are perpetuated by "who's mentioned when we talk about the booze, fights, drugs or dope addicts" (ibid.). These articulations, of what it is like to be "raised under Government System / Where you don't live, you're just existing," strike a similar chord in the diasporic aural imaginaries of the new immigrant youth (10). In his song, "The Reason Why," Azim addresses his life growing up in "Motherland Kyrgyzstan," where when a child turns ten, "He's the man, the soldier of this life" with "no choice … no voice, no opinion / On the streets chillin" (10). Azim's expression of street life as a struggle for survival parallels that of life on the streets of Winnipeg. In "Cruel Committee," Two Young describes the strategies for survival on the street, from prostitution to panhandling (11). The street is another imagined world that the youth frequently articulate in their lyrics. It is an imagined world that transcends boundaries and borders, a place found in any city across the globe. While most expressions of the street in the hip hop songs of *Winnipeg Child* point to the harsh realities of violence and racism, the street also creates a "space of identification" that resonates with youth both within and across different neighbourhoods and expands their ways of "thinking about the world" (Ibrahim 2009, 237). The final, and most illuminating, imagined world vocalized by the youth of Winnipeg Child is the "promise land" (Winnipeg Child Program 2009, 14). The youth speak of the promise land as an imagined (promising) future world free of racism, sexism, poverty, hunger, child soldiers, and violence, an inclusive world based on equality and unity that the youth imagine striving towards.

The youth's description of the promise land constructs an image of an empowering, decolonized world united by peace, love, and comradeship. It is an imagined future that the youth see themselves working together to build, not a future promised to them by someone else. Unlike the term "promised land," which reflects religious and colonial discourse and bespeaks of past (and continuing) broken promises between Indigenous peoples and the Canadian state, notably over (promised) land and unhonoured treaty agreements, the term "promise land" invokes the youth's agency in constructing their own promising future. The biblical roots of the image of a promised land conjure the reality of decades of destructive church- and state-imposed policies and practices, from forced Christianity and compulsory schooling in residential schools, to the criminalization of sacred ceremonies such as the Potlatch, to the state appropriation of land and the imposition of the reserve system, to the over-incarceration of Indigenous people, especially male youth. In playing upon this notion of the promised land, the youth's imaginings of the promise land as a positive and productive future world additionally evokes an image of a past and current world that has been (com)promised, divided, and usurped by a colonizing dominant power.

In exploring how a hip hop aural imaginary cultivates the work of the imagination, it is instructive to consider the strategies of cultural resistance embedded in the language and music of hip hop. Kalyan (2006, 254) identifies four main strategies: a rearticulation of history, a redressing of a history of wrongs, an assertion of identity, and a call for something different. In "What Does it Mean…" Illaztic addresses the traumatic history of colonization and the devastating impacts of residential schools with a reworking and rearticulation of traditional Indigenous life. In the refrain "What does it mean to be aboriginal?" Illaztic sorts through various articulations of what being Aboriginal has come to signify in Winnipeg, expressing what it feels like to be "looked at as a criminal to [being] ashamed if you wasn't traditional," and concludes, "I'll never know unless I look / What does it mean to be aboriginal?" (*Winnipeg Child* Program 2009, 9). The repetition of Illaztic's refrain in seeking and asserting Indigenous identity is what Kalyan (2006) refers to as a process of cultural translation. In his analysis of the Hawaiian hip hop group Sudden Rush, Kalyan reiterates Homi Bhabha's (2004) explanation of cultural translation. Bhabha maintains that culture is translational "because spatial histories of displacement" complicate the question of "how culture signifies, or what is signified by culture" (as quoted in Kalyan 2006, 244). Kalyan analyzes the translational aspect of Hawaiian identity in the hip hop lyrics of Sudden Rush and locates the assertion of Hawaiian identity through the repetition of the lyric, "What is a true Hawaiian?" This is strikingly similar to Illaztic's refrain and suggests the shared quest for asserting identity. Other statements of identity in the music of *Winnipeg Child* centre on the communication of identity in opposition to the violence, hate, and dreamlessness of the street as the youth imagine themselves as agents of change, with "the world in [their] eyes / the future in [their] hands (*Winnipeg Child* Program 2009, 13). In "The Reason Why" Azim affirms, "Now when I rap, can you hear the confidence in my voice / Can you see it in my eyes / Cuz I see it in my choice" (10).

Furthermore, the aural imaginaries of *Winnipeg Child* constitute a collective imaginary. Appadurai (1996, 8) speaks of the imagination as a "property of collectives" and argues that "part of what the mass media make possible, because of the conditions of collective reading, criticism, and pleasure," is a "'community of sentiment,' a group that begins to imagine and feel things together." Correspondingly, Kalyan (2006, 246) observes that hip hop lyrics have the capacity to express "solidarity against oppression and colonization, constituting broader social identities of resistance that transcend racial divisions by rearticulating history from positions of common marginalization." Through the collaborative process involved in producing the hip hop music of *Winnipeg Child*, the Indigenous and new immigrant youth discover the connections between their local struggles of violence, racism, and oppression, and those experienced by youth in different countries around the world. This is not to diminish the impact of local histories, issues, and conditions but, rather, to emphasize the ability of youth to recognize their common struggles, allowing them to collectively imagine "alternative worlds and counter-globalizations" (249). This collective aural imaginary is especially apparent in the song "Together Together," co-written and performed by four members of the group, who express solidarity in their collective imagining of a global promise land. Mandela sets the tone of the song: "What's wrong with da world / People keeping dying / people keeping lying / even you see da kids crying" (*Winnipeg Child* Program 2009, 14). Azim steps in: "We need it over sease [sic] / we need it over here / Let's build a better future now / So after many years, millions of children can live a life / Withouta fears, withouta guns and tears … / Just imagine, country got no revolution and corruption / better days / where war is not an option / Well, here my friend, hold my hand to the promise land" (14). AMR concludes the song with his commentary: "Complexion and colour we don't have to fear / Immigrants and aboriginals be working together to make a decision for the world / boy or girl, young or old" (14). "Together Together" is a fitting example of what Pennycook (2007, 85) calls message or conscience rap, a genre of hip hop that "takes overt political stances against racism [and] violence," a genre defined in distinction to the misogynistic lyrics of gangsta rap.

The juxtaposition of this imagined future world with the gangsta rap lyrics of "Cruel Committee" reveals the contradictions embedded in hip hop culture (Marsh 2009a, 117). Whereas the lyrics of "Together Together," with its emphasis on unification and harmony, demonstrate "a politics of resistance" (ibid.), the lyrics of "Cruel Committee" reproduce a discourse of authenticity that relies on negative stereotypes and problematic gender relations. In "Cruel Committee" Krayzee, for example, advises: "Better be listening to what I'm dish'n out / Do'n this just to let you know what I'm all about / All about money bitches tracks" (*Winnipeg Child* Program 2009, 11). Examining these songs side by side highlights how, in addition to enabling a site of resistance, hip hop culture perpetuates problematic stereotypes, notions of violence, hyper-masculinity, and sexist gender roles through a discourse of authenticity (Marsh 2011, 151–3).

It is important to consider the songs and lyrics of *Winnipeg Child* within the context of their performance as it illuminates the embodied aspect of performing. Drawing on Richard Bauman and Charles Briggs's (1990) understanding of performance as "a frame that invites critical reflection on communicative processes" (quoted in Pennycook 2007, 74), Pennycook argues that, as an embodied performance, hip hop calls attention to language as social action. In this respect, I argue that, through the act of performing, the youth of *Winnipeg Child* invite their audiences to reflect critically on what they are trying to communicate. This relates to Pennycook's point that the significance of the idea of performance is not in the spectacle per se but "in the interactions that performance calls forth" (77). Pennycook stresses that the shift from the performative to the transformative is crucial for approaching performativity as neither simply "the playing out of public roles nor the acting out of sedimented behaviour, but the refashioning of futures" (ibid.). In the concluding hip hop song of the performance, the youth gather together, arms outstretched, inviting the audience to join them in singing the refrain of "Together Together." Through the hip hop songs and performances, the youth enact their views against racism, concerns for social justice, and visions for social change, seeking to engage the audience in a reciprocal dialogue. The audience's responses are positive and palpable as they rise to their feet, clap their hands to the music, and join the youth onstage. Thinking through the notion of performance as interactive in the context of

Winnipeg Child, it becomes apparent that the act of performing hip hop not only opens up a space for forming new and resistant identities among marginalized youth but also allows them to translate how they see and make sense of the world and to engage the audience in a dialogue about social change and transformation.

CONCLUDING REFLECTIONS

Although I conceptualize the hip hop aural imaginary as a positive transformative process, there are some troubling aspects of hip hop that require comment. Popular media discourses on hip hop generally concentrate on its violence, misogyny, and racism. Academic critics of hip hop acknowledge these problematic aspects and argue that, while elements of hip hop's authenticity may lie in violence, "this does not render hip-hop itself inherently violent" (Pennycook 2007, 85),[9] nor does it deny its potential to express greater social consciousness and "progressive politics" (Newman 2009, 195; see also Marsh 2011). As discussed in the first section of this chapter, current research documents the expressive and transformative potential of hip hop.[10] In "Under Construction: Identifying Foundations of Hip-Hop Feminism," Whitney Peoples (2008, 21) maintains that, "beyond the problematic of demeaning women [through] its incontestable misogyny, hip hop provides a space for young black women to express their race and ethnic identities and to critique racism." This observation is consistent with the responses of the female youth in the CCAP Hip Hop Project. In the interviews, they told stories about their experiences of racism and discrimination, both as immigrant newcomers and as youth living in the inner city. They also affirmed the importance of expressing their thoughts and feelings through hip hop and collectively performing in front of a public audience for other immigrant and Indigenous youth as well as "for white Canadians" (Youth End-Interview #10).

The youth's collaborative achievement in creating and staging *Winnipeg Child* captures the work and positive impacts of the hip hop aural imaginary. Interacting with a live audience was especially meaningful to the youth. They wanted to connect with their audiences, feel that they were being heard, and advocate for social change. One youth spoke of the energy exchanged between the hip hop performers and the audience, describing it "like ping pong, like you give them energy, and you get back energy" (Youth End-Interview #4). This youth felt the audience members, especially new immigrants, understood what he was trying to communicate. He explained: "Immigrants that had to go through the same thing, you know, and they understood me. Even the native people, like they're not living in paradise here, you know, they are still going through struggles. So they understood me." In particular, the youth recognized the value of performing for other youth who felt marginalized: "The [reserves] and the kids that are from different countries who feel like they don't belong when they come here because of their culture, I want to do it for those groups" (Youth End Interview #6). The youth also spoke of the support and empathy they felt as a result of working together on the Hip Hop Project. This brings to mind Marsh's (2006, 92) finding that "shared anxieties, excitements, and responsibilities" and not "essential qualities of sameness" elicit bonding among participants in a project. Admiring the talent of one of the co-participants, one youth realized the power of hip hop to convey a sense of a common struggle: "And it's cool. He makes people understand what it's like to go through struggles" (Youth Interview #8). Finally, the youth spoke of the emotions they inspired from the audience: "A lot of them cried, a lot of them were touched, a lot of them were happy. Yeah, it was very real" (Youth End-Interview #6). These comments suggest that the hip hop aural imaginary has a powerful expressive capacity. Through the work of the aural imaginary in creating and performing hip hop music, the youth gained a sense of agency and began to envision their place in the world, imagine new worlds, demonstrate their value to the broader community, and call for change.

NOTES

1 The CCAP art studio first opened its doors in downtown Winnipeg in 2000. Over the years, Edith Regier, artistic director and founder of CCAP, has developed a variety of projects in a number of locations from the inner city of Winnipeg to Island Lake in northern Manitoba to Nepal. Consistent with its art practices, CCAP gathers diverse groups of people together to share stories, lived experiences, and culture and "to engage their imaginations and their voices in dialogues about social change locally and globally" (Crossing Communities Art Project n.d.). Information about the history and work of CCAP, including the Hip Hop Project and the Evaluation Study, can be located at the CCAP website.

2 Funders included: National Crime Prevention Strategy Community Action Fund, Canada Council for the Arts, Manitoba Arts Council, Winnipeg Arts Council, Neighbourhoods Alive!, and the Winnipeg Foundation.

3 I had the privilege of working with the youth, first as a volunteer at the outset of the intensive training period in November 2008 and later as a research assistant from January to August 2009. I was also one of the co-investigators of the project evaluation prepared for the National Crime Prevention Strategy Community Action Fund. As a member of the evaluative team, I participated in all stages of the research process, including: the construction of interview guides, conducting interviews with youth participants and project mentors (e.g., contracted artists, course instructors), transcribing audio interviews, and editing preliminary drafts of the report.

4 Edith Regier, who is also a visual artist, designed the Hip Hop Project and played a key mentorship role throughout all phases of the project as well as staging the final public performances alongside the artistic director of Winnipeg's Contemporary Dancers. CCAP staff and seven contracted artists worked with the youth, mentoring them in a wide range of art forms. The mentors represented a diverse group of artists, coming from different cultures, race/ethnicities, ages, genders, and skill sets.

5 It should be noted that all six students completed the course with grades ranging from B to A+.

6 At the beginning of the project, there was an informal preliminary survey undertaken with the youth to gather some background information (e.g., their interests and community involvement).

7 While I focus on the hip hop music and performance of *Winnipeg Child*, I understand that hip hop includes a wide range of cultural practices, such us MCing, DJing, graffiti art, breakdancing, fashion, language, style, knowledge, and politics. I am also aware of the problematic aspects of referring to hip hop or hip hop culture in the abstract as a "singular and monolithic" form and recognize that there is a plurality of hip hop cultures (Alim 2009, 2–3).

8 Alim's use of the term "nation" to describe this global community is interesting, exemplifying Anderson's identification of persisting discourses of nationalism; yet, the term "community" seems better suited to Alim's description of the global hip hop nation and its fluid borders.

9 Pennycook's (2007) argument is threefold. First, there are many different genres of hip hop, gangsta rap being only one of several types of rap, and many different realities presented in "reality" rap. Second, in view of the audience of gangsta rap, which he defines as white, suburban, middle-class youth, Pennycook contends that this criticism requires reinterpreting gangsta rap "in terms of a white fascination with violence" (85). Third, within a

global context, the meaning and lyrics of rap must be reconsidered and recontextualized. He explains, "While hip-hop around the world may draw on aspects and styles of US hip-hop, the localizations of hip-hop as well as overt opposition to violence and 'bling bling' culture make rap in different contexts explicitly non-violent" (85). See Pennycook (2007, chap. 5), for his entire argument and analysis.

10 For more information, refer to Buffman 2011; Kalyan 2006; Lashua 2006; Lashua and Fox 2006; Low 2001; Marsh 2009a, 2011, 2012a, 2012b; Marsh and Petty 2011; Pennycook 2007; Potter 1995; and Proulx 2010.

7

A ROYAL STATE OF MIND

An Interview with True Daley

Mark V. Campbell

INTRODUCTION

True Daley was one of the founding members of the *Masters at Work* radio show in Montreal at CKUT 90.3 FM. Since her initial start in radio in Montreal, True has gone on to work in radio in Toronto and in television in Asia. As a young, black anglophone woman growing up in a Montreal suburb, True offers an interesting and unique perspective on hip hop in Canada during some of its earlier years. Having moved to Toronto and lived in Asia, True sat down to reflect on some of her earliest memories of hip hop in Montreal. Her insights and stories revealed the layered and complex ways in which the black female hip hop body must negotiate through differing levels of patriarchy, which are not always or solely perpetrated by men. Within the limited confines of her suburban upbringing, her anglophoneness, and her racialization, True relays stories of empowerment and of resistance with a decidedly feminist leaning. The intersections of race, class, gender, and, in the case of Montreal, language, meant True's personal development of resilience, career-focused skills, and racial consciousness were significantly channelled through experiences in the hip hop community. Particularly in the realm of journalism, as a radio and television broadcaster and writer, True's career has been marked by a number of high-profile successes. Despite her mother's disapproval and clashes with women in her teens and early twenties, True continues two decades later to hold a strong and progressive feminist

7.1 True Daley in concert. Photo courtesy of the artist.

politic, actively seeking to work with and support women in the hip hop industry.

Interestingly, True's spatial analysis suggested that feelings of belonging and her heightened racial consciousness occurred by "being around black people," something that was not a notable part of suburban life. Moving along a hip hop circuit, from Montreal to Toronto to New York and back, seems to have helped solidify, if not solely nostalgically, Montreal as home. Despite the racism that she "discovers" upon the influx of Haitian immigrants, True not only keeps Montreal close to her heart, she creatively designs an ode to her home town that she represents in classic hip hop fashion. New York holds a somewhat mythical spot in True's articulation of hip hop, much as it does for many non-American hip hop artists. Surprisingly, New York's importance as the birthplace of hip hop does not replace Montreal as the central focus of True's affections and feelings of home. Unsurprisingly, and this is probably due to her success in a number of realms, True continued to record, perform, and remain immersed in hip hop music for twenty years, demonstrating that hip hop was not a fad or simply an isolated moment in her youth. The interview below was designed to simply relay remembered experiences of growing up in Montreal's hip hop in the late

1980s as a way of uncovering herstories and bringing voice to some of the obscured and overlooked narratives that make rich Canada's hip hop inheritances.

INTERVIEW

MARK V. CAMPBELL: How did you get into rhyming?

TRUE DALEY: Well my old school name was Royal T, circa 1988, that's probably when I started rhyming. First of all, I do not have the typical story of "I grew up in the impoverished neighbourhood" and never had the "missing father" and all that other stuff. I pretty much had a Cosby show kind of lifestyle. I was the only black family on my street. And, I think at the time when I was going to high school it was all about Rock. Rock and Pop. I was listening to Bon Jovi, Depeche Mode, Mighty Lemon Drops, Skinny Puppy, The Cure, then I was also listening to White Snake, Poison, and Madonna and Prince. Then L.L. came through and then I started getting into hip hop. So, when I was starting in my junior high school years, all the kids were making fun, asking "What's this Rap music? This crap." They were insulting and it was embarrassing 'cause I didn't want to be associated with anything that they didn't like because I was the only black kid in my school and the black person on the street. As hip hop started to gain more popularity, the messages were so militant or socially aware or so-called "conscious" and that helped me with my identity. People were bringing back tapes, I had cousins that would go to New York – we were all dreaming about going to New York because I started learning about hip hop culture and New York through these tapes. My cousins and family and friends would bring back tapes because they would go every summer, but my parents hated the States – we never went. The closest I got to New York was Plattsburgh [laughs]. We'd go to Plattsburgh, New York [laughs].

MARK: So your cousins brought back cassettes, mixtapes to Montreal?

TRUE: They brought back cassettes, that's how I learned about DJ Red Alert, and I told my friends to tape the commercials, so the whole show would run. HOT 97 just all day, all night, just turn the cassette over and I would just listen. Listen to what people would call in and talk about, listen to the accent, listen to the hottest tracks, and there were so many IDs, the station IDs were so interesting and so different with so many guests. Once I heard these tapes I got excited and I started telling my mother, "I'm gonna move to New York, that's where I'm going to go, I'm just gonna move to New York" and move to the Bronx, you know, 'cause that's where it is, that's where black people are [laughs], and Spike Lee was coming out [laughs]. When I was growing up, we were watching a lot of eighties sitcoms and there weren't a lot of black people, then. There was *Diff'rent Strokes* came out and then *Facts of Life*, so I was trying to be like Tootie, and Kim Fields was my hero 'cause I was into acting. And so, the only time that I probably was popular, I was pretty much, I wouldn't even say I was a nerd, 'cause I wasn't that good, I was average in school. And I wasn't an athlete, and I didn't have a lot of friends, I just didn't. The neighbourhood was predominately wealthy, it started off Jewish and then ended up being an Italian and Greek neighbourhood, and they were very into their culture and very proud of who they were. And, very aware of their religion, their language, their homeland, you know? And um, my parents were more concerned with raising me as a Canadian and didn't understand how that alienation occurred. So hip hop gave me a sense of pride, gave me a sense of black pride. By the time I graduated high school I was blackity black black [laughs]. I was a bit militant and my mother thought I was out of my damn mind! I wanted to change my last name, my last name is a slave master's name.

MARK: Is this the effect of Public Enemy?

TRUE: Yeah, very much so, and interestingly enough I don't know how it happened, maybe when *Colors* came out, I think that's when I got caught up with the West Coast. I was like, "I love Ice T, I love this guy, what do I have in common with this man?" I'm living in a suburban home, I'm talking to my mother about the black plight and poverty and the ghetto, and she is looking at me and she is not getting it. You know, why would I cling to something like poverty or, you know, I remember telling her once, I would have rather had lived in a ghetto 'cause at least they know they are black. She was shocked out of her mind.

MARK: Wow, I can only imagine.

TRUE: Yeah, I wasn't allowed to visit from the suburbs to the city. I wasn't allowed to go to the city, my parents sheltered me. I wasn't allowed to go down to the 'hood right? To the neighbourhoods where you could just, we would cut school, me and a few black girls that I knew in neighbouring suburbs, we would call each other up and cut school so we could travel an hour and a half to go down where the black people were. We'd get a patty and cola champagne and be cool! 'Cause you couldn't get that! There were no Caribbean restaurants anywhere! There was no B.E.T. [Black Entertainment Television]. There was no *Rap City*, there was none of that! And all the hip hop artists that would come to Canada would always go to Toronto, they would never come to Montreal! It was so frustrating.

MARK: And this is happening in the late 1980s?

TRUE: Yes, in the late eighties no one was coming. If they were coming, I wasn't allowed to go. Hip hop I think liberated me, so by the time I got to college, luckily for me I started college around in the late eighties – eighty-eight, eighty-nine. This was the perfect time. I wanted to be an actor, my mother was not having that, neither was my father. They were not going to pay for me to prance around and quote Shakespeare, as they said. So I was at a loss for what to do.

MARK: What college are you going to?

TRUE: Sadly enough, I loved my college, but it was where the massacre happened, Dawson College, where this, a man came out wielding a gun and shooting several women. Ironically, he also came from my hometown Laval. So that's another issue, is I lived in the suburbs until I was eight years old in an area called Cote-St-Luc, which was, at the time, a predominately wealthy Jewish neighbourhood. My mother worked in a Jewish retirement home. My mother came to Canada as a housekeeper, as a maid, my dad worked in a factory. My father stopped going to school at nine. My mother may have completed high school and their work ethic was ridiculous. Growing up in the suburbs also gave me exposure to so many different experiences. I love the fact that I grew up there now, I resented it then. I grew up like many Canadians, there was no urban music radio stations, it was all adult contemporary radio, pop and rock. When I got to college it was to me, at that time, *A Different World* had just started [on television] and I thought it was a different world because it was predominately black. Dawson College had a creative arts program and social sciences and stuff, and that [was] where the majority of the black young people that I knew went. I had never been around so many black people in my life. I thought, everybody's just gonna be chillin' everything's going to be great! NOT! If you were not skinny like, I had a conscious issue about my body size because they would tease me at high school and now, people are getting butt implants. Or lip injections, right? I wished my nose was straighter, I wished my skin was lighter ...

MARK: Is this primarily because of your upbringing in Cote-St-Luc?

TRUE: No, maybe Laval, so I ended up moving to Laval when I was about eight or nine years old and living there till I was twenty-three before I moved to Toronto. Laval is the second largest island in Quebec and that's also where DJ Starting from Scratch is from. He went to Laval Catholic High School and I went to a school across the street.

MARK: So then how did you travel down to the *Masters at Work* radio show?

TRUE: *Masters at Work* started because I was going to college and a young woman, I'll never forget her name, Darah Edwards, she was a good friend of Mike Mission, she said, "You know," 'cause I used to host events. I used to host events and I had a big mouth and a lot of opinions. We had a student group called Black & Third World, and it was a student group, and we always had these political debates about the state of Pan-Africanism and other things.

I had the medallions and the nose ring, the hoop – my mother thought I had lost my mind. She had raised her daughter and then Royal T emerged [laughs] out of some mixtapes and a couple of music videos! Going up to Dawson was great for me in some ways because I got exposed to even more black people, to black culture, and felt more at peace with who I was. But I also got my first taste of the divisiveness and the competition and violence. Straight up violence, the things that people went through in high school, I went through in college. Girls were trying to beat me down, and the rumours, I was like shocked because I had not come from those neighbourhoods, no one had known me, so looking back I'm the new chick on the block.

Hip hop culture introduced me to three careers simultaneously: (1) as a broadcaster 'cause that was my first experience hosting *Masters at Work* for three or four years and then (2) [in] community activism because of the topics and the issues that were being raised in the music, [which] gave me a better understanding and I was majoring in political science, and (3) as a hip hop artist because I had a chance to not only be introduced to the music and the culture but at the same time [to] continue creating because I was immersed in it. So, if I wasn't performing or hosting, I was interviewing someone. So I was able to always be in the mix in that way. So, it was good, it was the best of times and the worst of times, like any major turning point in your life. Being female was hard enough, being from the suburbs I think that was worse! Because they just didn't want to give you any clout, so it got to the point where people, and every female emcee I know goes through this, where guys will literally come up to you and ask you, "Who writes your rhymes?" It is the most insulting thing! It's like, "I read books dude!" [laughs] I know how to write! You know, and no one can teach you how to flow. If you can't flow, you just can't flow [laughs]. So, even if somebody wrote something for you and you can't flow? What difference does it make? I think that it was my, so I went through a lot of pluses because I was very active in the community and I was hosting and I was emceeing and doing all these things on the radio. But if I was off the microphone the hate was so hard! It was so much! It was guys who, you know, the rumours were just ridiculous it was just ridiculous, it was really, really bad. It's actually, we look back and we're like, "oh, it's not that bad," but it's really traumatizing when all you have is your reputation as a young person and you're trying to, you're in love with your people and you're in love with your community and, uh, it's not as utopic as you'd expect. And then you are in hip hop culture, which is extremely competitive, you know what I'm trying to say? And everybody wants their moment to shine and here comes this chick ... you know what I'm trying to say? I can't even imagine what Michie's stories are like – hers is on some other level 'cause she is a star.

MARK: So when was your first live performance? The first time you got on stage as an emcee?

TRUE: The first time I was on a stage and I was an MC ... I think the one that I remember the most was probably when I was opening, when I formed a group. Because I did a lot of solo stuff, but I was always in the studio. Eventually, because I was in the studio, and I was on the radio, then the promoters started thinking about, you know, ways to get me on stage. I did a lot of community shows, but the one I remember the most was when I formed a group of girls in college called The Attitude Crew. They were a group of girls that I hung out with so we had a hype girl, we had dancers, we had two emcees, we were just killing it. And we wore all the same outfits and there was a place in the mall that would stitch whatever you wanted in it, it's all about your name right? Some people had fuzzy letters, we had stuff in cursive stitched on every piece of clothing and we were The Attitude Crew.

MARK: Are those the girls in that photo?

TRUE: So, we were The Attitude Crew, there was myself, there's a girl named Neesha Nee [laughs], Es-Gee, Kay Gee, Royal T, it was all the E's and we opened for Ice T. That was pretty crazy 'cause Ice T was my idol. I don't know why, looking back, why I had this affinity to like this [image of Ice-T as a] PIMP! [laughs] But, no, he's a legend, he's a West Coast legend! And I remember at the time he was with his wife, his black wife [laughs], not the new wife with the butt implants, the old wife, I think her name was Darlene or something and, ah, it was just interesting to meet this star, you know, and he was very humble and very sweet and very kind. So we opened for Ice T, [an] all-female crew opening for Ice T, and it was phenomenal.

MARK And did the crowd respond?

TRUE: They were great! People were not expecting us. I think when a female steps on the stage, first they're looking at what she look like, 'cause its predominately men. Okay, she's cute, now let's see if she can do something, the fact that you can actually do something overrides everything else. But, as a female, if you're not getting respect after your performance, male or female, chances are you're just not a good performer [laughs]. Some people talk about, "there's hate," there's this there's that, I don't think you should as an emcee wait for the audience to respond to you. Especially in a place like Toronto because they pride themselves on being this "screw face capital," which I think is the worst thing to pride yourself on. I remember an old manager said "you have to command the stage" you know, you have to control the audience, the audience cannot control you, you know? And if you're a great live performer you could be singing the alphabet people will love it. You could be cracking your voice, missing notes and stuff, but if you're just hyped on your own ish, I think people respond to that. If you're not begging them for the approval, you're just commanding the stage. You own it, and I think that, growing up, I think that emcees that grew up in the eighties, you know what I'm saying, are better emcees than people today who are just studio artists who wanna make a video and they can't tour, they can't do a concert, they can't engage an audience, they don't have people skills, they don't know what to do when the sound goes out, when the mic is crap, you know what I'm trying to say? When the CD skips, they have no clue what to do. I run an after school program and some of these young girls, you know, they expect everything to be perfect when things happen, and I'm like, "it's not going to be that way."

MARK: Yeah, you got to learn to move with the crowd.

TRUE: YES!!! And I really think that that is the blessing when most of these young people, who do they admire? They admire people that are in their forties. Like Jay-Z is for sure, what – mid-forties? I think I love that in a way, that hip hop is still here, it's still around, and that those who are really able to rock a crowd, ah, are those that came and grew up, it's kind of like you had a rite of passage. 'Cause we don't have that anymore.

MARK: What's beautiful, is to see De La Soul on stage these days, they can get up and they can rock a crowd. And they're rhyming about their family and kids, real life. They've been doing it for twenty years or twenty-five years ...

TRUE: I was hosting a show on CBC back in the day called *ZeD*, a pilot series, and I was able to meet them in Vancouver. They are veterans, there's swag, there's a certain level of swag.

MARK: When the mic goes out they know what to do. When there's no record, when the DJ doesn't show up to the show, they're rocking the crowd. I think Biz Markie was one of those people who were just rocking the entire show, records or not.

Switching gears now back to Montreal, do you think, or, from your experiences, was there an anglophone/francophone division?

TRUE: Yeah, like any city, like any society, artists are always impacted by what's happening and we are the storytellers, right? Any artistic medium that you use. To think about being a first generation Canadian of Jamaican descent, growing up in a province that, you know, was kind of shunned by the rest of the country that has a history of being rebellious. I mean the French are no joke [laughs]. So, we had a lot of clashes with a lot of new immigrants coming into the city and at first, when we were growing up, we were taught that it was a language barrier as to why we were not getting the jobs that others were getting. So, when you had a large influx of Haitians, and they themselves are not getting it [jobs], we're like "Oh Shit! Its Racism!" [laughs] That's when I think a lot of clashes started coming and then they started to pass the law Bill 101 where they said that, they said it was going to be bilingual and they wanted to preserve the French culture and language. You just woke up one day and everything was in French. People would not serve you, in stores, if you did not speak to them in French. That still happens to a lot of people who are tourists, much less if you grew up there. Toronto, to me, represented independence, especially for black people because I had never seen someone drive a bus that was Black in my life until I came to Toronto. I'd never seen a black bank teller until I came to Toronto. I had never seen any black person or persons of colour in any position of power, and what you guys may consider nothing major to us was major. It was kind of like the segregation in the South, where people just didn't bother with what was going on in the South 'cause the North was so bustling and stuff. Because we were so separate from the rest of Canadian society there was a lot of stuff that was going down that nobody really knew about. The drug scene in Montreal was no joke! It's like the Wild Wild West, you know what I'm saying? 'Cause you had a lot of the Jamaican gangs, and this is prior to the Haitians coming in. Then you also had the Hells Angels headquarters, like they are no joke! When you have Skinheads in Montreal its serious. I find that Toronto is just more diplomatic, very British, very diplomatic, everything's really polite and nice and maybe there's, uh, maybe there's a higher rate of white-collar crime?

MARK: How about experiencing Montreal as an anglophone?

TRUE: And that's the thing, you became rebellious, number one I'm black, number two I'm female, number three I'm an anglophone and my parents are Jamaican, like I'm not feeling it. So I ended up going to Toronto because the options for me were limited in what I could do creatively and also financially and I just felt very stifled. I did speak French but I didn't even, it's so funny the mental, I guess you could say mental chains that you have. I never spoke it because we were always told as anglophones our French wasn't good enough. So we just never spoke it. But we had been learning it and speaking it and understanding it our entire lives when necessary, so I come to Toronto and there were all these call centres and I'm getting paid like twenty bucks. You know what I'm trying to say? In the nineties per hour! Right? Just to answer stuff in French, I'm like "For real??" So that's how I made enough money when I was going to college in London, Ontario. But, Toronto taught me, I guess you could say, about the music industry. Montreal taught me about live performance, passion, creativity, and it was just much more sociable. It could be the bad weather that people clung together, it could be the political scene, we were anybody who was not anglophone if you were Filipino, black, whatever, you know, Asian, whatever, you clung to each other because you were the enemy compared to white Québécois. You were second-class citizens compared to white Québécois, so, ALL cultures got together and we were more unified. Montreal is a very small city. It's not spread out like Toronto, you could literally have your own scene in Brampton, it wasn't really like that. Everybody congregated pretty much in the same areas. So, coming to Toronto taught me that there was an industry. I learned about grants, I'd never known there were grants available to artists. This is where I was able to make my first music video, this is where I was able to, to do a lot of live performances. Honey Jam was crucial because it was a space where females could actually, you know, show their skills, 'cause nobody else was putting us on. As females, it's a fine line, you know, because most of the people you work with are going to be males and many of them, no matter how creative you are, if they're not getting something out of it personally or financially they don't really see a point. They'd rather spend all day in their studio with a bunch of whack dudes that ain't going nowhere than spend two hours with a female that actually has some potential, you know what I'm saying? If they are not going to get, you know, benefits, personal benefits, or financial benefits. So, if you ain't giving it up and you ain't got that much money? And you're trying to work in the studio, dude was like, "Meh," "I don't know," he'll just go chill with his boys. You know what I mean? So it's a catch-22, but Toronto definitely taught me about the business of it that's a pro and a con because I lost, I think, a lot of my creative freedom being here [in Toronto]. And when I lived in Asia and came back I think I got it back because I was able to kind of experiment and try different things. But I find you get put in a box, people are very limited in what they can expect from a person. I started doing some spoken word and they were like, "Well, are you a spoken word artist? Or are you a hip hop artist?" Then I started singing and they are like, "Well, are you singing? Or are you doing hip hop? Like what's going on?" You know? And "Which Crew are you with?" and "Which box can we put you in? And can you just stay there?" [Laughing] You know? That's how I felt.

MARK: So, were there other events that were happening in Montreal, besides *Masters at Work*, at the time?

TRUE: Well, Montreal in terms of the radio station, *Masters at Work* was the definitive radio show for hip hop. They were breaking new tracks, they were going to New York all the time, coming back with the latest stuff. I realized that some of my feminist ideologies were formed there. I remember I got into a major argument because one of the top promoters at the time wanted me to read a flyer talking about a contest for the best batty riders. At some show, I was supposed to read this flyer, and I'm like "I'm not reading it," and the DJ's like, "You gotta read, Royal T, you gotta read it." And I'm like, "I'm not reading it and I am not sitting here as a female talking about, call now!" "And whoever wears the best punny printa and best batty rider gets $50." I'M NOT DOING IT. The promoter got so offended, he came down to the station and it was going to get violent. He was basically demanding that I read it, and I was like, "Make me! Make me read it!"

MARK: Was he buying ads at CKUT?

TRUE: He may have been, who knows! He may have been buying ads at CKUT and that's great, I'm just not reading it. I told him, you can ask the DJs to read it, which was totally not going to happen cause the DJs are not reading shit! They played records. They're like, "We're not doing this reading, nah."

MARK: You know nowadays Mike Mission is speaking on the mic and he is somewhat hosting it.

TRUE: Yeah! Well, I mean I think they've had a few hosts since I've left. I mean, I can't play records, you know what I'm trying to say? I'm not trying to spin records, so, I mean I technically could if I HAD to. But I'm not a DJ and DJs are DJs for a reason, they speak through their music. Hosts are hosts for a reason, you know? It's one thing to be an emcee but it's another to know that it really, it pushed my journalism forward. And even though I took broadcast journalism and I did the hard news stories, most of my published works have been based on hip hop or other urban artists. But, I mean, I've interviewed Mos Def, I've interviewed Lauryn Hill, I've interviewed, who have I spoken to that really ... I've had the opportunity through either performing, opening, or interviewing, of meeting some of the greatest legends. Rakim was probably the first hip hop artist that I met. He came and did a concert in Montreal in I think it was eighty-nine, the first year I started college, and he was doing an autograph signing. I was like, this is RAKIM! And you know back in the day with breaking you had the black-and-white chequered, you know. So I had this white shirt and it had the black and white chequers across and it went up one arm and across the chest and down the other. I was like so B-girled-out.

I'll never forget, I had bicycle shorts on and this T-shirt or whatever, but then I had brought my shirt, right, and all I could say was, "Could you please sign it?" And Rakim looked at me and wrote "The R" right across the chest of my shirt, and I brought it home and I was just like, "Oh my GOD!!" Rakim is my absolute favourite emcee in the world! In terms of lyricism, in terms of swag, in terms of content. To me an emcee has to have a whole bunch of stuff, you can be a dope lyricist and have no stage presence, you could have a lot of stage presence and no content, and then, just on a female tip, it really helps if you're fly. Rakim had all of that, ALL OF THAT, and still has it, you know what I'm saying?

MARK: Did you see him perform that time in Montreal?

TRUE: I didn't get to see him perform. That's another thing, I was (A) broke, 'cause, I mean, my parents had money, I didn't have any money, I was constantly reminded of that. (B) I was not allowed to go to a lot of concerts! I was just not allowed, my parents were very strict, and so hip hop liberated me because technically, I gotta do the radio show. 'Cause that was the only way I could get out because my parents could actually physically find me – they tuned in and they listened to me, they knew I was exactly where I was. Lucky for me the show was at McGill University, the best university in Canada, or one of the best universities in Canada. It gave it a little [independence], they were like, "Oh well it's at McGill University. Oh, she's doing her show." And then I'll come home at three in the morning, right? So it slowly kind of liberated me because it showed them that, you know, it was the arts, and then it also showed them that it was a career because I was actually doing it. They didn't understand why I was doing it for free. My mother was always like, "Where's the money?" My father, though, is a person who, as I look back, never discouraged me from the arts. My mother was more concerned about whether or not I would make any money. But my father is the person who gave me my love of bass, if I don't hear bass in my music, if I don't hear like distorted bass in a music, I can't, I don't get the vibe.

MARK: Was he a sound system man?

TRUE: You know my dad was, I think, an aspiring DJ, I call him my number one selector. When I was leaving, you know, Montreal to go to Toronto, I told my mom I was going to ask my dad for his forty-fives, and she looked at me and laughed [laughs]. I have a better chance of driving his car across the border, right? And he gave them to me! My dad gave me his forty-five collection, and my mother, I don't think she'd ever seen him let anyone even touch his records. And that's when I knew my father respected my music. He never said anything and I didn't even know he listened to my music until years later when my mother said, "You know we tuned into your radio station, to your show, every Saturday, do you know that?" And he had never talked about it. I think he was really proud because I remember going to bed with the house jams! The beauty of living in a suburban home, house parties all over. The unfinished basement is where you had the jam! And all night you know, my bed is vibrating on the third floor of the house because of the bass and the speaker system. I think that's what I grew up feeling. So, every now and then, when producers give me beats, I'm like, "Yeah, those are really nice keys, really interesting stuff you do with Pro Tools, but, where is the bass!" And that's what I think, if you wanna talk about the difference between Montreal and Toronto, I feel that people in Toronto want to be entertainers or they want to be reputable entertainers. I think that in Montreal we just wanna throw down, we just wanna rock the house, you know what I mean? You wanna just burn it down! You know, there's this passion and this energy because we don't have money and we didn't have an infrastructure and we didn't have our own national or international stars.

MARK: You weren't trying to become stars.

TRUE: We weren't trying to become stars, we were trying to be dope emcees, trying to be dope, all, no matter what artistic genre, I think maybe it's the French influence or whatever, there's this sense of passion and integrity and uniqueness that you just can't get anywhere, we're not corporate because nobody's rich, we're broke. It's not a rich city, Quebec is a very poor province compared to other [provinces]. It sells electricity but, the average person in Montreal – the cost of living in Toronto [is] one of the highest, double maybe triple. So you are at a very grassroots level, and it's a beautiful thing because we worked just to pay our bills. And at 4:59 we're not doing overtime, we're not into all that, we're not trying to bring work home, I'm having a glass of wine, we're chilling out, we eating some good food, you know what I'm trying to say?

MARK: It's the European influence.

TRUE: Very European, we're not killing ourselves with work, in Toronto you will. You'll die! You'll die working! You have two/three jobs, you're working overtime, you're in debt, and so that affects, I think, how you approach your art. People will not do things collectively here [in Toronto] just because of the love of what they're doing. Everybody's got to get a cut, whether you're going to get paid for it or the government is going to pay you, but somebody better be getting some money out of this. New York, I think, is the best balance because people are hustling 'cause they want that money, but they don't sleep on somebody who has some potential. They're like, "You know what, you got something! I'll work with you." You know what I mean? 'Cause they see the money coming. Recently, I've been going back and forth to New York, I just recently performed in an all-female showcase called She's So Fresh and it's put on by this amazing woman called Blessed Roxwell and she has a music and media company called Jag Music – Just A Girl, music and media. I went down last summer just to visit a few friends and people and check out Eternia because Eternia is a friend of mine. She's been doing this stuff for so long and she relocated to New York/Jersey and I went down to visit her. I haven't rhymed, I haven't been on a stage rhyming in probably, maybe eight years or so. So seeing Eternia's rocking the house, and then she was like "True Dailey I'll give you sixteen bars." She was performing, MC Lyte was there, my idol, MC Lyte was there and Eternia was on the showcase and it was like a Labour Day weekend and she said to me, "You know if you want, you can kick sixteen bars," and I was like, "Hell yeah, I'll do sixteen seconds! I'm in Brooklyn! MC Lyte is here! It's summer, you're here!" And it happened and we caught that on tape and I think that, to me, is one of my most, I'm like, "Oh I still got it!" "I still got it!" So now that bug has hit me again. 'Cause hip hop to me was when I was frustrated and didn't know who I was and wanted to get a message out. Once I figured out who I was and once I understood how the world worked, I started writing slow jams and soul music and folk, you know what I mean? Did a little spoken word, now I'm like looking at the state of hip hop culture and I'm getting angry again. I'm seeing how women are demeaning themselves when they are in one of the greatest times to empower themselves. We no longer have to do the things that we're doing. But we're still doing it. So, its empowering to me when I go back to New York and I see the hustle and I feel the vibe, and MC Lyte has this great organization called Hip Hop Sisters.com and I was able to meet with her and some of the founding members of this organization, which is promoting hip hop culture amongst women emcees, DJs, etc. We ended up all meeting at the Studio Museum in the heart of Harlem. Meeting MC Lyte, seeing Eternia...

MARK: Gave you back your love of hip hop?

TRUE: Being in New York City, the birthplace, and visiting the Bronx for the first time, last summer and taking a little tour ... Going to an open BBQ in an open garden space in the middle of the Bronx, you know what I'm saying? The speakers are blasting and I'm like, I felt like I was transported, I never got to go to New York when I was sixteen. But I ended up visiting it when there's almost like a new renaissance, I call it the hip hop renaissance that's happening in New York right now, and just some serious, serious emcees have come up right now, and a lot of them are female, and they're killing it. So, that's sparking my energy. Steel sharpens steel [laughs]. I don't get that vibe in Toronto but I get it in New York, and I haven't been to Montreal in a long, long time, so, yeah, I think people need to get out of their city, you know? And just travel a little. We're really lucky as Canadians that we can travel, but I don't find a lot of people do it as much as they should. Not unless they got a grant to do it [laughing]. Or there's a gig, but I just went down to New York last summer just 'cause I wanted to go and because of that I ended up getting gigs based on the people I met. We had a conference call with Hip hop Sisters, and MC Lyte is on the phone, and I'm like "Oh My God!" "I'm on the phone conference with MC Lyte!" [Laughing] I just love it, I love it.

MARK: We're glad you're back.

TRUE: THANK YOU!

MARK: And I want your EP.

TRUE: Okay, I will give that to you, my EP is called "I used to love him: Hip hop's Inspirational Messages." You know what I'm doing? I decided because the track was originally recorded on my original EP years ago, and I hated the production on it. It made my flow corny, so then I rereleased it on a hardcore, like dancehall riddim, and because of that I decided I don't own the production so I gave it away, so I actually gave it away in New York, when I went down a couple of weeks ago at the She's So Fresh event. New Yorkers got the first, I think, twenty to twenty-five copies, because it was an opportunity to give it out! I redid an anthem from Montreal, I still gotta mix it again but, we did an anthem from Montreal called Royal State of Mind and I realized the play on words because, like Mount Royal like Mount Real, our landmark, Mount Royal. At the same time my name is also Royal T. So I did Royal State of Mind and I got this dude JD Keyz on the keys and I just did a little historical breakdown of Montreal – Jay-Z and Alicia, they inspired me. The track talks about so many great things about Montreal, the fact that Jackie Robinson broke the [colour] barriers of major league baseball playing for the Royals in Montreal.

MARK: Wasn't Oscar Peterson born there?

TRUE: Yes! We have Oscar Peterson, that's what I talk about:

Home of jazz greats and the fans stay loyal

Jackie broke the barriers while playing for the Royals

Weather so cold feel like you're living in the North Pole

But the liquor burns in our chest so much sooner than the rest…

MARK: Well thank you for so eloquently breaking down the differences between Montreal and Toronto, especially in the hip hop scene. The diversity within the country's many hip hop scenes is amazing to see and hopefully it's a catalyst, sparking creativity in different cities and pockets across the country.

PART THREE

Representation and Belonging

8

POST-NATIONALIST HIP HOP

Beatmaking and the Emergence of the Piu Piu Scene

Alexandrine Boudreault-Fournier and Laurent K. Blais

INTRODUCTION

Does hip hop still represent a "nation"? Can we frame hip hop within a nationalistic discourse or within the borders of a nation? This chapter questions the nationalist discourse often associated with hip hop both in the literature and in popular culture by focusing on an emerging movement composed of a group of people who propose a new form of collective imagining. In other words, the nationalist model does not accurately represent how their social network is conceived. Therefore, we adopt a post-nationalist approach to a contemporary musical practice that is rooted in hip hop but that is now influenced by an array of other movements, genres, and styles. The proposed alternative approach to how people imagine their belonging to hip hop allows us to develop a more nuanced and complex understanding of the emerging Piu Piu movement.

More specifically, we address the above-mentioned questions by looking at how a sense of network-based unity and community is established, constructed, and maintained by people who identify with hip hop and its tradition today. Piu Piu, an emerging beat movement based in Montreal, serves as an excellent example for looking at present and future dynamics surrounding the idea of how communities and collectives are shaped and reshaped. This is because Piu Piu represents an emerging scene that effectively relies on various networks of connection, circulation, and distribution. It moves fast, it does not have a specific common aesthetic, and it does not always identify itself as belonging to a hip hop tradition. In such a context, we wonder, what is the bond that unites a group of people together? And, in the end, are they really bonded together or do they just come closer momentarily, like floating bodies moving fluidly?

We propose to question the use of the nationalist paradigm to define the contemporary and collective imaginaries of hip hop. What we argue, in light of the data we collected in Montreal from the Piu Piu movement, is that the nationalist paradigm associated with hip hop follows the same trajectory as "the family" metaphor associated with black popular culture as well as "the resistance model" associated with hip hop in the 1990s (for instance Martinez 1997 and Forman 2002). Its decline is predictable. We do not argue for a multicultural Canadian hip hop nation or any other global nationalist belonging. On the other hand, we do not contend that our perspective will compete with the nationalist discourse. Like Erin Manning (2000, xxiv), who explores how cultural texts construct and deconstruct the Canadian nation, we rather "seek to foster more productive forms of articulating the sense of belonging than one that relies on the national discourse." Practices and discourses associated with Piu Piu allow us to explore the different logics (Straw 1991) articulated by this movement and to discuss a post-nationalist approach to hip hop represented by the emergence of new forms of collective imagination that are not based on a nationalist model.

HIP HOP NATIONALISM

Roughly speaking, from a political theory perspective, post-nationalism can be approached from two main lines of thought. The first, which comes from the globalization theory of the 1990s, relates to the idea that supranational and neoliberal forces are imposing themselves on the international market and that, as a consequence, the state loses its authority not only in the economic domain but also in other spheres of political and social life. In this vein, supranational forces threaten the national model of governance (see Hobsbawn 1991). The second approach is based on the following idea: the nation-state is simply no longer relevant to people's lives. In other words, people no longer attach much significance to the idea of nation in imagining their identities. Other forms of imagined communities are shaped according to one or more alternative models of identification. Therefore, we are left with a series of questions about how and where we reimagine ourselves (see Heller 2011, 27). If we transpose this second approach in line with post-nationalism to hip hop, we get a sense of where our argument lies.

Challenging the nationalist hip hop discourse implies that we foster a dialogue that includes other narratives and ways of framing a sense of commonness. However, it does not mean that we reject the nationalist sentiment altogether. This would be shocking when considering that the nation remains one of the most powerful references for the construction of a collective imaginary in the modern world. As Benedict Anderson (1991, 3) argues, "nation-ness is the most universally legitimate value in the political life of our time." Questioning the relevance of the nationalist discourse in hip hop allows us to reflect upon the meaning of this expression. Instead of taking nationalism for granted, we propose to look at its genealogy in order to argue more effectively why it does not coincide with the way actors in the Piu Piu movement articulate their sense of belonging. In this sense we follow Paul Gilroy (2004, 89), who questions using the trope of the family – an authoritarian discourse based on pastoral patriarchy, in which women are associated with the reproduction process – to legitimize a form of racial belonging that is ultimately more Americocentric than Afrocentric.[1] Black nationalism, Gilroy argues, "is a powerful subtext" (88–9), but it remains attached to black US history. Therefore, before we delve into how Piu Piu is imagined and shaped by some people who identify with this movement, we will recall how nationalism has been used in "hiphoplogy" and, more specifically, how it has been adapted to the Canadian context.

The idea of a hip hop nation is deeply rooted in an African American construct based on a Black Nationalist discourse that took shape in the United States. Black nationalism is complex indeed and cannot be represented as a monolithic entity. The presence of multiple views can similarly be applied to hip hop nationalism, even if, at the close of the 1980s, rap groups such as Public Enemy were especially successful at articulating hyper-politicized discourse surrounding a hip hop nation based on racial and class references (Watkins 2001, 380). The association of hip hop with politics (as opposed to religion) in the United States in the 1980s comes from the dissatisfaction of African American youth – the post-civil rights generation – faced with still-rampant racial hostilities that sideline them from the centre of social and economic activities (391).[2] Hip hop was then articulated as a form of political expression embedded within a discourse of unity, nationalism, and black fraternity and family.

The subsequent commodification of hip hop nationalism spurred on by a consumption-hungry youth culture challenged this equation. Some authors, such as Angela Davis (1994) and Paul Gilroy (2010), complain about the fact that hip hop is no longer so simply and directly bound to politics. Hip hop became increasingly commercial and mainstream, implying, for some, a less politically engaged type of popular cultural product. As Craig Watkins (2001, 390) has argued, "the commercial expansion of rap music contributed to the rise and fall of message rappers." Hip Hop is now part of the entertainment industry, and it "is now for sale to all buyers" (Kitwana 2005, xiii). As a consequence, there is a general perception that, through this transformation, the discourse associated with hip hop nationalism got eroded. However, this process of commercialization did not eradicate the connection between hip hop and blackness. Watkins (2001, 393) argues that the phrase "keep it real" does still mean "keep it black," "black inspired." Other authors, such as Errol A. Henderson (1996, 335), are more cynical in arguing that "the nihilism in hip hop and the glamorization of hip hop 'culture' really represents the absence of national culture."

This hip hop nationalist discourse, briefly touched upon here, is embedded within the United States's national and social history.[3] Let us move now towards how nationalist views have been expressed outside of the United States.

With the rapid spread of hip hop at the global level, a new discourse, still based on nationalism, emerged in "hiphoplogy" – and, to a lesser degree, in popular culture. What characterizes all this hip hop "appropriation" outside the United States, argues Tony Mitchell (2001b), is a shift from a more Afrocentric manifestation of rap as observed in the United States towards a multicultural, multi-ethnic expression based on the common experiences of diasporic (or local) movements. As Mitchell explains: "The rhetoric of the hip hop nation has enabled hip hoppers in more remote parts of the world to express a sense of the belonging to a global subculture of breakdancing, graffiti, writing, MCing, and DJing whose U.S. roots and origins are often, but not always, acknowledged" (33).

From this perspective, the "hip hop nation" is not understood as being limited to the United States's territory but as encompassing a more global sense of belonging that, in many ways, crosses the political boundaries of the world's nations. The discourse unifying this collective is built on the idea of shared forms of expression, aesthetics, and common historical roots (to varying degrees). The hip hop nation becomes a global phenomenon experienced at the local level through its cultural and social adaptation and transformation. Similar aspects might be observed when listening to rap produced in Mexico and in Japan. As a result, there is an ongoing relationship between the way hip hop at the local level relates to global constructs,[4] on the one hand, and to the United States in general – which remains a cultural reference for many hip hoppers – on the other.

Following this line of thought, the hip hop nation narrative is used in different national contexts. For instance, hip hop is transnational in Australia (Maxwell 2001; 2003), global in Japan (Condry 2007), and multicultural (Mitchell 2001b, 31; Chamberland 2001; LeBlanc et al. 2007), Indigenous (Marsh 2009a; 2012a; 2012b), multiethnic, multilingual, and postmodern in Canada (Alim and Pennycook 2007, 90). The argument defending the adoption of a nationalist paradigm for hip hop is based on the fact that hip hoppers imagine their collective belonging in this way. Maxwell (2003, 154) argues, for instance, that the idea of the nation emerges unproblematically among hip hoppers in Australia and that it is perceived as a positive category for thinking about collective individual identity. This reasoning has also been reported in the Canadian context and, more specifically, in the province of Quebec – where, needless to say, the notion of nation is politically charged.[5] The article "'Ch'us mon propre Bescherelle': Challenges from the Hip-hop Nation to the Québec Nation" by Low, Sarkar, and Winer (2009) serves as an excellent case in point. The authors defend their use of the hip hop nation expression and paradigm citing two main reasons: first, hip hoppers from Montreal recognize a unifying sense of hip hop community at different geographical levels; second, hip hop youth in Quebec feel they are part of a larger movement constructed through cultural dimensions that are mainly geared towards the United States and France. According to the authors, these two factors legitimize the use of the phrase "Hip Hop Nation."

Even if preliminary empirical data encouraged these authors (and others) to adopt the nationalist paradigm, we argue that using such a narrative naturalizes the cohesiveness that represents the nation, depicted as a harmonious and homogeneous entity (Manning 2000). There are multiple forms of hip hop expression, and the Piu Piu movement is a striking example of this diversity. We argue it is time to question the unity that is ascribed to the "Hip Hop Nation."

PIU PIU IN MONTREAL

The origin of the term "Piu Piu" can be traced back to a specific time and place. On Friday, 8 July 2011, one hundred people gathered at a loft on Wellington Street in the Old Port of Montreal. In the centre of the room, half a dozen producers were positioned in a "cypher" around a table on which lay a cluster of wires, computers, samplers, and other controllers.[6] At one point, VLooper, a Quebec City-based producer, stopped his performance and grabbed the mic to say (in English but with a strong French accent), "Hi, My name is VLooper and this is Piu Piu music."

The setting was the second edition of Art Beat, an intimate event of spontaneous creative collaboration centred on the city's "faiseurs de battement/beat builders." Sev Dee and Mark the Magnanimous, co-founders of the concept, have defined beat builders as "Human Beings possessing the ability of producing a rhythmic or harmonic arrangement or sequence with the use of new devices, beyond the limits or confines of technology, with the purpose of transmitting a specific message" (Art Beat Montreal n.d.).

First understood as a verbalization of the popular laser sound used repeatedly by the creators of Art Beat, Piu Piu stuck because of its multilayered possibilities of meaning. It quickly became the term used to describe anything related to the activities of a heterogeneous collective of Québécois "beat builders," originating from different cultural, linguistic, and musical scenes. "Piu Piu" also evokes "the sound of a flying saucer,"[7] a figure integrated into their logo and on beat tape covers (see figures 8.1 and 8.2). It stresses the importance they give to "the future," conceived here as an opposition to the "past" from which they want to secede. It's also presented as an "alert," a "wake up call" to force Montrealers to "become aware of what they have, what they are able to do,"[8] whether it be an affirmation of their uniqueness or their capability to participate globally in a larger contemporary global beat scene.

The "beat scene" has a very loose and diffuse history but is generally acknowledged as the rise of beat producers that started to create music recognized, discussed, and consumed for its own sake and no longer only as a support for rappers. Many beatsmiths from different

8.1 Smahh / Smi Le !?!, Return of the shroombap (2012). Illusration by Monk.E.

parts of the world forged the path of "beat d'auteur,"[9] but the Low End Theory night in Los Angeles contributed notably to shaping, expanding, and spreading the notion of "beat scene." Founded in 2006 by Daddy Kev, producer and head of Alpha Pup label, this weekly event has been revered as the "epicentre of the sound of instrumental hip hop" (MTV Network n.d.). Artists from around the world performed there, and its fame soon went global. The event now has official branches in San Francisco and Japan, and has spawned like-minded initiatives such as "Space Is the Place," a weekly event held every Wednesday in Montreal and oriented towards beat builders.

The first defining characteristic of Piu Piu is its displacement of the focal point of interest towards beat-based harmonies and rhythms, which were traditionally used only to support text (rapped or

8.2 Flying saucer logo used by Aïsha Cariotte Vertus and Philippe Sawicki to promote their documentary Piu Piu, a Film about the Montreal Beat Scene (2013).

scratched) or movement (dance). Art Beat events are among the first to have put Montreal's and Quebec's hip hop producers in the spotlight.[10] By centring a show on the needs and interests of the particular artist, the organizers (who are themselves "beat builders") shed particular light on an original way of conceiving the creation, live performance, distribution, and consumption of music.

Invited beat builders are welcome to play whatever they like, in any way they like, with whatever equipment they choose. There have been instances in which a beat builder in the cypher has played pre-recorded beats using Windows Media Player next to another jamming live on a sampler. Sev Dee sees it not only as a way to avoid discriminating against anyone but also as a way to express the core value of their conception of beat building, which they consider to be universal, from the African percussionist to the contemporary beat builder who uses refined technology.[11]

Despite the fact that a discourse of universalism and inclusion is strongly articulated within the Piu Piu movement, absences can be observed. To our knowledge, there are no female "beatmakers" who are active in the Piu Piu movement, as there are few in the Montreal electronic music scene altogether.[12] However, some women are significantly affecting the Piu Piu movement at large as musicians, photographers, critics, singers, and/or promoters. Aïsha Cariotte Vertus is one of the leaders of the Piu Piu movement. In addition to being a serious music head, she speaks at conferences, writes articles and blogs about Piu Piu, and organizes tours and exchanges with beatmakers mainly from France and the west coast of the United States. She also produced a film called *Piu Piu: A Documentary about the Montreal Beat Scene*, which attracted attention from the Montreal mainstream media. It is impossible to refer to the Piu Piu movement without mentioning her name. On the one hand, this shows that, even if there have been no performing female beatmakers present at any of the Piu Piu events up to this date, some engage creatively within the movement and have a strong impact on its development. On the other hand, it also shows that, despite the inclusive and universalist discourse articulated by some male beatmakers who identify with Piu Piu, there is a lack of women who participate as beatmakers. But again, this is not a particularity of this movement, which, from our observation, is open to women's participation as beatmakers.[13]

Art Beat refuses to circumscribe participants to a competitive context, a trait that ran counter to the Piu Piu community. "Other [beat nights] in Montréal are focused on battle, competition, that creates emotions which are not necessarily going with our philosophy. Our value, in fact, is to share everything,"[14] says Mark. It would be an exaggeration to say that all Piu Piu beat builders (there are around fifty active members) collaborate and interact with each other,[15] but in our fieldwork we observed that sharing, in various forms and permutations, is predominant. These sharing-related values live outside the Art Beat, which often serves as a meeting spot for artists who want to exchange and work with others. Friend requests on Facebook and the rise of interaction between artists following an Art Beat is an indication of the social importance of Art Beat on the Piu Piu scene. Likewise, it is not unusual to see an artist boasting, sharing, "liking," and commenting on another artist's production on Facebook, Twitter, or Soundcloud.[16]

In the same vein, Art Beat never put forward one particular beat builder. This means that all the beatmakers who participate at one Art Beat receive the same attention. Organizers bet on the composition of the cypher (very cohesive or disparate) to program and promote each edition of their event. Likewise, every participant, whether old-timer or newcomer, gets the same playtime. No one is paid, either: all producers "give" their time and their craft. This also mirrors the general practice of giving music away for free online (on platforms like Bandcamp or Mediafire). All Piu Piu community artists are not automatically invited to play at Art Beat. An informal selection process conducted by the organizers of the event (Sev Dee and Mark) determines who is "notorious" or interesting enough to be showcased at Art Beat. Sev Dee and Mark have also set up parallel events dubbed "Art Beat Revelation" for new talents who are not yet "ready" for the "official" gathering.

The relatively low importance given to the language used in Piu Piu opens many new possibilities. At the local scale, it permits a unification of creators and audiences from diverse (and generally isolated) linguistic communities. Traditionally, hip hop actors of the two official language communities have evolved in interconnected trajectories that have rarely met. Anglophones and francophones share the same venues, newspaper column, and festivals without mingling. Sikh Knowledge, from the English-speaking west side of Montreal, explains that he discovered KenLo on the internet and only later figured out that they were from the same city. "That was the first time I had contact with East Montreal,"[17] he admits.

The liaison point for artists and audiences in Piu Piu is not based on their socio-geo-linguistic belonging. For example, at Art Beat in June 2012 the event included white and French-speaking "de souche" artists (Phil Sparkz, Tommy Kruise, Smahh), Quebecers of African and Haitian descents (Jam, Alaiz Crew), a Latino (El Cotola), and a person of Indian descent (Sikh Knowledge).

The Piu Piu community reshuffles the socio-cultural-linguistic territories of the city by connecting people on a common ground of musical experience and practices. Charles, a Laval (north shore of Montreal) beatmaker, relates a discussion he had earlier with another beatmaker: "Last week, I was talking with Mady and I was telling him: 'Ah, the album that I played the most in my life is Slum Village's Fantastic vol. 2.' He looked at me and went: 'You know what? That's also the album that I played the most.' You know, without knowing it, we were from the same place."[18]

But we should not automatically deduce that instrumental music like Piu Piu is free of traces of the origin of its creators. Owing to the choice of sampling from different sources, producers' cultural backgrounds still mark their art. High Klassified, of Haitian descent, used an excerpt from a popular Québécois meme on his track "Snap." In doing so, he manifested his belonging to French popular culture,[19] something that contrasts with his English moniker and the English onomatopoeia with which he titled his track. The same goes for Sikh Knowledge, who sometimes uses cithara and oriental sounds on his tracks, undoubtedly asserting his Indian heritage.[20]

Without some of the linguistic "burdens" of language, the Piu Piu community aspires to go global, where local rap (both French and English) never managed to succeed. For Mark, Montreal hip hop culture even developed an inferiority complex: "Hip hop here in Quebec, we always have the feeling that we are late [compared to global trends]. I think Piu Piu is in fact a wake-up call for us and the others: 'Look, you think we are late, we collectively think that we are late, but in reality, if we want, we can be in advance.'"[21]

Piu Piu places Montreal-based creators in a network of the contemporary beat scene, which is structured across various local scenes whose fame spreads via the internet, specialized media, and tours. Maintaining relationships between actors in each city grants Montreal a rare chance to exchange on equal ground with creators from other metropolises, such as Los Angeles, Paris, London, New York, and Toronto.

POST-NATIONALISM IN THE CANADIAN CONTEXT

In her book *Paths to Post-Nationalism: A Critical Ethnography of Language and Identity*, Monica Heller (2011) provides an insightful socio-linguistic exploration of how a post-nationalist era, defined as post-modernist and post-ironic, characterizes the young Canadian generation – more specifically, young Canadian francophone minorities. It is in dialogue with her socio-linguistic analysis and with the post-nationalist Toronto School (Meunier and Thériault 2008; Cardinal 2012), represented mainly by the work of Monica Heller and Normand Labrie (Heller and Labrie 2003), that we develop our argument for a post-nationalist hip hop era. Our intention in adopting this approach is not to support the claim for a post-nationalist francophone minority in Canada; rather, we adopt some aspects of the post-nationalist school because it provides rich points of comparison with the ideal discourse of a "hip hop nation." It further allows us to develop a critical approach to the adoption of the nationalist paradigm.

Furthermore, post-nationalism, as represented by the Toronto School, provides two main significant advantages to our argument: (1) it fosters a Canadian exploration of the idea of post-nationalism and (2) it focuses on a "population" (la *francophonie*) that, like hip hop, cannot claim a homogenous territory. On a deeper level, Heller's work provides us with a framework for defining what we mean by post-nationalist hip hop.

Heller argues that the discourse of the nation is transformed by a new globalized economy. "La *francophonie* is in flux," she argues, "Ideologies of language and nation are confronted with new ideologies of language as commodity, and the role of the state is in question" (Heller 1999, 357). In other words, there has been a shift in perception, an ideological rearrangement, from the way a collective is imagined within French Canada as a nation to the way a collective is viewed within the broader Canadian *francophonie* that is more complex and permeable, and where language can serve as one good among others on the market.

These ideological shifts give rise to tensions, which can play out in different places. One of the sites of tension, namely, the one between post-national irony and the anxiety provoked by globalization, can be resolved not only through the language practices of francophones (Heller 1999) but also, and more interestingly for us, through forms of cultural production (Heller 2011).

Heller further addresses how the forms of cultural production should be approached as post-nationalist. She maintains that these forms of cultural expression are characterized by the mundane, by what is everyday and ordinary – what she refers to as ironic postmodernism. She mentions three main features associated with the post-nationalist sensibility: first, it embraces "globalized heterogeneity and mobility"; second, it implies "defanging English, playing with the vernacular and other hallmarks of Romantic nationalism"; and third, it makes "terrible fun of the purists" (Heller 2011, 183).[22] She uses two examples – namely, Franco-Canadian singer-songwriter-composers Dano LeBlanc and Damien Robitaille – to illustrate her argument. In both cases, LeBlan and Robitaille are attached to their identity categories,[23] but they make fun of the serious militancy and purist nationalism associated with earlier generations. They resist anglophone domination but they master English perfectly. They represent an ambivalence in which they both not only adhere to their Franco-Canadian identity but also make fun of purist nationalist sentiments. They "can no longer make revolutionary consciousness-raising music, literature, or theatre" Heller explains, "The time for that has passed" (189).

In the following section, we challenge the hip hop nationalist paradigm, as developed here, in highlighting certain features of the Piu Piu movement that we associate with a "post-nationalist sensitivity," to echo Heller's expression. In other words, we develop a *critical* approach to the hip hop nationalist paradigm in highlighting other forms of collective imaginaries.

POST-NATIONALISM AND PIU PIU

Piu Piu remains a marginal form of expression within hip hop, although it is attracting a growing number of young producers who listen not just to hip hop but to anything they can get their hands on. Piu Piu belongs to a hip hop tradition but its producers, and, by extension, its consumers, do not show any obligation to be loyal to it. Why would they? At the end of the day, being in and out of Piu Piu is not something that is clearly defined and articulated. People who listen to Piu Piu might listen to other musical tendencies; they follow trends and emerging groups at a fast pace without necessarily confining themselves to Piu Piu and its associated beatmakers. This is despite the fact that they do show an interest – often a strong one – in the Piu Piu movement. Their loyalty to Piu Piu is not exclusive. There is a common narrative addressed by beat builders: Piu Piu belongs – to varying degrees – to a hip hop tradition, but, at the same time, there is a strong sense that it represents an explosion of hip hop's aesthetic norms.

The elusiveness of Piu Piu's collective identity does not mean that there is no Piu Piu imaginary or sense of group cohesiveness. However, we wonder: What is the glue that binds them together, even if momentarily?[24] In order to explain why Piu Piu corresponds to a post-nationalist hip hop phenomenon and, subsequently, why we chose to adopt a critical approach towards the national paradigm in hiphoplogy, we develop four main features in dialogue with Monica Heller's description (see previous section).

Linguistic Value

The Piu Piu collective imaginary is not based on a common language. As mentioned previously, no intrinsic linguistic value is attached to Piu Piu. Being in the post-everything wave, Piu Piu is an example of a post-rap phenomenon. Although some rappers and singers (including women) adopt Piu Piu's explosive norms, beat builders do not produce beats with the aim of adding lyrics to them. The goal is for their beats to stand as an art form in their own right.

Research studies on language and hip hop are numerous (e.g., Alim and Pennycook 2007; Alim 2002 in the United States; Low, Sarkar, and Winer 2009; and Sarkar and Allen 2007 in Canada), and the idea of shared common language and linguistic patterns indeed contributes to creating this sense of nation. Language is a major factor in national cohesion (Giddens 1984), and it is therefore not surprising to notice that the main post-nationalist intellectual trend in Canada (the Toronto School) comes from a socio-linguistic approach. Similarly, hip hop collectives are shaped by the language factor (for instance, the hip hop francophone world; see Durand 2002), although English is most often taken for granted as the "natural" hip hop lingua franca.

Even if producers and consumers of Piu Piu music constantly play with the vernacular, the linguistic component of this art is not what unites them. On the contrary, what is powerful about Piu Piu is its absence of lyrics and linguistic attachment; it successfully crosses linguistic boundaries.[25] As Musoni explains: "What I like about the beat is that it unites people together. First, it's universal because there is no language; it brings together the whole world. Everybody can feel it, understand it ... and they can relate to it. Also, it does not have a message. I don't know about the others but for me, it's just something that – how could I put it? – welcomes you."[26]

Musoni suggests that Piu Piu has the power to cross linguistic boundaries because it is an instrumental type of music. According to him, beat music is universal not because it serves as a form of language but, rather, because it can be appreciated independently of one's linguistic (not to mention ethnic and cultural) background. As a result, one's linguistic knowledge is not perceived as an obstacle to fully appreciating beat music.

Postmodern Irony and Detachment

The "Piu Piu" label was proposed spontaneously and was at first perceived as a joke. By reducing his artistic demarche to an onomatopoeia, Vlooper anticipated its potential critics, parodying what a neophyte would perceive superficially from his music. In this sense, using "Piu Piu" to describe electronic experimental music is a lot like saying "boom boom" to describe electronic dance music. The fact that this ironic appellation stuck with beat builders who identify with Piu Piu shows well the general spirit of joking, self-depreciation, and frivolity that pervades the scene.

Vlooper also plays a major role in Alaclair Ensemble, a rap group that serves as another excellent case study for illustrating the extreme irony characterizing not only Piu Piu but also a broader movement of producers (and rappers) on the hip hop scene today. Alaclair Ensemble is a super-group formed with members from Montreal and Quebec City. Most of them also had successful careers on the provincial rap scene before uniting under the same banner. They are closely affiliated with the K6A Crew, whose members also include Sev Dee and other beat builders who are regularly showcased at Art Beat. They are therefore intrinsically linked to the Piu Piu community and are among its most visible ambassadors.[27]

Alaclair created a vernacular universe in which these beat builders constantly mix the contemporary Quebec reality with rewritings of historical events. They are pleased to repeat that their music should be called "post-rigodon," which they define as a "cultural dialectic" between the "oral tradition of Lower Canada and contemporary American music" (Alaclair Ensemble n.d.b.), principally the music scene of "Detroite" led by influential producer J. Dilla, who died in 2006. They revived the concepts of Upper and Lower Canada, a division established in 1791, to talk about Quebec and the rest of Canada. They renamed Stephen Harper "Stivon Harpon" and dubbed him CEO of the colony. They are obsessed with the Patriots of 1837–38, a group of native English- and French-speaking settlers who wanted to gain independence from the British Empire. They have publicly read the Patriots' declaration of independence many times on stage, at award shows, and during other events. One of the rappers even performs under the moniker "Robert Nelson," referencing the English-speaking leader of the movement. In the context of a sort of historical science fiction, Alaclair Ensemble tries to imagine the present day as if the Patriots had defeated the English and managed to establish a Lower-Canadian Republic in the mid-nineteenth century. They have invented their own flag (purple and orange with the maple leaf pointing towards the bottom to represent "Bas-Canada," which in French means "low" and "bottom" – see figure 8.3), composed a national anthem, created a detailed glossary of neologisms (Alaclair Ensemble n.d.a.), and even offered a downloadable "passeport Bas-Canadien."

Surprisingly for some, the group never positioned itself in favour of Quebec's independence. It is drawn to the Patriots' idea of collaboration between individuals of different tongues and cultures in order to promote anti-imperialist and pro-republican ideals. This interpreta-

8.3 "Bas-Canada" flag by the Alaclair Ensemble. Courtesy of Alaclair Ensemble.

tion of the Patriots' movement is different from that of the *souverainiste* groups, which often associate their struggle with the cause of the Patriots.[28]

By separating the Patriots from the present national question, and by reinterpreting Quebec's history, Alaclair Ensemble manages to take with a grain of salt (and a few laughs) the "real" constitutional, identity-related and linguistic situation that links and divides Canada, Quebec, Montreal, and other places. By appropriating and playing with history, Alaclair Ensemble attempts to dislocate the strong cohesion of traditional "nationalisme québécois" (predominantly French, Catholic, white, and aimed at independence and social democracy) and reshape it to make it fit its vision and desire for contemporary Quebec.

Although Alaclair Ensemble was quite successful in finding an audience, the group shocked some people who strongly identified with Quebec's French rap scene. "Oui bonjour???" a member of the HipHopfranco online forum (the virtual town hall of the French rap community) sums up the grievance against Alaclair Ensemble: "I guess Alaclair could be considered 'humoristic,' but I see it more like guys that are having fun pretending to suck. Maybe it would be less frustrating if they were random dudes, but it pisses me off to know that they all are great lyricists and that they are intentionally bad just to be 'different'" (Hip Hop Franco n.d.).

It is interesting to point out that this commentator sees Alaclair Ensemble as being voluntarily bad (instead of reproaching its lack of talent and effort). This is a sign that the group's demarche is on the frontier of norms and practices. By discrediting its intention to be "different," this forum user expresses that Alaclair Ensemble rappers are wasting their talent in trying to go somewhere other than in the direction of reinforcing and reiterating a tradition.

Locality

What we observe with the Piu Piu movement is a devaluation of local belonging as a marker of authenticity and realness. Even if locality remains a focus of identity, the idea that one has to be born and raised in Saint-Michel to be authentic and real is lost.[29] This association was very strong among rappers from Montreal until recently, and it remains prominent in certain circles but not Piu Piu. Producers such as High-Klassified live in Laval (the dormitory neighbourhood on Montreal's north shore). He constantly makes cracks about his city on Facebook (ironically, we agree). The hood in Montreal as a marker of authenticity has lost its strength, relieving much tension in hip hop regarding who can and cannot "keep it real."[30]

Therefore, at the same time as local and urban belonging has lost its power of authenticity, a reimagining of the city has become a key component of how beatmakers relate to and follow each other. A beatmaker is not from Canada but from Montreal, Toronto, Los Angeles, or Detroit. A configuration of the city, which often extends its official boundaries, becomes the site of belonging. At the international level, Laval automatically becomes Montreal.

Also, living in Montreal does not mean that one cannot take part in a beat scene located elsewhere. In fact, many beatmakers and Piu Piu consumers from Montreal maintain a close relationship with beatmakers and house productions located on the west coast of the United States. Many imagine themselves as being part of what is happening in Los Angeles. They organize travels there and invite beatmakers from the West Coast to their events in Montreal.

This form of cosmopolitanism is articulated through what seems to look like a constellation of places and spaces instead of a map of nation-states. Here we refer to a graphic representation designed by Nate James that sparked many comments on the Web at the end of 2011 (see figure 8.4). This guide (for lack of a better term), called "A Comprehensive Guide to the Beat Generation," is a constellation of 120 beatmakers from around the world whom James considered as

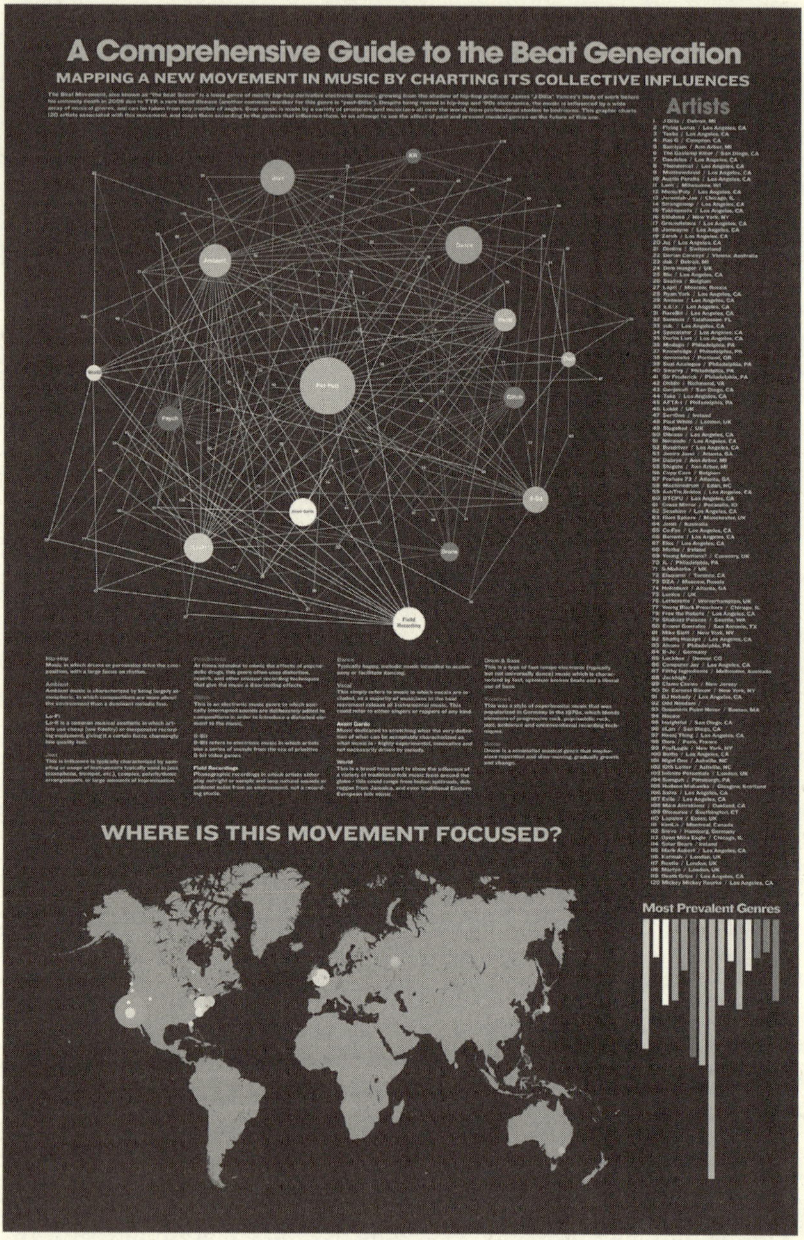

8.4 "A Comprehensive Guide to the Beat Generation" by Nate James. Courtesy of Nate James.

belonging to the Beat movement. The guide provides an alternative mapping, a total reconfiguration of how beatmakers imagine their relatedness and, by extension, their collective. James drew lines connecting all the beatmakers depending on their stylistic influences, ranging form Electronic to Dubstep. The result is an extremely complex figure made of planets all related to one another by lines of different colours, with each coloured line connecting an individual artist to a "planet" of musical genre (Ambient, Lo-Fi, Jazz, Psychedelia, Glitch, 8-Bit, Field Recordings, Dance, Vocal, Avant-Garde, World, Drum & Bass, Krautrock, and Drone). On the right side of the constellation is a list of the beatmakers, their city and country of residence, and a corresponding number that one can relate to a position in the constellation. It is striking to observe how this constellation is much more vibrant, flexible, and fluid than the more traditional geographic configuration shown below, under the title "Where Is This Movement Focused?"

Temporality

Strongly influenced by science fiction, ninja slow-motion effects, and video games (among others), Piu Piu producers aim at creating the sound of tomorrow, the sound of the future. Like a flying saucer, Piu Piu is about being fast and instantaneous. It is not about permanency and durability. Developing a futuristic sound is integral to Piu Piu aesthetics; the rhythm is broken, it slows down and increases again.

According to Will Straw (1991, 374): "different cultural spaces are marked by the sorts of temporalities to be found with them," and "the 'logic' of a particular musical culture is a function of the way in which value is constructed within them relative to the passing of time." Therefore, the temporal "logic" of Piu Piu refers not only to its futurist sound but also to all the discursive patterns that locate this cultural space within the present but are projected towards a highly technologized future. This temporal logic is also articulated within networks of music circulation and distribution that Piu Piu producers decide to adopt, along with a fragmented "apparatus" (Grossberg 1984, 236) that contributes to the construction of affective alliances (Straw 1991).[31] These networks, which have their own temporalities, influence how the sense of belonging, even if momentarily, does take shape.

Erin Manning (2000, xxx) argues that time – constructed as linear and in evolution – is a narrative that is delineated by the containment of the nation-state. Interestingly, Manning adds that alternative ways of organizing time can generate new narratives, "new modes of being in common" (xxxi). The networks within which Piu Piu producers and consumers (and a large section of the Piu Piu generation) interact influence their relationship with their surroundings. For instance, our interviewees did not hesitate to post our questions on Facebook and chat with friends during our interviews. We do not criticize this new conception of social life and, subsequently, how social relations are conceived and normalized, but we recognize that they involve new ontologies of how time and social relations might be constituted, depending on one's presence in a flux of social milieus.[32] As a consequence, this sense of being in common is multiplied and does not necessarily depend on physicality. Networks are constructed and deconstructed with one click of a mouse, and these connections do not rely on national boundaries.

THE PIU PIU LOGICS

In the previous section, we mention the idea of temporal "logic" borrowed from the work of Will Straw (1991). By extension, the "logics of change" – how musical terrains become linked with new values – also discussed by Straw, is relevant to our argument. Straw maintains that what is meaningful to the logic of change is how social differences such as gender and race are associated with the building of audiences that identify with particular musical terrains. Similar to works that adopt articulation as their theoretical framework for looking at popular music (such as Middleton 1990; Gilroy 1993; and Wade 2000), Straw explores how musical terrains are continuously redefined by a series of values. Hip hop, for instance, has been (and, in certain circles, still is) a strong defender of Black Nationalism and political activism; it has also been associated with pleasure and mercantilism. Hip hop, like other musical practices, is complex and heterogeneous. Piu Piu is one example of such diversity – even if not mainstream, it is a centre of attraction for many people who do feel the (often strongly expressed) desire for sharing, in a broad sense.

Heller (2004) also explores how social and economic transformations that occur at different levels influence the way people construct their linguistic belonging (or wish to belong). Pressure brought on by globalization has generated new ways of imagining *la francophonie*, not essentially as a Canadian unity but, rather, as one aspect among others of one's identity. Based on Heller's work, it is obvious that *la francophonie* has followed some logics of change.

We argue that the nationalist approach of referring to hip hop as a collective no longer represents (if it ever did, outside the United States) how this musical terrain progresses in accordance with its "logic." We also explain our reserve in adopting this paradigm by assessing the term's genealogy and associated ideological components, which cannot be easily transposed to every context, location, and cultural practice. In other words, we argue that the nationalist paradigm for hip hop cannot be taken for granted.

To finance some of its activities and events, in the fall of 2012, Art-Beat held a sale of T-shirts displaying the slogan "Do you. Piu Piu." One of the first elements that caught our attention is that the slogan is divided by a period rather than by a question mark. In this sense, "Do you. Piu Piu." becomes not a question, such as "Do you belong?" or "Can you do it?" but, rather, an invitation to join the movement, to express one's real essence, to "Be yourself." and "Do it too." In other words, it is an invitation to be unique, a call for self-determination – "Become your own nation!" This illustrates another bridge that is articulated by Piu Piu. Here, the collective imaginary is not built on the hip hop nation but, rather, on the cultural practices that characterize it: beatbuilding. There is a horizontal type of imagined collective that is constructed among individuals – beatmakers and their followers – scattered across a constellation of sites rather than a hip hop culture affiliation. This "beat generation" is based on the idea of sharing practices and aesthetics that are associated with the production and consumption of beats.[33]

The discourse of universalism expressed by many Piu Piu beatmakers is indeed utopic: the emergence of new imagined collectivities entails the establishment of boundaries, which, by extension, implies both the inclusion and exclusion of some players. We observed fractions within the broader beat scene in Montreal, and Piu Piu represents one movement among others. Those divisions, which are based on language, education, and aesthetics (among others), are forces that do have an impact on the shaping of this imagined collectivity. Furthermore, the scarce presence of women beatmakers is reproducing an ongoing gender pattern within many spheres of the hip hop culture.

But the logics of Piu Piu are not stable, and inclusions and exclusions are not fixed. We hope that this chapter shows how Piu Piu is a moving constellation of networks that are continuously remodelled. We are aware that some of the logics we mentioned in the previous section (language, irony, temporality, locality) are open, broad, and permeable. Some could argue that they do not allow us to construct a solid collective imaginary, as nationalism would. Our answer to this is: Good! The collective that builds up Piu Piu today is unstable, volatile, fluid, and abstract (like a flying saucer, if we may suggest the analogy). We cannot propose a model similar to what nationalism aims to achieve because what we observe is a complex, fragmented, emerging, and segmented "sensitive affiliation," to echo Straw once again, rather than an imagined identity that is based on long-standing but obsolete matrices.

NOTES

This article is based on ethnographic fieldwork and fifty-one interviews conducted in Montreal in 2011 and 2012. Investigation was funded by the project Music, Digitization, Mediation: Towards Interdisciplinary Music Studies, a European Research Council (ERC) research project based at the University of Oxford and headed by Professor Georgina Born.

1 Here we refer to Gilroy's argument to emphasize the fact that the family trope is tied to US nationalism. However, we are also aware that black feminist intellectuals strongly denounced the use of the term "family" to refer to Black Nationalism because of its implications for black women, not to mention its dangerous eugenic presumption. See, for instance, Collins (2006).

2 Henderson (1996) provides a detailed account of the emergence of Black Nationalism and its association/dissociation, through history, with the hip hop nation.

3 See also Alim (2002), who refers to hip hop national language in the context of the United States.

4 For instance, Pan-Asian in Morelli (2001) and francophone in Durand (2002).

5 The question of nation in Quebec is closely tied to the independence movement and the more general argument that the province of Quebec should acquire a different status from the rest of Canada. The debate on the status of the province of Quebec was particularly animated in 2006. At the time, the prime minister of Canada, Stephen Harper, introduced the following motion: "this House recognizes that Québécois form a nation within a

united Canada." This motion aimed at defusing another motion that had been put forward by the Bloc Québécois (in favour of independence), stating that the "Québécois form a nation." Harper's motion was adopted with 266 voices in favour and 16 against, while the proposition of the Bloc Québécois was rejected with 233 voices against and 48 in favour. The status of the province of Quebec within Canada is a recurrent theme in Canadian politics.

6 A "cypher" refers to a circular gathering of a group of people. "Cyphers" are common in freestyle sessions where each participant improvises rhymes in turn, from left to right.

7 Interview with Mark the Magnanimous, 3 November 2011.

8 Interview with Sev Dee, 3 November 2011.

9 Onra, Madlib, J.Dilla, DOOM, and Flying Lotus were often referenced during our interviews with Piu Piu artists.

10 Turf Builder was an event at which beat builders could bring a CD of their production to Scott C, the initiator and DJ of the evening. Although it was open to the public, the vast majority of the attendees were beatmakers. Still, Sev Dee claims that Turf Builder is "one of his principal inspirations" for Art Beat. Interview with Sev Dee, 29 November 2012.

11 Interview with Sev Dee, 2 December 2012.

12 Regarding the electronic/digital music scene(s) in Montreal, Valiquet (2012, 14) writes that "there is a fairly persistent pattern emerging in which women are afforded only limited access to 'high' technological practices and knowledge" and that, consequently, "the gendered division of labour in musical institutions has also contributed to the repression of aesthetic innovations made by women". Studio XX (n.d.) is a bilingual, feminist artist-run centre in Montreal that promotes women's creative actions with the technological landscape in order to address this pattern (example provided by Patrick Valiquet, personal communication, 15 May 2013). Also worth mentioning is Rodgers's (2010) book, which aims at disentangling the assumption that technology and music are male domains. See also Marsh (2012b).

13 One concrete example: ABF (co-author of this chapter) applied to become a member of a restricted group of beatmakers living in Montreal on Facebook. As the leader of the group thought ABF was a beatmaker, he answered her request right away, welcoming her among the rest of the group and announcing that she was the first female beatmaker member. He was disappointed to learn that she was actually "just" an anthropologist.

14 Interview with Mark the Magnanimous, 3 November 2011.

15 Interview with Mark the Magnanimous on the Art Beat Montreal website (Art Beat Montreal n.d.).

16 A social network dedicated to sharing music and mixes.
17 Interview with Sikh Knowledge, 1 December, 2011.
18 Interview with Charles, 16 November, 2011.
19 The track contains an excerpt from the popular YouTube video "Juste une fois au chalet," viewed over a million times, in which an old man accused of incest contradicts himself rather comically in front of a reporter. The expression "Just once at the cottage" has gone viral and has become integrated into Quebec's popular culture.
20 Sikh Knowledge's parents are from Punjab, India. He constantly refers to his Punjabi background on Facebook. He also mentioned it on many occasions during our interview (1 December 2011). His Indian heritage has a central impact on the aesthetics of his music.
21 Interview with Mark the Magnaninous, 3 November 2011.
22 Heller (2011, 181) also puts it in those terms: "making peace with the ordinary and everyday, not letting English and the vernacular freak us all out, and taking a bit of distance from the high drama of nationalism."
23 Dano LeBlanc is from Moncton, New Brunswick, and Damien Robitaille is from Lafontaine, Ontario.
24 A wide literature in music studies and anthropology addresses similar questions. See, for instance, Born (1993) and, more recently, Born (2013).
25 We are aware that other cultural forms of hip hop expression have the potential to cross linguistic boundaries – dance is one example.
26 Interview with Musoni, 16 November 2011.
27 They released three albums in 2011, one of which was called *Un piou piou parmi tant d'autres*.
28 For instance, the Patriots' flag is often seen at *souverainiste* protests. Also, Victoria Day was renamed Patriots' Day by a *péquiste* government in 2003.
29 Saint-Michel is a neighbourhood located in northern Montreal. Approximately 42 percent of its population is composed of immigrants – mainly from Haiti – compared to an average of 28 percent for Montreal (De Coninck 2004).
30 This is not the case in all Canadian cities. Marsh (2011) shows that in Regina, Saskatchewan, "keepin' it real" binds young Aboriginal males associated with gangsta rap to space, place, and capitalism, and, by extension, to ongoing colonialist discourses that promote patriarchy and racism.
31 Grossberg (1984, 236) defines apparatus as being composed of musical texts, practices, and economic determinations.
32 We would like to thank Professor Line Grenier for her insightful comments regarding this point of analysis.
33 Unlike previous beatniks, however, they have little interest in exploring America's back roads.

9

LAST NIGHT A DJ SAVED MY LIFE

Hip Hop, Cultural Continuity, and First Nations Suicidality

Margaret Robinson

INTRODUCTION

In 1991 I was a seventeen-year-old Mi'kmaw woman in my first year of university. Having snuck into the campus pub, I was enjoying some curly fries when a news story came on the television about the Public Enemy song "By the Time I Get to Arizona." The white reporter warned that the song advocated violence against the government before playing a clip of the video. That afternoon I walked to Sam the Record Man on Barrington Street and, for the first time in my life, bought an album on speculation. As I listened and relistened to the tracks on *Apocalypse 91 ... The Enemy Strikes Black*, one thought kept recurring in my mind: I wish *we* – by which I meant Indigenous people of Canada – had a Public Enemy. I did not know then that Melle Mel was Cherokee, nor could I have foreseen how many Indigenous hip hop artists would emerge within the next decade, as if in answer to the need that I, and other Indigenous youth, had for music that spoke not only *to* us but about our lives.

In this chapter, I argue that hip hop can be a conduit through which Indigenous people[1] – especially youth, but others as well – maintain our sense of cultural and personal continuity, enabling us to construct a comprehensible and livable Indigenous identity in the present, and to imagine a viable future. Using a social aetiology of mental illness lens and a textual hermeneutics rooted in critical theory, I offer supporting examples from Indigenous hip hop artists such as Reddnation and Slangblossom. I propose that Indigenous hip hop, as an art medium, can support the mental health and wellness of its participants and fans by offering Indigenous identities and cultural expressions that are appropriate and meaningful in a contemporary urban environment.

URBAN INDIGENOUS PEOPLE AND CULTURAL IDENTITY

Indigenous critical theorist Sandy Marie Anglas Grande (1999) notes that iconic images of Native Americans are frozen in time. The "noble savage" stereotype of Indigenous people as so close to nature that we essentially *are* nature is supported by the general isolation of reserve land in Canada, basically putting Indigenous communities out of sight and out of mind for the white mainstream. Paul Nadasdy (2005) argues that such stereotypes do real damage to Indigenous people, erasing the reality of our lived experiences, reducing the diversity of our lives to caricature, and creating a standard of authenticity that is impossible to attain. So pervasive are such stereotypes that Indigenous Canadians may not be recognizable to our fellow Canadians, or even to one another, unless we match the image of us presented in film and television. As a result of stereotyped iconography, Grande (1999, 307) argues, "Indians remain virtually invisible and relatively absent from the collective consciousness," and, as a result, we face greater challenges than other racialized and marginalized groups in "complicating and re-humanizing" our subjectivities.

Such invisibility can lead others to doubt our authenticity as Indigenous people, limiting our social support, and resulting in serious psychological and political problems. Scholars have noted the degree to which First Nations involved in land claims in Canada and the United States have had to prove continuity with our ancestors, often defined as a lack of change from early post-contact lifestyle (Lawrence 2004; Proulx 2010; Tennant 1990). Mi'kmaw scholar Bonita Lawrence (2003, 23) provides the example of the Gitksan/Wet'suwet'en case, in which: "the plaintiffs were continuously presented as contemporary interlopers whose claims to Indigenous rights were invalid because they were not 'the same' people as their ancestors were – because they held paying jobs, lived in houses, consumed pizza and other European foods, and in general lived contemporary lives."

Evidence of cultural hybridity, especially the adoption of colonial culture, has often been perceived as discontinuity, leaving us simply a collection of individuals with Indigenous ancestry. This should not be surprising since it has long been the goal of colonialist governments to "get rid of the Indian problem" (Library and Archives Canada 1920, 55) by absorbing Indigenous people into the Canadian mainstream, erasing our distinct identity. For Indigenous Canadians resisting assimilation, culture has tended to be seen as something that needs to be reclaimed in a reified form rather than developed.

Métis anthropologist Craig Proulx (2010) notes that the development of Indigenous culture is limited by ignorance of the role played by cities in Indigenous life and by the association of authenticity with a lack of change. As a consequence of this ignorance, David Newhouse and Evelyn Peters (2003, 6) report: "Aboriginal people who chose to live in cities are seen [within Canadian popular culture] as an anomaly or as people who have turned their backs on their culture." The alleged incompatibility of the concepts "urban" and "Aboriginal" (or "Indigenous") are the result of government policies designed to displace Indigenous people from cities and consolidate us on rural reserves.

Contrary to our rustic stereotype, over half the Indigenous population in Canada (54 percent as of 2006) make our home in an urban centre, and this figure is expected to increase by 42 percent within the next fourteen years (Statistics Canada 2006, n.p.; Aboriginal Affairs and Northern Development 2007, 5). Framing urbanization as a move to alien territory is disingenuous since, as Newhouse and Peters (2003) remark, many of our Canadian cities were originally areas of settlement or meeting for Indigenous people. There are 120 urban reserves in Canada, representing one out of every four reserves (Frood 1999, xiv). Framed in development discourse as a "springboard into the mainstream economy" (Aboriginal Affairs 2008, n.p.), urban reserves may challenge the geographic frameworks within which colonial readings of Indigenous youth are shaped (Marsh 2009a). Contrary to stereotypes of Indigenous people as languishing in cities, reports indicate that Indigenous culture in our urban communities has become stronger, rather than weaker, over the past five years (Environics Institute 2010, 2).

For many non-status Indigenous people, assimilation is a survival strategy. Without status recognition Indigenous people cannot lay claim to reserve housing, educational support, or health care (Tulk 2008). As a result, non-status First Nations and Métis people are significantly more urbanized than are those with Indian status (Ristock, Zoccole, and Potskin, 2011). My own family has lived in an urban environment for over five generations. As a result of urban migration, Indigenous people face the challenge of making our traditions and our history relevant to our contemporary lives. What does it mean to have a special relationship with the land when I live in a city where actual soil is seldom visible? How do we stay connected with our histories and cultures if we have migrated to a territory that is not our own? And how do we acknowledge the effects of colonialism on our lives without being overwhelmed by an inheritance of grief and trauma for which we are not prepared? The section that follows outlines the psychological importance of identity and culture for Indigenous people, particularly as such resources buffer against the risk of suicide.

CONTINUITY AND YOUTH SUICIDE

Personal continuity is the ability to construct a sense of oneself as a person, undergoing change over time, with a trajectory into the future. Psychology professors Michael Chandler and Christopher Lalonde (2008, 226) note that personal continuity helps adolescents struggling with tumultuous change resist suicide: "Young people recurrently lose and typically regain faith in their own future as a predictable part of the usual identity-formation process, and these recurrent transitional moments leave them especially vulnerable – in ways that other age groups are not – to the risk of suicide."

The importance that Chandler and Lalonde attach to personal continuity is confirmed by their research with adolescents admitted to a psychiatric facility over an eighteen-month period. They observe that "all but two ... of the actively suicidal participants seriously tried, but consistently failed, to ... justify a sense of personal sameness in the face of change" (227). When personal identity is disconnected from past and future, the self that suicide removes scarcely registers as a self at all.

The performative identities available within hip hop culture (e.g., DJ, MC, b-boy) may serve as supports for personal continuity, enabling youth to adapt an identity with pre-set meanings, histories, and futures as a stop-gap measure when self-continuity breaks down.

Through its tradition of autobiography, real or fictional, hip hop can enable youth to make a comprehensible personal narrative by providing a template for how negative experiences can be integrated into a story of positive self-identity. Hip hop scholar Mickey Hess (2007) has noted the importance of autobiography within hip hop, particularly stories that narrate a rise from poverty to wealth. Tales of criminal involvement, violence, or police harassment highlight the centrality of struggle to the hip hop performance persona and provide a counter-narrative to stories that position black artists as disempowered victims of white exploitation. Such stories can serve as prototypes for how Indigenous youth might create meaning from their own experiences of cultural violence and colonial oppression, sketching out a perspective on their past that counters that provided by dominant narratives and creating a trajectory that points in a new direction. As Brian "B+" Cross suggests, through hip hop, "you can conjure a past, you can imagine a future" (Tate et al. 2006, 41).

While not all hip hop is autobiographical, and some first-person narratives are fictional, Hess (2009, xiv) observes that "hip hop artists tend to link their first person stories to specific geographic locales," enabling them to represent their region. Regional identity may be meaningful even for people not living in the area. In 1996 I worked as a youth mentor for an educational and work training program in the Halifax Regional Municipality. For a while I tutored youth from local group homes in math and reading, and they schooled me on the music of NWA, Tupac Shakur, and Snoop Dogg. Most of the young men in class identified with the West Coast hip hop scene, adopting the hand signs and clothing despite living within a day's drive of New York. The continuity of a geographic locale, even on the other side of a continent, taken up through the hip hop tradition of representing, may provide a sense of continuity (past, present, and future) that is not yet experienced on a personal or cultural level.

Culture is one of the sources from which the particulars of identity are formed. When culture is consistently undermined, as Indigenous cultures in Canada have been, then the foundation upon which personal continuity is built cannot support us. As Chandler and Lalonde (1998, 193) put it, "the grounds upon which a coherent sense of self is ordinarily made to rest are cut away, life is made cheap, and the prospect of one's own death becomes a matter of indifference." Those of us who rarely see our lives accurately represented, rarely see our contributions acknowledged, and who struggle under the weight of stereotypes that over-write both our history and our present experiences, may feel so erased that our absence would be barely noticed. Suicide may seem our only option for leaving a mark of our existence.

Chandler and Lalonde (1998, 2008) reviewed youth suicide rates in British Columbia's First Nations and Tribal Councils from 1987 through to 2000. While half the communities had suicide rates that were five hundred to eight hundred times the national average, the remaining communities had no suicides at all. Further, they discovered that communities with the lowest suicide rates also had the highest rates of cultural continuity. Cultural continuity is the extent to which cultures connect to their past and secure some control over their future (Hallett et al. 2007, 1). Chandler and Lalonde theorize that cultural continuity reduces suicide by providing youth in crisis with a sense of place and the promise of a future.

Chandler and Lalonde (1998, 2008) identified numerous elements associated with a clinically significant reduction in youth suicides: active resolution of land claims; self-government; control of systems such as education, health, and child welfare; a First Nations police and fire service; language preservation; access to cultural facilities; and women in key government leadership roles. James Burgess Waldram (2004) has observed that these measures might be described more accurately as aspects of cultural *change* rather than continuity. What these factors do assess is the degree to which particular Indigenous communities are actively engaged in preserving and restoring, not simply our historical culture – that is, our "traditional" ways of doing things – but our identity as a people with a cultural inheritance and a collective future. If cultural and personal continuity serve as a buffer against suicide risk in Indigenous youth, would we not be remiss if we failed to make use of the cultural resources in contemporary art forms such as hip hop?

Like other cultural groups marginalized by the dominant white colonial discourse, Indigenous Canadians have turned to alternative sources of truth. Rap scholar Roger Chamberland (2002, 306) described rap as a mode of expression that, while it emerged as a black art form, was rapidly adopted by "immigrants and disenfranchised people" in urban Canadian centres. Reflecting upon my own experience, I suggest that hip hop can function as a point of Indigenous cultural access, offering identity support and stability during times when self-continuity is in crisis. By the term "hip hop" I refer not only to the music but also to the dancing, graffiti, and graphic arts that take up the hip hop aesthetic, technical arts and production, and the fan cultures that have grown up around the arts themselves (Price 2006).

While hip hop is often portrayed as a youth culture, its longevity has resulted in multiple generations of people who have grown up within it. Dj Kool Herc, a pioneer of hip hop, was born in 1955, and Afrika Bambaataa, the grandfather of hip hop, was born in 1957. Wab Kinew, now leader of the New Democratic Party for the province of Manitoba, was also the 2009 winner of an Aboriginal Peoples Choice Music Award for best Rap/Hip-Hop CD. Kinew notes that while his relationship to the music changes over time, his bond with hip hop remains strong: "Twenty years deep into my love affair with this music and culture, the things I'm doing are different than when I started listening to it. Today I'm raising kids, building a career, learning how to be an anchor for the people around me. Yet hip hop is still here, telling me the same thing it did back then: I hear you, I am your voice, I understand, because I'm going through it, too" (Kinew 2012).

While suicide rates are disproportionately high among Indigenous youth, accounting for 22 percent of all deaths among those age ten to nineteen, suicide also accounts for 16 percent of deaths among adults age twenty to forty-four (Kirmayer et al. 2007, 21). As Kinew argues, hip hop may provide a sense of identity and connection that can support Indigenous people across our lifespan. By its longevity, it can become a shared language that facilitates communication across generations. In the sections that follow I argue that Indigenous hip hop provides not only Indigenous youth but also older adults with a sense of group and cultural belonging, offers us a critical vision of contemporary Indigenous identities, and makes particular futures imaginable.

HIP HOP AS A RESOURCE FOR CULTURAL AND PERSONAL CONTINUITY

Christopher Lalonde (2006, 52) expands the concept of resilience to include not only "individual coping in the face of dire adversity" but also "the ability of whole cultural groups to foster healthy youth development." Five aspects of hip hop offer resources for fostering such resilience. The first is hip hop's accessibility in terms of cultural and financial capital. The second is hip hop's hybridity, which enables artists to incorporate elements of historical Indigenous culture (e.g., language, traditional dance, and music) into contemporary artistic expression. The third is hip hop's status as a recent art form, its association with urban culture, and its resulting ability to affirm Indigenous culture as authentically contemporary. The fourth aspect is hip hop's use of critical politics, present since its inception, and the space thus created for artists to elaborate a postcolonial politics grounded in Indigenous experience. The final aspect of hip hop that I want to suggest supports identity resilience is the centring of Indigenous subjectivity, finding universality in our specificity.

Hip Hop's Accessibility

Key to hip hop's growth and longevity has been its relatively low start-up cost. Charity Marsh (2009) notes that hip hop culture offers a variety of artistic entry points. "For many of these arts practices," Marsh observes, "one does not need formalized training; in fact, hip hop cultures all over the world pride themselves on their DIY sensibilities" (119). In its rawest form, one can perform solely with the power of the human voice, as was done in the beginning on the street corners of the South Bronx. Given the poverty that is endemic to many Indigenous communities, hip hop's low cost makes it highly accessible. Median incomes for Indigenous people in Canada are 30 percent lower than are those for other Canadians (Wilson and MacDonald 2010, 3), and data from 2000 indicates that 55.6 percent of urban Indigenous people live in poverty (Canadian Council on Social Development 2003, n.p.).

From the early days of "The Message," commentary on urban poverty and its impact has had a place within hip hop. For those of us whose lives are similarly marked by poverty, hip hop provides a mirror, enabling us to feel represented, heard, and understood (Marsh 2009a). This mirror can also become, in the words of William Butler Yeats (1936), a lamp to illuminate social realities. In valorizing the strength that can emerge from straitened circumstances, hip hop artists help reduce the stigma of poverty, verbalizing and mainstreaming what is often a private shame. For those Indigenous youth struggling with poverty and its associated problems, hip hop can provide a sense of solidarity not found in mainstream Canadian culture. Hip hop stories of want, loss, violence, and pain, while grim, may contribute positively to young people's mental health by reducing their sense of isolation and alienation.

As an industry, hip hop also offers the possibility of meaningful employment. Reddnation, established in 2000, has garnered awards from the Alberta Aboriginal Music Awards, the Aboriginal Peoples Choice Music Awards, and the Canadian Aboriginal Music Awards. Their song, "When I'm Gone," in which one of the verses is directed at the MC's young daughter, posits hip hop as a job, albeit one with an almost quasi-religious appeal:

I'm a tell you what this hip hop meant to me when I'm blessed
It was an outcome to help me when I was in stress
It was made in the Bronx but it was felt in my chest
Brooklyn! Yeah, they did it the best
But then some weak cats got in the game and left it a mess
Restoring this hip hop was always part of my quest
It introduced me to people from east to west
It put food on the table and fed us the best
It bought you your bike, your clothes, and your favourite dress
So if you ever need daddy remember me through this.

In this verse, hip hop is a survival industry, akin to hunting and fishing, yet the lyrics also portray the music as a source of comfort. And, as the song speculates on the MC's death, his art is offered as a way for his daughter to remain connected to him. In this way, hip hop promises a legacy that may extend beyond lives shortened by poverty and oppression.

The increasing affordability of the technology of production and dissemination has fed the underground hip hop industry. The accessible do-it-yourself nature of hip hop culture – whether music production (e.g., song writing, rapping, DJing, beat production), art (e.g., graffiti, tattoo, graphic novel art), dance (e.g., breaking, turfing, krumping), or clothing (e.g., design, production, reconstruction) – enables one to participate as an artist as well as a fan (Marsh 2012c). One can record rhymes, design beats, and capture and edit video on a home computer. And the internet enables artists to draw and build a fan base outside of a major label deal or to address one's message to a mainstream audience (Marsh 2009a).

The venue for exploring autobiography, politics, and culture that Indigenous hip hop offers is refreshingly free of governmental gatekeeping. One does not need a membership card to claim belonging to Indigenous hip hop – indeed, the genre includes artists who are non-status, Métis, or mixed-race. Indigenous hip hop culture has developed without the supervision of a federal government department or individual band councils. Bonita Lawrence (2004) has outlined how inequities in legislation, combined with the use of blood quantum and cultural immersion tests, have disproportionately excluded Indigenous women and their children from Indian status. As a result, many Indigenous women cannot gain access to our oral traditions, ancestral land, or cultural resources, making it harder for us to resist assimilation and colonial domination. By disregarding Indian status, Indigenous hip hop may begin to heal some of the wounds to personal and cultural identity that have been inflicted by the status system.

However, hip hop is not immune to the dynamics of oppression and may even do some wounding itself. Several authors have condemned hip hop's failure to be critical of patriarchy, its tendency to uncritically adopt and promote misogyny and sexualized violence, and its suppression of the female voice (Young 2008; Peoples 2008; Pough 2004). Kendra and Renee King (2009) have argued that if hip hop is to be a vehicle for change it must, among other things, provide space for politically and socially conscious women rather than relegating us to being the sexualized Other. Indigenous hip hop is not immune to these issues. Charity Marsh (2012b, 196) notes assumptions that hip hop is a "masculinized culture" and reports gendered differences in how students engage with hip hop, with male students tending to take centre stage while female students lay down beats. Given that Indigenous women have a suicide rate of 30 percent, compared with 19 percent in the general female population (Kirmayer et al. 2007, 24), women experiencing a crisis in personal continuity may choose to endure hip hop's misogyny rather than go without its cultural support.

When Indigenous hip hop enshrines misogyny, heteronormativity, and rigid stereotypes of masculinity, it endorses values that, in many cases, are antithetical to those of our ancestors. Such choices also risk alienating Indigenous women, lesbian, gay, bisexual, trans, and two-spirit people, and men whose gender expression does not fit the norm. Reddnation's song, "This Is for My Doggz" is a prime example:

"This is for my doggz that know how to get down in poppin tags / This aint' for the snitches, bitches, pussies, hos, or fucking fags."

As a two-spirit woman, it is disappointing to find one of my sources of Indigenous identity nourishment polluted with misogyny, sex negativity, and homophobia, which I see as colonial influences. Given how people with intersectional identities experience multiple interlocking oppressions (e.g., racism, colonialism, sexism, homophobia, etc.), being alienated from Indigenous hip hop and the cultural support, contemporary Indigenous identity, and social inclusion it offers is a serious health issue indeed.

Incorporating Historical Indigenous Culture

Chandler and Lalonde's research demonstrates the importance of active engagement in preserving and restoring Indigenous identities, and emphasizes the role culture plays in supporting personal continuity. Hip hop's openness to hybridity creates space for Indigenous artists to rework aspects of our tradition in hip hop style. As Edmonton-based DJ CreeAsian observes, "A lot of people that I know are able to incorporate traditional dance steps and traditional languages" (Gainer 2012, n.p.). Christina Verán et al. (2006, 278–9) describe the role that hip hop's hybridity plays in making aspects of Indigenous culture relevant to youth: "Rap lends itself as a motivational force and context in the promulgation of indigenous languages and group identity, for peoples as diverse as the Maluku of Indonesia to the Sami of Norway. Culturally significant sources too – think whale calls, as employed by Greenlandic Inuit DJs from the tundra-fied streets of Nuuk – provide rich soundscapes to remix indefinitely ... Even Dine (Navajo) b-boys on the res have related corporeal movements and rhythms of breaking and uprocking with their own styles of more traditional powwow dancing since the early 1980s."

By reframing our traditions as the materials of contemporary Indigenous art, hip hop frees us from the rigidity of fundamentalist approaches to culture that equate authenticity with lack of change. The mental health effects may be particularly positive where language preservation is concerned. Hallett, Chandler, and Lalonde (2007) found that suicide rates dropped to zero in communities where half the band members had a conversational knowledge of their Indigenous language. Incorporating throat singing, traditional dance, or language into hip hop expands the number of venues in which Indigenous people can perform and enact our identities. The presence of traditional dances or language in hip hop art may also provide points of familiarity for our elders, calming fears that hip hop is a sign of assimilation and facilitating conversations between the generations.

Such hybridity enables Indigenous artists to work with the specificity of our Indigenous cultures. Traditional Mi'kmaq quillwork designs taught to me by my father can be reworked with a hip hop aesthetic into graffiti or tattoo art. The art exhibition *Beat Nation: Art, Hip Hop and Aboriginal Culture*, describes itself as presenting "unique cultural hybrids that include graffiti murals with Haida figures ... and hip hop performances in Aboriginal dialects" (The Power Plant 2013, n.p.). By making space for our distinct cultures, hip hop may help Indigenous Canadians develop an identity that feels relevant and meaningful while countering stereotypes that portray all Indigenous cultures as essentially similar. By providing space for Indigenous artists to take up and transform our historical inheritance, hip hop helps us to be Indigenous in authentic yet fully contemporary ways.

Authentically Contemporary Indigeneity

Jonathan Williams (2007) argues that authenticity has been an integral part of the hip hop genre since its inception. Hip hop authenticity, according to Williams, has been variously defined as constituted by degrees of classed blackness, by independent and underground status (versus "selling out" to a major label), or by technique, with MCs who can "rock the mic" being authentic regardless of their racial or class origins (2–9). The issues of authenticity within hip hop – intersecting as they do with class, race, gender, sexuality, and other markers of identity – echo and interact with measures of authenticity that Indigenous people already negotiate.

At the heart of the concept of personal and cultural continuity is our ability to assert that our self or our culture is, despite changes over time, the same self or culture it was previously. Paul Gilroy (1991a, 1991b) argues that black culture is hybrid, confounding simplistic definitions. Gilroy, and others, have used the phrase "the changing same" to describe how black art, rooted in African religion, responds to the constantly shifting experience of racialization and exploitative co-option by whites (Jones 1971; Gilroy 1991a, 1991b; MacDowell 1995). This concept may be applicable to Indigenous culture and artistic expression, rooted in tradition, but changing and evolving in response to practices of colonialism, exploitation, and erasure.

Whether our sameness is like that Amiri Baraka (Jones 1971) proposes, rooted in an essentialist notion of being (i.e., in the blood), or is more akin to a postmodern production of the "racial industry" (Butler 1993, xxv), matters less than what the emerging sense of continuity can provide. In this case, I argue, such continuity offers a potentially life-saving authenticity, however complicated that authenticity may be to live in our contemporary settings. Imani Perry (2004, 89) emphasizes the significance of the community as "an identifying and authenticating force," which can serve as a buffer "against claims of artifice." As a culture in the sense that Perry uses, hip hop may have resources for people whose Indigenous authenticity is challenged or whose access to Indigenous culture is curtailed.

Due to associations of Indigeneity with prehistory, fostering a sense of Indigenous identity that feels simultaneously authentic and contemporary requires negotiating a myriad of reified concepts of Indigenous essence. In speaking to an increasingly urbanized Indigenous audience, hip hop has risen to the challenge. Litefoot, a Native American MC, asserts, "I'm going to press the issue of recognition until the world sees that we're still here and not running around in beads and buckskin" (Thompson and Johnson 2001, 48). Although rural hip hop, sometimes called "hick hop" (Berkes 2004), exists, hip hop emerged in an urban context and has tended to be seen as an urban art form. These origins bring with them a claim to modernity that can help counter the stereotype of the noble savage, which portrays us as irrational, immature, primitive, and undeveloped. By its very newness, and its association with urban living, hip hop can make Indigeneity visible as a contemporary way of being, however hybrid, fractured, or multivalent.

Yet in placing such a high value on personal narrative, the hip hop industry has elevated some narratives, particularly those reporting criminal exploits, to a high status. Whether such narratives are accurate reportage or archetypal posturing, there is a danger that the image of the "gangsta" (playing with stereotypes of excess) will reinforce still current and problematic images of Indigenous Canadians, who are already heavily criminalized (Rudin 2005; Marsh 2009a, 2011). In countering the noble savage stereotype, hip hop risks reinforcing the stereotype of the "ignoble savage," representing all that is violent, indulgent, and criminal. Hip hop offers us a platform for responding to such stereotypes as well as a venue for a complex and nuanced reflection on how criminalized industries such as drug selling or sex work, and experiences of incarceration, are an ongoing reality for many Indigenous Canadians (Bruckert and Chabot 2010).

Hip hop's political expression extends beyond the lyrics of particular songs to clothing and graphic art. Winnipeg's Dead Indians has a merchandise line that features an image of "Chief Wahoo," the racist mascot of the "Cleveland Indians" baseball team, retired after the 2018 season, with his eyes crossed out. Indigenous performance artist Skeena Reece combines British colonial regalia and fetish corsetry with traditional Haida design, producing a subversive political message: "The regalia's red-and-black ceremonial cloak is embroidered, as is typical, with buttons – but in the shape of a silvery hand grenade. And the work is fronted by a Thunderbird distributing AK-47 guns to Native warriors. Reece plays havoc with notions of terrorism, violence and the defense of rights and land in the last setting you'd might expect it – inside Vancouver's respected art gallery, housed in the former city court house" (Ball 2012, n.p.).

In addition to being its own art form and industry, Indigenous hip hop fashion can make Indigenous people visible to one another by enabling the more subtle cues of our identity to be read. The visibility of a Reddnation cap, or the Electric Powwow T-shirt of Ottawa's A Tribe Called Red, allows those of us who get read as white (in part because we do not match the colonial iconography of Indigeneity) to subvert this privilege. Such wearable art helps counter our cultural invisibility and facilitates connections across differences of racialization.

Hip hop video production provides a platform for representing Indigeneity in ways that are nuanced and complicated. The video that Reddnation produced for its song "Fabulous" asserts a sense of cultural continuity that is decidedly contemporary. The video begins with shots of brick buildings in Edmonton, Alberta, evoking a gritty urban feel. Over these images appear the words, "There was a fire that no one could put out. They called the fire Reddnation." The chorus of the song can easily be read as part of the hip hop tradition of self-assertion:

We ain't (We ain't)
Ain't going nowhere (Nowhere)
'Cause we're right here. (Right here. Right here. Yeah we're right here)
We fabulous (Fabulous)

And we're dangerous (Dangerous)
Most crews can't handle us (Handle us. Can't handle us. Can't handle us)

Reddnation, "Fabulous," *Now or Never*

In the same way that the name refers simultaneously to the group and to Indigenous people as a whole, the aggressive confidence of the lyrics can be read as applying to us (the Red Nation), undercutting stereotypes that portray us as a tragic, doomed culture. In the tradition of James Brown's "Black and Proud," Reddnation's lyrics invite Indigenous listeners to join in the call and response, asserting that *we are fabulous*. As the song says, we may indeed be dangerous. And if the past two-plus centuries have proven anything, it is that *most crews can't handle us* – certainly not colonial governments.

Hip Hop as Political Expression

Traditions of narrative storytelling, personal biography, and political critique have been present in hip hop from the beginning (Hess 2007; Bradley 2009). When taken up by Indigenous artists, these traditions provide a venue for reflection on experiences such as substance abuse, suicide, gang violence, and colonialist projects such as the residential school system or the Sixties Scoop. Charity Marsh (2012c) has called this political reflection "narrating colonialism." Such politics are evident in the lyrics of Montreal's Slangblossom:

My style's gravity because I broadcast attraction
I'm a red man in the crowd yelling aloud that it's time for some action
We went from peace pipes to crack pipes
I attack type or act tight, ask my folks to act right
Blaze the weed to black lights
While white judges tell the brothers to pay their debt to society
I'm wondering when society's gonna pay its debt to us
You better admire me

Slangblossom, "The Hate," *Convulsions*

One of the most exciting aspects of hip hop's political potential comes from its status as a global art form. Edmonton's DJ CreeAsian observes: "It doesn't matter what culture you are, what religion, what colour of skin, hip hop is for everybody. It's a global language" (Gainer 2012). Hip hop enables us to share experience and politics with people around the globe whose lives have also been affected by colonialism, exploitation, white supremacy, and genocide. The *Beat Nation* art exhibition "brings together artists from across the continent – from the West Coast as far north as Alaska and Nunavut, as far east as Labrador and south to New Mexico – and reveals the shared connections between those working in vastly different places" (The Power Plant 2013, n.p.). As Marsh (2012c) notes, "What we are seeing over and over again is this recognized shared collective experience of marginalization, of persecution, of rebellion, celebration." In drawing performers, artists, and fans from disparate regions together, and enabling mutual affirmation and critique, consciousness raising, and celebration, Indigenous hip hop events may be as significant as other large-scale Indigenous cultural events, such as powwows.

The global nature of hip hop reduces the significance of the border between Canada and the United States, and reveals commonalities between Indigenous lives north and south of the 49th parallel. The words of Short Dawg, from Highland California, reiterate a familiar history of colonial settler-Indigenous relations:

> As I'm riding through the plains, I see my people in chains
> And these children all got hunger pains
> Shit won't change while all these rich people still bitches and complains
> That I own a little land and it's tax free
> Ask me and I might reply nasty
> Fuck you. The house that you live in is mine too
> Where you stand and behind you
>
> Short Dawg Tha Native, "Rez Life," *Short Stories*

The psychological impact of belonging to a culture that has been subjected to continuous systemic oppression cannot be simply brushed aside. Numerous scholars have described how experiences such as land loss, incarceration in the residential school system, or the Sixties Scoop affect not only the immediate survivors but also their children and grandchildren (Wesley-Esquimaux and Smolewski 2004; Mitchell and Maracle 2005; Nelson 2012). This experience has been termed "intergenerational trauma," and some scholars, such as Maria Yellow Horse Brave Heart and Lemyra M. DeBruyn (1998, 60), suggest that the high rates of suicide, homicide, domestic violence, child abuse, and alcoholism within Indigenous communities are "primarily the product of a legacy of chronic trauma and unresolved grief across generations." By providing a venue in which Indigenous people can process this trauma, express our anger, and grieve publicly for our losses, hip hop may serve a function similar to that of other art therapies.

Centring Indigenous Identity

Mickey Hess (2009, xiv) notes, "just as hip hop authenticity centres on a continuum of tradition and innovation, artists must also prove themselves both local and universal." The regional representation that Hess articulates enables Indigenous youth to claim a multitude of regional identities and provides them with a foundation through ties to hip hop traditions emerging from those locales. In addition to a regional belonging, participants may see themselves as belonging to a global hip hop culture, even if such citizenship is complicated by barriers of sexism or homophobia.

Craig Proulx describes Indigenous hip hop as reaching into a primarily Indigenous audience, while simultaneously reaching out to non- Indigenous others (Landzelius 2006). This dialectic enables Indigenous hip hop to "communicate and educate about processes of colonialism, empowerment, and identification" (Proulx 2010, 40). The process of reaching in accords the Indigenous listener a rare experience – seeing ourselves presented as the norm. Indigenous hip hop provides a venue whereby those of us who are usually the *object* of media gaze can become *subjects*: to be creators of our own images rather than consumers. The work of artists such as Reddnation problematizes iconography that portrays us as obsolete, while centring Native subjectivity. The title of its June 2010 release, *Grown Folk Muzik*, plays on the genre of folk music, while undercutting stereotypes of Indigenous people as infantilized:

> Yeah … Reddnation!
> Big boy music
> We're coming
> You know it you bro and we holdin' it down and we ride
> A grown folk gonna fight for every ounce of pride
> And persevere when he's beaten down he's gonna rise
> This is grown folk muzik
>
> Reddnation, "Intro (Featuring Pen Pointz)," *Grown Folk Muzik*

Reddnation's lyrics show a variety of implicit listeners: competitors, fans, insiders and outsiders to hip hop. Yet it is the moments when the group speaks directly to its Indigenous audience that seem to me the most promising, as the term "Native" takes on a quality of universal human subjectivity that, though present in many of our Native languages (the Mi'kmaq, for example, refer to ourselves as "l'nuk," meaning "the people"), is absent from the national discourse in which Indigenous people are peripheral at best. In addressing his audience, Madjikal (Keith Laboucan) raps, "Every time I come and hit you Natives the hardest," and later, "Because you heard it before, Native don't get confused," centring the Indigenous listener and marking the work as a conversation among insiders. This recentring of Indigenous subjectivity stands in stark contrast to the normalization of white settler identity.

While placing Native subjectivity front and centre is promising as a support for Indigenous identity, the practice also risks narrowing the definition of Indigenous in ways that can exclude those already culturally marginalized by colonialism and assimilation. Reddnation's use of the term "Native," for example, used to distinguish its own work from that of competing MCs, can express and reinforce measures of Indigenous identity against which non-status Indigenous people constantly struggle. In "Truth Be Told" Madjikal raps:

> They ain't got enough style to get it poppin' like me
> They ain't got enough skill to get it on with Keith
> They ain't got enough dough to buy out the bars
> They not Native enough to bang with these stars
>
> Reddnation, "Truth Be Told," *Now or Never*

As a woman who received recognition of my Indian status under Bill C-3, claims that one can be "not Native enough" hit rather too close to home. The presence of identity rulings is a disappointing dilution of hip hop's inclusive promise, yet may be an inevitable by-product of identity politics. One solution lies in the multiplicity of subject voices made possible through hip hop's use of first person narrative. Reddnation's "Who I Am" track asserts the power of Indigenous (in this case, Métis) identity:

I'm not afraid to say who I am, where I'm from, or what I stand for
Culture, people, pride, unity, mind, identity, history, community
***
Yo, They used to tell me, "know your place"
And all the TVs, nah, they won't know your face
No radio plays and no VIPs
No red carpet treatment, "Let's see IDs," Man, please!
It's 2008, I'm in a position of power and you can't hate
I'm a doctor, a lawyer, the captain of my team,
And I'm an entrepreneur who's just capturing my dream
And every day ain't easy, believe me,
Many masquerade, concealing their feelings
All the while I never lost who I was
There'll forever be Métis pride in this blood.

Reddnation, "Who I Am," *Grown Folk Muzik*

The lyrics illustrate both the erasure of Indigenous people from mainstream media and the class domination that has accompanied colonialism. While the song represents the group's own experience of struggling to obtain airplay and being singled out for security checks, the lyrics can also apply to those of us attempting to escape cycles of poverty through efforts and means (such as university education) that have sometimes been deemed evidence of assimilation. The confidence of the song's MC can serve as a placeholder for those of us whose identities are not yet so strong. As Professor of African American Studies Imani Perry (2004, 89) has argued, listener identification can be facilitated through shared life circumstances, aspirations, or "language, clothing, and body politics of the artists, who operate as cultural signifiers." Such imagined similarity enables the listener to participate vicariously in the strength of the artist – a life preserver for those of us suffering through a crisis of personal meaning and continuity.

CONCLUSION

It is easier to demonstrate the health value inherent in physical aspects of hip hop, such as breakdancing. Yet if hip hop does support personal and cultural continuity, then it may be an important resource for mental health as well. Indigenous hip hop constitutes a cultural resource that facilitates the narration of a continuous self and enables us to challenge dominant metanarratives of Indigenous people as degenerating and self-destructing. Hip hop artists reframe Indigeneity as creative, powerful, and authoritative, asserting pride in the strength and resilience evident in our having survived repeated and ongoing attempts at cultural and physical genocide. Hip hop's tradition of self-reflection and personal storytelling provides a model by which individual Indigenous people – especially youth – can construct our own tales, drawing our disparate experiences into a story that makes sense for us. As an industry and a growing art form, Indigenous hip hop offers a future in which Indigenous youth can imagine themselves and in which many eagerly wish to participate (Marsh 2009a).

Educational programs have already discovered the benefits of incorporating hip hop into their curricula. The Toronto District School Board, for example, included hip hop as part of its language curriculum at D.A. Morrison Middle School, incorporated hip hop styles into its dance program for Grades 4 and 5 at Broadacres Junior High in 2012, hosted a series of motivational talks with Maestro Fresh Wes (aka Wes Williams) at eight schools in the Greater Toronto Area in 2010, and examined the lyrics of Somali-born hip hop artist K'Naan in a unit that looked at the experience of child soldiers (Lyonais 2013; Broadacres Junior High 2012; Miller 2011). After school programs such as Literacy through Hip Hop, or Lost Lyrics, expand the educational potential beyond the boundaries of the school day (Lyonais 2013). Such programs might have clinical applications as an art therapy that enables youth struggling with depression and suicidal ideation to find the solid personal and cultural ground upon which to live confidently.

In describing the effect of her Interactive Media and Performance Labs at the University of Regina, which offer training and access to a multimedia studio, Charity Marsh (2012c) reports, "we've seen grades rise, we've seen young people stay in school … Now we're seeing all of the young people that have been participating talking about seeing themselves within the university setting." While educational attainment is an important marker of both physical and mental health, the ability to imagine a future for the self – to integrate previous changes in identity, practice, location, social context, and culture – may be a life-saving effect.

NOTE

1 Throughout this chapter I use the term "Indigenous" to refer to First Nations, Inuit, and Métis people of Canada, regardless of whether or not their Indian status is recognized by the federal government.

10

REPPIN' RIGHT

K'naan as Diasporic Disruption in North American Hip Hop

Salman A. **Rana** and Mark V. **Campbell**

> I come with all the baggage of Somalia – of my grandfather's poetry, of pounding rhythms, of the war, of being an immigrant, of being an artist, of needing to explain a few things. Even in the friendliest of melodies, something in my voice stirs up a well of history – of dark history, of loss's victory.
>
> K'naan, *New York Times*, 2012.[1]

One can excuse early hip hop culture for being hyper-local. The origins of hip hop culture, while tangentially connected to global processes, were for the most part forged in the largely abandoned post-industrial barrios of the South Bronx. In fact, one could say hip hop's local focus has been influenced by the prepubescent competitive masculinities of street gangs like the Black Spades and the up to forty other territorial and street-prowling youth groups. Graf writers also signalled the importance of geography, neighbourhood, and space with the importance of going "all city" by bombing subway cars that criss-crossed all of New York City's boroughs. Between nightclubs in Manhattan and the parks of the Bronx, hip hop culture's American origins are very much about place, space, and race. Unsurprisingly, the globality of hip hop has been achieved within the confines of nation, where processes of representing one's local environment have been central. The concerns of an emcee from Dakar or Sao Paulo are, and continue to be, very much about achieving social justice and equity, defeating corrupt political structures, or maintaining control over one's identity.

By opening this chapter with a quote from K'naan's reflective op-ed in the *New York Times*, the goal is to illustrate the ways in which notions of diaspora, or diasporic sensibilities found within Canada-bound emcees from Continental Africa, are productively disruptive to normalized ways. These emcees, including K'naan, Shad K, Spekwon, and several others, expose the limited ways in which the discourse of the nation gets deployed and easily reproduced within hip hop musics. The "baggage" K'naan claims, and from which he refuses to disassociate himself, is emblematic of a particular strategy of authenticity that ruptures the nation as a hegemonic mechanism and moves beyond hip hop's hyper-local tendencies. K'naan's unwillingness to hide or ignore his "baggage" is both a modality of representing one's self in a very orthodox hip hop way and a way of diasporically disrupting both the power of the national space and of discourses in mainstream hip hop music. There is nothing innocent about the nation and its mechanisms of ordering its populations into disciplinary modes designed to reproduce the status quo. The challenge that diasporas have brought to the door of the nation has been the ability to make borders porous, to illuminate the fluidity and flexibility of identities, and to question the assumed all-encompassing power of the nation.

Hip hop's emergence in the United States has found ways to fit neatly into the discourse of the nation, often rearticulating popular values exalted by the nation, such as conspicuous consumption. With a central focus on surviving the tumultuous machinations of a bankrupt New York City and then the ravages of Reaganomics, one cannot expect racialized American youth on the margins to be engrossed with the concerns of Dutch, Cuban, or Canadian hip hoppers: attention to one's local situation has been central to the task of making life livable within the confines of post-industrial urban life. Representing, or r*eppin*', as a specific strategy of hip hop artists, involves deep ethnographic analysis of one's neighbourhood as well as an honouring of those who contribute to an emcee's artistry via the "shout out." The forms of reppin' are often locally based analyses and observations that bolster the importance of one's surroundings and neighbourhood. The nostalgic, and in some cases traumatic, memories of life from within Continental Africa work to provide emcees with liminal perspectives within hip hop culture. As outliers, Canadian-based emcees of Continental African inheritance provide an important voice in hip hop culture, a voice that moves beyond the nation through critiquing mainstream hip hop discourses over-invested in the concept of a nation as the central pivot point of a politics of representation.

In what follows, we move through the music K'naan produced between 1999 and 2012, providing a discourse analysis of the ways in which diasporic sensibilities productively expand and challenge dominant ideas of hip hop culture in the public sphere. Diasporic sensibility is defined here as being concerned with "the texture, gesture, form, content and indeed the underlying politics of various utterances of cultural expression" (Walcott 2006, 12). Both in his music and, more important, in his public appearances, K'naan refuses to confine his work and persona to a strictly local or Western perspective. Beginning with his first release "Soobax" in 1999, and supported with an interview with CBC Radio in Toronto and his underground remixes and releases, this chapter demonstrates how K'naan exposes both national and local constraints and boundaries of the nation and hip hop culture, both creolizing and subverting some of the dominant discussions in mainstream American hip hop.

DIASPORIC DISRUPTIONS

K'naan's willingness to utilize his music as a way of "getting his message out" aligns well with the histories of black expressive cultural forms. K'naan's aesthetic embeddedness within the art of rhyming and his adamant political orientation demonstrate a black cultural diasporic sensibility, where the political, artistic, and economic spheres of life are negotiated in ways that trouble or "seek revenge" on modernity (Brennan 2008; Gilroy 1993). While the glamour and glitz of the pop music did not appear to seduce K'naan during his earlier music, once his success with "Wavin' Flag" was imminent, he soon found himself justifying his "like" of pop music.

In seeking ways to connect K'naan's music and public persona, diaspora becomes a useful tool as it forces us to rethink the borders of nations and nationalisms while also paying attention to the shifting relations between citizen and state (Evans and Mannur 2003). Diaspora provides a useful theoretical frame to examine K'naan's music and aesthetic gestures because it allows us to connect K'naan's work with global political transactions and discourses that do not fit neatly into the Canadian national narrative. K'naan's unrelenting criticisms of Somali warlords, his nostalgic yearnings for a prewar homeland, and his almost complete disengagement with dominant tropes in North American hip hop renders flaccid previously rigid notions of the nation.

Following Jenny Burman (2002) as she riffs Martiniquan theorist Edouard Glissant, the investment in diaspora here is an investment in the poetics of relation, connecting seemingly disparate ideas across borders. With significant Somali migration to Toronto post-1991, much of the Canadian landscape of blackness and diaspora has been dramatically rearranged. The difficult relationships newcomer Somalis experienced with Toronto police and the mainstream media was very much about, and still is, a certain kind of anti-blackness (Cole 2016). The early 1990s was the beginning of a much wider definition of blackness in the Toronto diaspora space, which had been previously dominated by various forms of Afro-Caribbean cultures and, at times, an Afro-Canadian blackness from Halifax. Outernational yearnings, as Burman (2002) calls them, were no longer simply circulating along the former triangle of trade. East Africa now became part of the imaginary in Toronto's diasporic cityscape, with Somalis arriving in the largest numbers in the early 1990s followed by Eritreans and Ethiopians later in the decade.

As a high school drop out K'naan experienced the "push out" effect that black students in Toronto face, an experience that had more to do with existing tropes of blackness than with anything specific about being Somali (Dei 1997). Part of the process of becoming black, as Awad Ibrahim (1999) has explored, involves being exposed to the negative tropes, the low expectations in the school system, and the societal effectives of anti-blackness, such as over-policing and blatant criminalization. Often, it is popular culture, and hip hop specifically, that produces dominant representations of black culture to which young people are exposed while negotiating and developing their personal identities.

When geographer Katherine McKittrick (2002, 33) claims, "the black diaspora illustrates how the politics of location – geographical, linguistic, and imaginary – is importantly rooted in a politics of (un)belonging: rooted, routed, and rootless geographic tensions," K'naan's work immediately comes to mind. Between both Toronto and New York, physically and psychically in Mogadishu, K'naan's diasporic sensibilities forces listeners to consider black life in a non-Western location. Both through signification and through creolization,

K'naan tackles issues such as violence in hip hop music by reflecting back on his days as an adolescent in Mogadishu. K'naan's work diverges from Clifford's (1997, 244) assertion that diasporic communities are automatically concerned with creating a "home away from homes." Instead, by engaging with hip hop's cultural debates within North America, K'naan intervenes to present the case of Somalia as an area of the world where the severity of people's lives are comparatively worse than what is depicted in the representational topics American hip hop music popularizes.

By intervening in and creolizing the topical issues debated in North American hip hop, many of which Tricia Rose (2008) focuses on in *Hip Hop Wars*, such as misogyny, violence, and race, K'naan reorients and points the listener's focus towards his former homeland. Undoubtedly, issues of nostalgia, trauma, and home colour the music of K'naan, yet these concerns make rich the kind of critiques of North American hip hop in which he explicitly and implicitly engages and that his audiences can also read in his work. Commenters, who appreciate K'naan's "vintage bohemian look," are quick to voice their displeasure with "bling culture" and are eager to find ways to amplify his difference from other more mainstream hip hop artists (Intini 2005; Shapiro 2009). In fact, headlines such as "A War Weary Rapper with More Street Cred Than 50 Cent" or "Somali Rapper K'naan Schools American MCs" serve to de-link K'naan from some of the tropes that cast a negative shadow over the hip hop industry. When paying close attention to the works of K'naan, what becomes clear is that his focus is on Somalia and geopolitics, not on refashioning already problematic and highly localized North American representations of blackness found in hip hop musics. It is this divergence from more local concerns found in hip hop musics that is central to the accomplishment of his artistic political vision, which casts a Somalia beyond the question of war.

By being embedded within hip hop culture from the global North, yet by remaining steadfast in discussing and illuminating the issues for Somali people as part of the global South, K'naan's music and politics are productively disruptive. Songs such as "T.I.A.," "Somalia," and "Soobax" encourage a re-examination of the kinds of citizen and nation-state relationships we find commonplace within mainstream hip hop music. K'naan's diasporic sensibilities, his concern for "home," and his mixture of politics and entertainment provide a fresh perspective on some of the more embedded discourses within mainstream hip hop that are intimately connected to the nation-state. Yet, in all of the disruptive work K'naan's sensibilities produce within hip hop circles, he still adheres to specific representational practices within hip hop culture.

REPRESENTATION, REPPIN'

> It might sound arrogant or stupid ... but I feel so outrageously authentic at what I do that the question of selling out or not selling out doesn't even enter my head. I think people who worry about this must already be worried about their true credibility. I'm just interested in, How do we get my message out?
>
> K'naan 2010, qtd. in *Fast Company*

Nas's 1994 track "Represent" is somewhat of a canonical work as this song and his debut album, *Illmatic*,[2] capture the encoded nuances from which much of hip hop culture's symbols and meanings are derived.[3] Nas opens the track with a detailed ethnographic account of his surroundings:

> Straight up shit is real and any day could be your last in the jungle
> Get murdered on the humble, guns'll blast, niggas tumble ...
>
> The streets are filled with undercovers, Homicide chasin' brothers
> The DA's on the roof, tryin' to watch us and knock us

Nas aligns himself with street culture, describing both his peers and the predators among whom he lives. In the next verse, Nas describes himself as an extralegal "type of fella," highlighting his high school dropout status and his fashionable dress code – his stylized "walk with a bop." By the end of the track, Nas honours his peers by shouting them out, celebrating the community that raised him and nourished his skills. Nas calls out names of relatives, producers, and friends as he also provides a geographic connection to the spaces that he represents, the projects, and other city spaces that hold meaning for him and his peers. Nas's "Represent" is an ethnographic, biographic, and geographic survey that highlights where and how meaning enters his consciousness. This track's critique of social institutions such as law enforcement and the school system cements "Represent" as an accurate portrayal of the ways oppressed African Americans relate to their openly biased institutions, which structure black histories and lives. Rather than have Nas's track operate as a mechanism for generalization or stereotyping, we use "represent" as one example of the instability between versions and interpretations of a term that informs cultural studies work. The definition of representation that comes out of cultural studies is interested in reading the ways in which information is positioned, particularly by mainstream social institutions and media outlets. A politics of representation in its earliest articulations primarily sought to counteract the ideas and images circulated by mainstream media and to secure a way to understand how meaning is made. Accordingly, representation is the way in which we understand meaning to be transmitted through signs and signifying practices. It is the way in which meaning is given to the things depicted rather than a literal reflection or distortion. According to Stuart Hall, representation is an active process that is constitutive of the image or event it portrays (Hall 2002). Representation points to the ways in which we come to know through the framing practices of others, such as the media or others with power. Discourse and language are the basis upon which two people can share in a specific understanding of something. At stake in the practice of representation is not only the power to define but also the kinds of social and political possibilities that come from how one's dress, race, or language is made to take on social meaning. If, as Hall claims, "nothing meaningful exists outside of discourse," then meaning comes after the process of representation (ibid.). Thus, in this case, representation as articulated is a discursive positioning of images or events through which a desired meaning can be discerned.

In contrast, Nas's "Represent" and hip hop's discourse around representing focuses on capturing the lives of people who relate primarily to hip hop culture and street culture and critiquing social institutions as a secondary activity. To represent in the same fashion as Nas is to present an image or notion of an individual, group, or space that both expresses and relies upon a system of values and meaning that is alternative to prevailing dominant meaning-making institutions. For example, when an emcee is reppin,' they use a rhyming style that demonstrates one's ability to engage in important signifiers (such as spontaneity or indirection) within the African American vernacular tradition (Smitherman 1977). It is between these two approaches, a politics of representation and hip hop's practice of reppin,' that I look for diasporic constructions and notions of home. Practices of reppin', then, signal within this work the convergence and continued oscillations between the sonic/oral techniques of representing and a political concern with the meaning-making tactics of the nation and dominant media.

If we turn to Murray Forman's (2004) definition of "representing" within hip hop culture, another notion of representation is articulated. Forman asserts that "representing … involves creating a broader profile for the home territory and its inhabitants while showing respect for the nurture it provides" (208). While Forman connects representing with the discursive construction of the "hood as home," he also explicitly highlights the ways in which those who nurture and support the community are highlighted within rap discourse. I would add to Forman's description that various ethnographic analyses by emcees vividly paint pictures of how marginalized communities imagine and self-fashion themselves within the machinations of otherizing hegemonic texts and social landscapes. For example, Nas self-fashions his ability to represent by describing himself as "rapping with a razor under my tongue" or "walking with a baseball cap turned backwards," both modes of self-fashioning on the margins of dominant society. In this way, hip hop creates images and makes meaning that is more than geographic, relying on the connection between self, space, sound, and style.

By enmeshing a cultural studies academic term with an "illegitimate" hidden transcript (Scott 1990) from the streets, this chapter examines the space of meaning-making where reppin' and representation intersect and speak to one another. While there is nothing written, to date, that connects Nas's "Represent" and Stuart Hall's politics of representation, the double entendre implications of these terms, together, provide a useful framework within which to read Afro-diasporic temporal innovations of making home. Our use of the term "reppin'" is meant to capture the aforementioned acts of reappropriation, identity juggling, and temporal meaning-making manoeuvres and linguistic innovations. This rhetorical move, "offer(s) a strategy for the construction of modern temporality" (Weheliye 2005, 83), suggesting a viable space of analysis if we are to think of the ideological overlap between reppin' and representation.

If we look broadly at how images of black Canadians, or, specifically, Afro-Caribbeans, in Toronto are positioned and criminalized as belonging to somewhere else, one can understand the struggle for representation of black populations in Canada (Walcott 2001). Openly discriminatory immigration policies and institutionalized racism (think here the effect of zero tolerance policies in Ontario schools), including the well-circulated historical myth that "Negroes" could not bear the harsh Canadian winters, that accompanied early racist Canadian immigration legislation are all representational strategies that produce a narrative of Canadianness that does not include its black populations. Shadd's frustrations exemplify how black people are "othered" within the representational regimes dominant in Canada's discursive practices of imaging itself. In her article, "Where Are You Really From? Notes from an 'Immigrant' from North Buxton, Ontario," Shadd (1994), a fifth-generation Canadian, elaborates her many encounters in which she is imagined as coming from elsewhere. The otherizing that takes place within the nation is vividly and well documented in the works of Foster (1996), Clarke (1997), Philip (1992), Walcott (2001), and Puplampu and Tettey (2005).

Yet, while an all-encompassing distorted and pathologizing picture of inherently violent black culture is painted, Afro-diasporic populations are neither silent nor overdetermined. Reppin' by Afro-diasporic youth in Toronto can be read via the independent hip hop records produced in the city. Turning towards hip hop's creative acts in the city is important, as Murray Forman (2004, xviii) reminds us that, in rap music, the "city and its multiple spaces" are the foundation of rap's cultural production. More specifically, the city is made audible via explicit citations and digital sampling as the "aural textures of the urban environment" are reproduced (ibid.). Forman's formulation of representing and Hall's understanding of representation neatly overlap, allowing for an interpretation of hip hop culture's meaning-making power.

The meaning making Hall (2002) highlights as constitutive of representation involves precisely the activities hip hoppers engage, but through processes that are designed and defined within the realm of hip hop culture. Some of these processes, as detailed by Forman (2004), include shout-outs to one's crew; frequent references to specific streets, spaces, and boroughs; and digital sampling of the city. This last technique, digitally sampling the city, frequently involves capturing the sound of the subway or, in the case of Scarborough emcees, capturing the sounds of the Railway Transit.

Reppin' captures the slippage from "high" academic discourse to the actual meanings that circulate in the streets. Thus, image representation and meanings are not solely created by institutions but are also challenged by creative communities. In the alternative meaning-making worlds of creative arts communities and subaltern populations, poor does not necessarily correlate with disempowered and blackness does not solely correlate with criminality. In this way, reppin' highlights the oppressed as agents and operates as a counter-narrative to the insidious attacks on Afro-diasporic urban life by mainstream media. Importantly, reppin' signifies, in an Eshu kind of way in this book,[4] the indetermination at the crossroads of academic theorization and hip hop street signification.

The dominant narratives of capital accumulation, individualism, and black criminalization are both reflected and refracted in activities of reppin' so that "keeping it real" can mean recycling narratives with a criminal residue or relaying life in the 'hood as it is understood. Reppin' in this sense is slippery, but it is useful because it captures temporal innovations, sometimes demonstrating how the dominant logic is subverted. For example, if we look at K'naan's remix of the popular Kid Cudi track "Day 'N Night," we see that he dislodges the meaning of this song by talking about the pirate situation off the coast of Somalia instead of engaging Kid Cudi's very North American weed-smoking adventure. K'naan rhymes:

> dayless nights, I see pirates in the ocean late at night
> they roam around and can't wait to fight,
> watch out for pirates roaming late at night (at at at night).

Revising Kid Cudi's original chorus:

> Cuz day and night
> The lonely stoner seems to free his mind at night,
> He's all alone through the day and night,
> The lonely loner seems to free his mind at night (at at at night).

K'naan's version, "Dayless Nights," uses the same beat as "Day 'N Night" but instead focuses on the geopolitical situation in Somalia. K'naan takes on the persona of a Somali pirate and a Somali civilian, highlighting the perils of landmines and the possible hunger of pirates at sea. K'naan is "keeping it real" in a hip hop sense, representing his reality growing up in Mogadishu and the plight of his people; he is representing, in a sense, his 'hood.

Similarly, if we turn to "Soobax," K'naan's first release with the independent label Track & Field, what immediately becomes clear is that the song is meant to engage both English- and Somali-speaking audiences and turn their attention to the plight of his homeland in the global South. "Soobax" is a Somali word meaning "come out with it," in reference to the hiding warlords and gunmen in Mogadishu. By releasing a track with a Somali-language title, K'naan immediately distinguished his music as something more than the same cliché narratives found in American rap musics.

In the song K'naan critiques the warlords who have ripped Somalia apart since the fall of its central government in 1991. Much like the black public sphere Mark Anthony Neal (2013) discusses in length in *What the Music Said*, K'naan circulates Soobax in a global black public sphere amplifying an ethical violation, admonishing the Somali warring factions, and daring them to come out and face the consequences of their actions. "Soobax," like so many other black expressive forms, moves seamlessly between the political and the aesthetic, and between national borders, evading a simplistic presentation of the issues. "Soobax" begins by utilizing African American vernacular:

Basically, I got beef
I wanna talk to you directly
I can't ignore, I can't escape
And that's cause you affect me
You cripple me
You shatter my whole future in front of me
This energy is killing me
I gotta let it pour like blood, soobax

In the chorus of "Soobax," K'naan's lyrical tirade continues in Somali:

Dadkii waa dhibtee nagala soobax (you've exasperated the people so come out with it)
Dhibkii waa batee nagala soobax (the troubles have increased so come out with it)
Dhiigi waad gubtee nagala soobax (You've spilt the blood so now it rolls in balls, so come out with it)
Dhulkii waad qubtee nagala soobax (You've burnt the root of the earth, so come out with it)

The video for Soobax, shot in Eastleigh, a Nairobi slum that has become home to many Somali refugees, featured what appears to be an abandoned school bus colourfully adorned in graffiti. Absent from the video are the cliché signifiers of hip hop music videos, such as scantily clad women, displays of excess, or celebratory alcohol. What we do see replacing the "crew shot" of (usually men) jostling for camera time are the men, women, and children of the Eastleigh community, dressed in hijabs and everyday clothing.

Hip hop music becomes a vehicle for K'naan as his multilingual rhymes centre on his very diasporic political concerns, allowing him both to stand out as a breath of fresh air in hip hop music and to gain a niche audience while also troubling some of the ways hip hop music aligns with nation-state views and values. Lester Spence's (2015) *Knocking the Hustle: Against the Neoliberal Turn in Black Politics* captures well the ways in which American hip hop has become complicit with neoliberal logic by reproducing its logics within the mentality of "hustling." K'naan's movements between his diasporic home in Canada, his political concerns in Somalia, and his global performance touring schedule demonstrate the very loose ties between the nation-state and his diasporic citizenry. For K'naan, the politics of his location in the global North affect and extend his message in ways not possible in the global South, and we see K'naan's global reach extend with his World Cup relationship with the multinational corporation Coca Cola.

WAVING FLAGS

K'naan's career took a dramatic leap into the international limelight when his song "Wavin' Flag" was selected by Coca Cola for the company's 2010 World Cup global marketing campaign. Touring eighty-four countries in nine months, K'naan's sanitized version of "Wavin' Flag" was authorized by Coca Cola minus the original lyrics, a "violent prone, poor people zone" and "struggling, fighting to eat" (Prince 2010). Despite being virtually censored by his marketing relationship with Coca Cola, K'naan found a way to read his situation as productive. He claims: "I saw it as an opportunity to reach more people … I don't work for Coke or anything; what I do is my music. This was a really great opportunity for them to use my song, without compromising my integrity as a musician. This is what I write, these are the songs I make. I'm happy about it" (as quoted in Prince 2010). As an artist whose music refuses to operate within the ideological or narrative boundaries of a particular nation, the irony of "Wavin' Flag" is not lost here. The most well known symbol of nationhood, the flag becomes a metaphor by which K'naan attempts to raise awareness of Somalia's plight. Like a rhizomatic root, which Glissant (1992) theorizes as one that extends and finds connections, K'naan's "Wavin' Flag" (with marketing help from Coca Cola) creates sets of relations around the national symbol of a flag. His audiences, as citizens of various countries and World Cup fans who clearly rally around the nation, are all brought into relation as they understand power and disempowerment through the lens of the nation-state.

The "Celebration Mix" of "Wavin' Flag" featured eighteen different versions of K'naan's song with A-list artists from various countries, such as David Guetta, David Bisbal, and Drake, along with upbeat instrumentation. One could say from the position of raising awareness about life in Somalia (or the global South in general) K'naan was successful in sharing his views, with "Wavin' Flag" reaching the top two position on the Billboard charts in several European countries. By collaborating on remix versions with various stars in the African, Asian, European, and Latin American countries, K'naan's diasporic routes globalized his message, which was rooted in the realities of Somalia. The commercial success of "Wavin' Flag" around the world best demonstrates how K'naan's diasporic sensibilities evade a top-down hegemonic narrative of the nation-state. For example, despite his living in both Canada and now the United States, neither traces of the American Dream narrative of rugged individualism nor traces of the language of Canadian state-sponsored multicultural celebration can be found in K'naan's original "Wavin' Flag." In fact, it is a willingness to represent Mogadishu in a manner that honours the realities of the life there that steers K'naan away from reproducing dominant Canadian or American narratives. K'naan's local focus in a global context and on a global stage allows him to produce music that resonates beyond borders and nation-states. At the level of the nation-state, K'naan's "Wavin' Flag" is an important intervention, both relying on the nation as an ideological formation and refuting it as over-determining his message. In more popular terms, K'naan's other songs are decisive incisions into dominant thinking, particularly within popular culture and its recent import of hip hop.

WHAT'S HARDCORE?

K'naan's outsider status, as one who seeks to represent the struggles of the global South, provides him with a unique perspective when tackling the pervasiveness of the masculinized posturing in American gangster rap. "What's Hardcore" is K'naan's frustrated rebuttal to an abundance of performances of gangsterism he finds congesting BET programming.[5] With feedback from Somali communities in Minnesota, Toronto, Ohio, and elsewhere, K'naan felt it important to critique tales of gangsterism and the glorification of violence in American hip hop music. Utilizing the perspective of someone from the global South, K'naan is quick to question the screwface demeanour of rappers as well as the excessive boasting of the murders one commits. Instead, K'naan relays the experiences of those in the "Third World" and of war and violence. "What's Hardcore?" provides hip hop fans with another perspective from which to understand and contextualize the images of black death and violence with which they are bombarded on BET and websites like World Star Hip Hop.

K'naan finds hardcore posturing "not special," and he is disinterested in the demonstration of privilege he sees with the excessive jewellery and the expensive cars. K'naan reads the conspicuous consumptive patterns of American rappers as a sign of privilege, a reading that is often in direct contrast to many rags to riches narratives. It is the very formation and reproduction of the rags-to-riches mythology that underpins much of what constitutes popular or mainstream hip hop. Such stories are simply refractions of the "American Dream," the "pull oneself up by one's bootstraps" mentality. Therefore, when 50 Cent titles his album *Get Rich or Die Trying*, or when Jay-Z rhymes about his life in the Marcy housing projects while still ranking in the Forbes list for wealthiest rappers, we simply see a variation of the American Dream being played back in slightly altered ways. K'naan, as a refugee who fled a war-torn country, refuses to narrowly subscribe to one of the dominant narratives in American hip hop.

Instead, "What's Hardcore?" widens the frame of the discussion, allowing the very American frames – to be precise, the United States's histories of fabricating and promoting a sense of pathological blackness – to become clear.[6] The marketing of mainstream hip hop and the very overused representations of 'hood life and mass incarceration are exposed as relative and very Western in their attempts to market oppression, pathological blackness, and black death. K'naan's music and analysis help to expose "realness" in American hip hop as a subjective and geographically contingent American social construction. K'naan's critique in "What's Hardcore?" falls just short of narrowing in on the larger problem of corporate media representations of African Americans, focusing instead on the dominant trope of hardcore gangsterism in American hip hop music.

K'naan's highlighting of the lack of governmental services such as police and ambulances in Mogadishu serves to underscore the vast wealth of Western societies and the privileges, like hospitals, to which those posing as gangsters may have access. In contrasting a city like Mogadishu to any Western city, "What's Hardcore?" encourages a re-evaluation of the terms and images by which mainstream American hip hop promotes itself. Importantly, it is the production of relatively difficult living circumstances for television networks like BET that K'naan critiques, using the war-ravaged Somali as an example of how much worse life is for those of the global South.

As quoted in the opening of this chapter, the baggage K'naan claims to carry around with him, like his grandfather's poetry, is in fact a critical disposition nurtured by his outsider status. It is K'naan's willingness to combine his Somali roots and his diasporic routes into tools for comprehending the contemporary moment in North American popular music that transforms his critiques into serious charges levelled again a Western music industry. In a moment of rare cockiness, K'naan brings his diasporic sensibilities to bear on the proliferation of gangster rap. He claims, "If I rhymed about home and got descriptive I'd make 50 Cent look like Limp Bizkit." By reppin' Mogadishu, K'naan is both able to avoid reproducing the dominant tropes in American hip hop and to provide a contextual frame within which residues of national narratives embedded within the story of 50 Cent are illuminated and refuted. The idea of the violent black male, the rugged individual who can achieve the American Dream, and the gangster posturing that is so well funded by mainstream media are both called into question by K'naan's unwillingness to accept American hip hop's tropes as objective reality.

CONCLUSION

K'naan, in his music, interviews, and live appearances, is consistent in his focus on his homeland and the plight of Somalia. His at times nostalgic renditions of life "back home" clearly place him at the crossroads of roots and routes, of past and present, and between the global North and the global South. Diasporically wandering between discourses, narratives, nations, and ideological formations, K'naan disrupts some of the neat formations that align popular hip hop musics with the dominant narratives in their host countries. By deploying a politics of reppin,' K'naan finds ways to authentically share his reality, his 'hood, with the rest of the world. By capitalizing on his marketing relationship with Coca Cola, K'naan's "Wavin' Flag," revised and censored for the 2010 World Cup, provided him with a global reach to spread his message.

Prior to the success of "Wavin' Flag," K'naan regularly leveraged his interview opportunities with mainstream media to discuss the situation of warlords and gunmen in Somalia. In particular, one striking example is his willingness to utilize a Canadian Crown corporation, the Canadian Broadcasting Corporation (CBC), to discuss warring factions in Somalia rather than his latest album. Inside of the nation-state, and even directly utilizing a state apparatus like the CBC, K'naan routed his interventions into the public sphere and into the music industry through his diasporic sensibilities, yearnings, and desires for home. By reppin' Somalia on tracks like "T.I.A.," "Somalia," "Wavin' Flag," and others, K'naan maintains a relationship with one of the core features of hip hop music – honouring the networks and surroundings that contributed to their artistry.

Despite the massive success obtained via "Wavin' Flag" and his more recent censoring, K'naan allows us to see how the nation-state is intertwined with the reproduction of national narratives and dominant discourses via popular music. The outer-national reaches and connections of K'naan's music are productive in their disruption of the relationships between nation-states and its citizenry. By reppin' right, K'naan honours his past in Mogadishu and disruptively intervenes in American hip hop to challenge and present us with more expansive ways of imagining diasporic life in the global North.

NOTES

1 A version of this op-ed appears in print on 9 December 2012, on page SR7 of the New York edition with the headline: "Censoring Myself for Success."

2 Nas is one of hip hop's premier emcees. He rose to prominence in the early 1990s and released his first album, *Illmatic*, to critical acclaim in 1994. Nas has been praised for the depths and complexities of his rhymes, which focus on the inner workings of dispossessed life in the Queensbridge projects in Queens, New York. Topics on *Illmatic* range from the incarceration of his peers ("One Love"), commemorating fallen community members ("Memory Lane"), to the perils of life in New York City ("New York State of Mind").

3 "Represent" has appeared as "representin'" or "reppin'" within hip hop music. See Smif N Wesson "Tims in hoods check" or Jim Jones "Reppin' time."

4 Eshu, or Esu, is the trickster who sits at the crossroads in Yoruban-based religious worldviews such as Santeria.

5 See interview on the Daily Motion website (Daily Motion n.d.).

6 The Moynihan Report of 1965 is just one such example that builds on the negative images created by the film *Birth of a Nation* and a horrific blackface minstrelsy industry in the early decades of the 1900s.

11

“THE HIP HOP WE SEE. THE HIP HOP WE DO.”

Powerful and Fierce Women in Hip Hop in Canada

Charity Marsh

It’s not about being a woman in hip hop, it’s about, are you practising your skill? You know, did you develop your craft? And I think that if we can really encourage people to develop their craft, and their awareness, and their intelligence, that might help us to differentiate between the commercial hip hop that we see, and the real hip hop that we do. And that’s all I try to do as a woman.

Kia

BLURRED LINES: AN INTRODUCTION

During the past twenty years, as both a popular music scholar and a feminist, I have embraced the often uncomfortable task of publicly refuting overly generalized feminist and anti-feminist critiques of particular genres (pop, electronica, hip hop), women artists, and their fans. Through this work, I have problematized the frequent dismissive analyses that suggest women have sold out, are perpetuating gendered norms, are ensnared within the capitalist desiring machine, or lack any agency or critical voice. These superficial readings fail to take into account the complexities of the material world in which we live; they lack the imagination to ask tough questions about women’s subjectivity or to see how communities are always fraught with contradictions. These kinds of surface analyses do not allow for a multidimensional existence. In short, they refuse a fully developed subjecthood. Nevertheless, I am not naively suggesting that popular music should be consumed in a vacuum without a critical lens. As it has been clearly demonstrated throughout *We Still Here*, hip hop musicians, genres, and fans should not be dismissed based solely on the idea that they embrace or lack an overt feminist perspective. To engage with the nuances within an analysis of hip hop is imperative.

Similar to other popular music genres, hip hop is complex. In 2008, Tricia Rose (2008. ix) claimed: "Hip hop is not dead, but it is gravely ill. The beauty and life force of hip hop have been squeezed out, wrung nearly dry by the compounding factors of commercialism, distorted racial and sexual fantasy, oppression, and alienation." Hip hop is enacted within a patriarchal, colonial, capitalist world, which is in constant need of critique and ongoing dialogue. Indeed, as many of the previous chapters illustrate, hip hop has the ability to give voice to the disenfranchised, disrupt power relations, and cause trouble for hegemonic systems, while simultaneously existing within an industry filled with bias and ever-present sexist and heteronormative narratives. Indeed, if we are to heed Rose's comments, hip hop has fallen from grace. As Rose has so eloquently stated, this fall is due to capitalism and its fetishes and perversion of desire. But even though hip hop is "gravely ill," one could argue, the women who are the subjects of this chapter are breathing new life into the genre.

Shaped by experiential reflection and narratives of feminist activism, I turn to the stories of a multifaceted group of five women who participated in a round-table discussion at the Raincity Rap Festival in Vancouver, British Columbia, during the fall of 2013.[7] Although I draw on a specific conversation, this chapter highlights the experiences and struggles shared by many women artists living and creating hip hop in Canada. Focusing on their strategies of how to move beyond the aforementioned blatant contradictions and sexism existent within hip hop culture, it becomes apparent that JB the First Lady,[8] Kia Kadiri,[9] Kim Sato,[10] DJ She,[11] and Andrea Warner[12] gravitate towards grassroots activism as a means to challenge the unequal power relations of commercial hip hop while producing herstories that place empowered and fierce women at the forefront of local hip hop cultures. These stories provide rich narrations of hip hop, including a fuller subjecthood for women. They bring to the forefront questions of loneliness and the resourcefulness and creative strategies these women come up with to uniquely navigate the gendered politics of hip hop. Elaine Carol, creator and producer of the

Raincity Rap Festival, brought this group of women together. Initially planned as a biennial festival, Raincity Rap was a multidisciplinary conference of hip hop music, dance, art, and culture. This festival, which began in 2011 and was held one more time in 2013, was one of the significant contributions made to Vancouver's arts scene by Elaine Carol, the artistic director of MISCELLANEOUS Productions, an interdisciplinary arts organization located in Vancouver. Working collaboratively with community-engaged professional artists and socially and culturally diverse groups of youth, MISCELLANEOUS Productions creates hip hop-oriented performances in music theatre as well as various arts events. Coming from a community arts-based perspective, this festival challenges conventional ideas about hip hop arts projects and attempts to cultivate important dialogues about hip hop cultures, her/histories, politics, performances, business models, mediations, and issues of identity and representation.

The inaugural festival focused on the history of hip hop culture in Vancouver and included panels on the business of hip hop and the music industry in Canada, along with a panel dedicated to the history of hip hop in Vancouver.[13] A number of important figures in Canadian hip hop culture took part in the discussions, including Sol Guy, Ndidi Cascade, DJ Flipout, Chin Injeti, Red1, Emotionz, and JB the First Lady. The theme of the 2013 Raincity Rap Festival and Conference shifted to "the art of Canadian hip hop" and its distinct place in urban music and culture in Vancouver and across the country. There was also a change in format for the second festival, including the introduction of one-on-one in-depth public interviews with hip hop artists Maestro Fresh Wes, Kinnie Starr, and Chin Injeti, along with a panel focused on the music industry and a roundtable discussion entitled, "Clear Lines: Powerful and Fierce Women in Hip Hop."

Even though a number of years have passed since the last festival in 2013, the stories told by the participants continue to be relevant to understanding what it means to be a woman participating in hip hop culture in Canada today. Their stories connect with the current #MeToo campaign and provide further understanding to the ubiquity of gender inequality and sexual harassment in the music industry, and, more specifically, within the realm of hip hop in local scenes as well as on national and international stages. The themes of this conversation focus on shared experiences as well as multi-pronged strategies for working within (and against) a music culture that still clings to hegemonic norms bound up within a discourse of patriarchy. Through an articulation of the differences between the "commercial hip hop [they] see and the real hip hop [they] do," these fierce women focus on the impact of role models and mentors; networking opportunities; access to gear, technologies, and knowledge; as well as figuring out how to navigate systemic harassment by people within the industry, audience members, and the hyper-masculinized lens through which hip hop is represented in the media.[14]

EXPOSING TRUTHS

> Twenty-thirteen has not been a terribly kind year for women in music, or for how women have been portrayed … It seems like we should be past the conversation about degrading women, musically and in music.
>
> Andrea Warner

Naming the roundtable "Clear Lines: Powerful and Fierce Women in Hip Hop" provides a feminist context and a particular lens for the discussion. Following an introductory statement on hip hop and feminism, each participant was asked to describe some details and/or experiences explaining what it was like to participate within the culture of hip hop. Their stories are compelling and provide narratives of frustration, indignation, heartbreak, and celebration. Kim, Kia, and Tara spoke about their hip hop origins, reflecting on the lack of hip hop within their local environments and the complexities of relating to a particular hip hop vernacular, style, or discipline (i.e., Dancing, Rapping, DJing). For Kia, hip hop was foreign to her, looking and sounding nothing like her life. She explains:

> I hated hip hop when I was fifteen and sixteen, I absolutely hated it. I thought it made no sense; I didn't understand it at all. I didn't understand why people were talking to me like "Hey! Yo! What's up!" My little brother was trying to get me to listen to Public Enemy and it was the big, you know, black man, black woman, black baby! Well, we grew up in Victoria, and I was one out of fifteen hundred students, and I was the only black person in my whole school. So, I didn't really have a connection to being black, or black culture or black music, any of that. I was a figure skater listening to classical music while my brother was trying to get me to listen to rap. And it wasn't until I was nineteen that I

11.1 Round-table participants. Photo courtesy Miscellaneous Productions/ Chris Randle.

> met my first black friends in Victoria, and they basically explained to me what it was like to grow up in Oakland and to really experience racism. Racism to me in Victoria was, it never really came across, because there is not enough black people to get upset about it, you know. There's a lot more racism against Asian cultures and against First Nations people than there is really against black people. So, I didn't really have a connection to it. I didn't understand it.

Her experience of racism was hidden in the lack of diversity among people living in Victoria. Kia's introduction to hip hop culture was set against her own experience of blackness in a location of whiteness. Thus, it was initially challenging for Kia to identify with a culture born out of the social conditions of an American urban black experience. This lack of connection was shared by Tara, whose identity also played a role in how she engaged with hip hop and the music industry early on:

> I'm queer. I'm a female, and I'm a person of colour. So right there that's three checks on the minority card. And I really relate to what Kia said because I grew up in Prince Edward Island and I was the only person of colour in my province for eighteen years. So I mean, I've really had to learn some ninja skills throughout my life to be able to manoeuvre through many spaces and I've somehow managed to wind up in the music industry in Vancouver, and it's been a really interesting experience.

The necessity for Tara to learn "ninja skills" to navigate hegemonic norms associated with sexuality, gender, and race is telling. As Kia describes above, hip hop is a culture bound up in authenticity, which is enacted through race and gender, and particular codes of conduct. Kia is both critical of and drawn in by these kinds of gestures:

> But my friend, who actually ended up teaching me how to rap, got out of the struggle and the streets and the gangs in Oakland by becoming a graffiti artist and then getting his art degree. And, he really explained to me the appreciation of the culture. And, I developed a respect for it because I was like, people are just speaking their voice, and you have no right to tell somebody that they can't tell their story. And if their story involves violence and guns and women being portrayed in a certain way, then that's their story and they have the right to voice that! It's how we internalize it [that matters]. But it really created this division from myself ... I absolutely refuse to listen to [commercial hip hop], it sickens me when I hear it ... I don't care if the beats are good. I don't care if people are just saying bullshit. I don't want to listen to it and I don't. But, it really creates this divide because I was raised as a strong woman, because I wanted to develop my craft and when I did get into rap, I just loved it. I thought it was fun, it was great! And so I would go to shows, but people still looked at me for the first however many years of my career, and they're like, "Yo! Yo! Kia! Yeah! What's Up!" and I'm like, "Why are you talking to me like that?" I don't use "yo" in everyday language, and I don't get all like, "Yeah, alright homies." And I really didn't connect to hip hop culture. I just liked to rap, and I like poetry, and I really just developed that. (Kia)

How one reads and identifies with hip hop (or, for Kia, rap) highlights the ongoing tension between the perception of what is "real" and "authentic" as opposed to "commercial" or "apolitical." Understanding hip hop through this sort of false binary is concerning. Critical, thoughtful, and highly political content has certainly been part of commercial rap in some instances, just as some of the most misogynist, homophobic content can be found in the underground or non-commercial hip hop. And yet, for this group, the differences between commercial and more authentic sounding or "conscious" hip hop plays heavily into the question of gender and sexism in hip hop.

For Andrea, a journalist who spends a lot of time thinking and writing about popular music, many people in the music industry are still getting away with too much, especially in commercial hip hop. She explains:

> It really strikes me that in the same year that gave us Angel Haze, who I just think is remarkably cool, we also have Rick Ross rapping a line about raping women and being pleased with himself. We have "Blurred Lines," which, I know that not everyone agrees, but I think is one of the worst atrocities, particularly its music video. And then you couple that with Kanye who, in almost every single music review that I read of the album,[15] praised its daringness, its willingness to look at racism, its sonic challenges. I think that the album does all of those things, but it's also, perhaps one of the most sexist albums he's ever put out in his career. And these are all men who are around my age, thirty-four or so, who have been raised within a sort of "post-feminist" world – who typically have been raised in feminist households by single mothers. And I feel that this is a wilful degradation of women. This is knowing that it's wrong and deciding to make horrific statements about women's worth, body parts, physical violence or the hint of physical violence. These are things that I don't understand why there is a place for them currently.

Unpacking this "wilful degradation of women" and the space it is given within hip hop is at the heart of this conversation. Although this is not unique to hip hop, there is something quite troubling within the history and ongoing discourse surrounding hip hop and its explicit lyrics, its heteronormative hyper-masculinity, and its continual subjugation of women, that demonstrates a need for serious disruption. How does one reconcile the significance of a feminist upbringing and enacting a "wilful degradation of women"? Andrea goes on to suggest, "[we need to realize] that you can enjoy music, you can even enjoy the beat of a song, but I think we need to have conversations about lyrical content. I think we need to challenge these notions of people saying again and again and again that women don't count as much as men; women don't have the same value as men."

Similar to Kia, and to some extent Andrea, Tara attempts to limit the amount of media and commercial hip hop she takes, stating: "I feel I have to filter what I ingest from the media because it's just absolutely overwhelming and, to a point, disgusting … I work in a nightclub, I see enough sexual exploitation of women in my job. I don't need to ingest that in my recreational time." For Tara, combatting sexism in the music industry needs to be a collaborative approach where everyone steps up. "It's a fiery topic for me. I think it's an important topic to consider and come to some type of solution as to how we, as all people in the Industry, take a stance and share that with our peers, with the people that we teach. And, to just open the dialogue and say, 'this is not OK.'" Calling into question the pervasiveness of sexism and misogyny within hip hop, working collaboratively with peers to critique and offer alternative narratives, is one way forward. Moreover, the value of encouraging women to be at the forefront of navigating sexuality in a way that respects consent, desire, and autonomy is critical.

CREATING AND SUSTAINING FEMINIST SPACES

> Hip hop has been a place of belonging. Hip hop has been a place of giving power to my voice. Hip hop has created spaces I've never imagined; hip hop has created a sisterhood that I dreamed of and became reality, manifested.
>
> JB

Prior to the event I asked the panelists to consider how, from a global hip hop perspective, hip hop continues to be drawn on as a strategy for resistance and understood within a politics of empowerment. Hip hop and its arts practices have the potential to give voice to young people around the world, but the question remains: How can we speak about hip hop as a culture of empowerment while so many women continue to be excluded, marginalized, objectified, and vilified by its participants, whether they are producers, managers, club owners, musicians, or audience members, within hip hop culture itself? How do we come to terms with and move beyond such blatant contradictions bound up within contemporary hip hop culture? Historically, hip hop was about reclaiming public space and that public space excluded women and girls. With this context of hip hop in mind, I asked the participants what kind of strategies they have adopted, created, and discovered, whether that is an avoidance of particular aspects of the culture, filtering, dialoguing, and seeking mentorship, or taking on the role of mentors, which is valuable and important.[16]

When discussing strategies for empowerment and full participation within hip hop, many of the panelists spoke to the need for knowledgeable role models. For Kim, the dancer of the group, hip hop dance (including break, locking, etc.) classes or teachers were not easy to come by in her childhood and early teen years. For her, it was initially a purely DIY venture, where she practised and performed at parties. Kim relays her excitement regarding the first time she was introduced to hip hop as a possible practice in her ballet school:

> Finally, a teacher came to my ballet school and she was a hip hop teacher ... And she basically had us do a hip hop class but I was in my ballet clothes doing hip hop. So, I had my pink tights on and I put on biker shorts because that was cool at the time so really not cool at all, but I still had my pink ballet shoes on and she was just looking at us going, "Does anybody have running shoes here?" And for some reason nobody else did but me. ... But once I got the taste of learning it from somebody else I was like, "Ah, I have to be in her class every week." So I sought her out. I went and got a T-shirt and made my mom buy me some sweatpants, and I came to her class and said, "Hey! Do you remember me? I was that girl in the ballet class," and I was like, "In my running shoes? And I loved your class." [From then on] I was in her class every week, and I just fell in love with it. I loved the movement, but it was the commercial side of [hip hop dance]. And what I was doing, what I grew up with was, you know, the real stuff, like the nitty-gritty, like the partying, the community. But I got really into the commercial side of hip hop and I started studying that for years and years and years and I was heading down to L.A. and wanted to be a backup dancer for Janet Jackson, and I thought, "This is the coolest!" And I'm like, "Yeah! Awesome! I'm gonna become this amazing professional dancer!"

Having a role model who was a knowledgeable teacher in one form of hip hop dance changed the path for Kim. She was introduced to a more "commercial" form of dance, and, thus, her goals shifted, along with her repertoire of dance movements and expectations for a future in dance.

The power of seeing oneself as an artist, or being able to identify with someone who is a rapper, a DJ, a B-girl, a graff writer, cannot be underestimated. As was evident from JB's story, the impact of coming across other Indigenous hip hop artists empowered her in a profound way:

> My mom did her amazing best. And ... she'd always say, "Go to the Friendship Centre, where the Native people are and they'll have resources and they'll help you out no matter what." And at that time I walked into the space and I saw Kinnie Starr, Ostwelve, Manik 1derful, and Skeena Reece ... When I saw these performers talk about Native pride and being proud of where they came from, talk about colonization, decolonization, I said, "You know what, one day I wanna do that! I want to inspire someone to be proud of who they are!" And that's what I did.

JB identified with these artists and, moreover, began to cultivate her practice within a supportive environment. For her, many of these artists became both mentors and role models. She explains:

> I became engaged and there was a place called Knowledgeable Aboriginal Youth Association, and they had a recording studio for Aboriginal youth. And one of the youth workers was like, "You got rhymes!" and I'm like "Peshh, no! For real?" and he's like, "Yeah, you got rhymes," and I was like "OK!" ... I'm a very passionate speaker, and have lots to say, and he said, "Put it into hip hop!" That was Curtis Clear Sky and he [participated in the UN Messengers of Truth programming]. He really helped me find that within myself ... So I'd always volunteer and help out, and then I got mentored into working for a non-profit all the way up to executive director for Knowledgeable Aboriginal Youth Association. And to see that movement through hip hop and to see these voices where we said the mandate of our organization was to empower youth and give youth a voice, representation, participation. We did that through hip hop; we did that through music, and we had a recording studio.

Giving back to the community is something that all of these women share. In spite of their circumstances or experiences of sexism, these women feel strongly about the need to be empowering role models and to provide alternatives to what is offered up in mainstream hip hop culture. After Kim's experience of gender discrimination and gendered violence within the industry during her time in Japan, she returned to Canada to recover and establish a more productive environment within which to create and mentor. She explains:

> It was a horrible thing, and I had to process what happened to me in that moment, and it was a really big lesson of where the industry can be very malicious and manipulative. And when I came home to Canada I decided that I wanted to start helping other people through this, through my story, and I basically started building myself back up as a woman in hip hop dance and break-dancing. I discovered and re-fell in love with hip hop culture. I realized what I loved about dance was the community, the people, the friendships, the stories, everything that I'm sharing with everybody, and the culture of it. And I went back into break dancing, found myself, back to being a beginner, taking baby steps all the way through. Breaking is hard! So, I went through that whole process of rebuilding myself with people from my community. In the industry, people were curious about what I was doing so they were really following me to break dancing practice. All these girls, but they didn't know that I actually, I was so passionate about this, I honestly loved this stuff and it gave me power. It helped build me back up. I found who I was; I identified myself through being a B-girl, and then I found the other styles. I started popping. I started locking, and now I'm not breaking as much because I'm getting older and it hurts my body. But I've fallen in love with locking, and that is the first street style before breaking came along. Started in the West Coast and started studying this, I seek out my forefathers, and I'm so lucky that they are still around and I can call up the people that created all these party dances or created locking, and I still have a really good connection with that. But on the other side, with the whole taking care of the community, everybody now in this community calls me "Mama Kim" because I'm a nurturer and I love to nurture people.

This push into a role of nurturance is also highly gendered and fraught with complications, and yet, it is a role that many women find themselves in or take on as a way to give back or make change within a culture that they love and want to make better.

During our conversation, the participants offered up a variety of other strategies used to confront sexism within the industry. From her position as journalist, Andrea offered up a particularly profound example, one that leads us back to how one reconciles one's own sexist attitudes, performances, and presentation within hip hop culture with the rest of one's life, which includes families, culture, and upbringing:

> I was asked to do an electronic piece on a dude that was coming through town [who has] horrific content in his music. Like, the videos, everything, like everything about it is really, cartoonishly oppressive. And so, I decided that if I was going to do this piece I was going to ask him about women, and I wanted to know, "Who are the women he respects? What did your mom ever do for you?" I asked him exclusively about women. … "Which women do you like in music? What do women mean to you?" And this was the entire interview and he was very confused at the end of it. I didn't feel personally the need to confront him and say, "OK, I think your music is mostly quite disgusting." I just thought, let's only talk about women, and he was so thoughtful about women. He loves, allegedly, women. His mom took him to music school, he did all these things, he listens to all of these different women. It was completely contradictory to the music he makes and I personally wanted to showcase that contradiction. So, this has been my strategy now, if I come up against someone whose musical content I find deplorable, I specifically ask them only about women throughout the whole interview.

This strategy is one way to jolt someone out of the comfort of presenting a typical hip hop story. As a tactic, it makes things unpredictable and asks for something more, challenging an artist to connect one's celebrity persona with a more personal narrative, and perhaps even calling up a sense of responsibility for one's actions.

Tara's tactic is to enact confidence and stand your ground:

> It's kind of like. "OK, so I want this gig, what do I need to do, ABC, to get it?" And I generally know I'm gonna come up across some

> kind of bullshit along the lines of dealing with men in the industry. And, whether it's the simplest thing of somebody's management, promoters, sound tech, what have you, I think it's just been a matter of being confident and putting your foot down and being like, "No, I'm sorry but this doesn't work for me," and having an intellectual adult conversation and saying, you know, as an artist this is what I'm here to do, could you please also do your job, and we can move this along quickly?

These kinds of sexist attitudes are not only found within hip hop, and yet there is still a need for knowledge sharing and strategizing in order to address and begin to dismantle them. One way to challenge this kind of sexism is through information gathering. For example, Kia discusses the importance of being educated and knowing your rights:

> And there was a cool article about how there are the big electronic DJs that tour all around and make so much money on each gig. You know, like thousands of dollars, and they're going around, and 90 percent of the music that they play has women singing the hooks in their songs. And they make a lot of money off these songs and most of the women that are in that position are getting paid a couple hundred dollars to go in the studio and sing and they kill it. So, it's about educating women as well. It's like, "Hey, you know what, you have to know your rights too." You go into that session, and you ask what you are paid, and you get paid what you're worth. Don't just sign away and say, "Oh, sure, yeah I'll do it because you're my friend." Well then, you're not being smart, that's not good business, right? But there's also still this mountain, and it's not just women in music, it's women in many powerful positions. It's women in business, it's women in banks, how many people sitting in that top 1 percent are women? It's not a lot, it's still a large battle that we're waging against men. Not that it's a fight, "I want to have that power," but just an awareness that we're still not on the same level, and I think that carries across whatever art form we are doing, whatever we are talking about. It's something that needs to be taught to the women but also taught to the men too. It's just like, you can't just put us in these positions of sexualized roles and take the good out of it, right? And make all the money yourself. I don't know, it's a strange dynamic that I think we've created for ourselves, but again, I think it all comes

> back to letting your skills speak for what you do, and that will come through, at least it has in my experience.

RESPONSIBILITY, RESISTANCE, RECLAMATION ... NOURISHING THE ROOTS

> Hip hop has been a place where I could express my cultural views but in an urban setting. Looking at hip hop and seeing all of the different elements from dancing to arts to DJing to storytelling, has been a direct parallel to my Indigenous cultural ways and elements that I'm supposed to engage with as each and every one of us has a gift. And for me, my gift was storytelling and bringing that power to my voice through hip hop and spoken word.
>
> JB

Mainstream, commercial hip hop is often slick and seductive. And yet so many representations that are so prevalent in commercial hip hop play into stereotypes and normative codes of gender, race, and sex. In spite of this, hip hop as a politics has been taken up by many disparate groups of youth worldwide as a critical strategy of resistance.[17] As has been discussed in a number of the previous chapters,[18] hip hop is a cultural form through which many Indigenous youth are articulating contemporary lived experience and making sense of current colonial-settler relations that exist within Canada.[19] Certainly, JB tells an incredible story of empowerment and strategy. Hers is a story that demonstrates the amazing capacity of hip hop to allow for the incorporation of both local and cultural politics. And yet, there is this ongoing blatant contradiction of oppression and empowerment within hip hop, and, rather than pretend it does not exist, this contradiction is something we have to acknowledge and theorize. Hip hop can be both a productive and a disruptive space, as is evident in Kia's story:

> Over the years, as an artist, I found that I didn't really like the direction of the music industry, and I didn't want to be involved with it. It was very manipulative, it was very abusive, it really tore me apart. After I finished my first record, it was almost to the point that I didn't want to listen to it anymore because of all the negative things that came from that experience. People wanting to just use you as a catalyst to get their message out. And I see that in

> the same commercialization of hip hop music and culture, and it saddens me.

As a way to resist this kind of "commercialization," Kia changed directions and began to focus on working with youth:

> And so I really went the route of working with kids, because it's OK, if you start with them young and you just teach them about the real roots of hip hop and the real roots of expression and creativity and give them that power, and that tool. Then that's going to be something that's more fulfilling for me. So now I like to work with youth, and I like to share that experience with people. And I don't even touch on the other aspects of it, the commercialized hip hop. I don't go to the clubs, I don't, and it makes me sad when I see kids dancing like, we were talking about this backstage, in a sexual manner, and they have no idea what they are doing, they're just mimicking. And so it's like, well, that's pretty sad that they can't mimic those nineties dancers that were all about dancing and fun or [when I see people] putting dances together, and it really brings it back to that community level, that gives me a bit of hope that hip hop can be, can rise above the contradictions that we are seeing in the industry.

The complexities of women's participation in the music industries and what it takes to gain status were also discussed as some of these very contradictions. As she describes in the quotation I used to begin this chapter, Kia believes in focusing on the development of one's craft first. She offers:

> You know, there are a lot of women that strive to be stars. And they want to be seen and they want to be heard, but they do it in these ways that go against really the empowering part of being a woman, which is just to get your expression out and your voice, not necessarily do it with your body, you know? And I think a lot of the men in the industry look down on some of the other women because they're not excelling at the skill. It's not about being a woman in hip hop, it's about are you practising your skill ... And that's all I try to do as a woman ... And I think we really have to look at the whole picture of being a musician as not just being good at your craft. It's the balance that we create in our

> lives, right? So you have to be good at music, you have to be good at business, you have to be professional, you have to show up on time, you gotta know your equipment, you gotta build and be a real person.

The multifaceted aspects of paying attention to balancing responsibilities and to the social codes of being a professional musician or artist within the culture were also emphasized by the other participants. It is this kind of ethical engagement and musical citizenship that is also pitted against the process of commercialization. Tara adds:

> As for hip hop right now, I kind of dipped out of being interested in hip hop I'd say in like 2002, because I really feel, I'd say like '99 moving forward is when consumerism started to kick in, and commercialization of hip hop was really starting to become prominent. I relate to Kim, coming up in the nineties and everything was about good vibes and parties and like "this is our culture and our music," and, at a certain point, I really feel like somebody in an office, sitting at a desk on a phone said, "OK, this is going to make us a lot of money! This is how we exploit this, and flip it and make a profit from it," you know? And, here we are, these kids coming up in the nineties thinking, "This is us, this is our culture, this belongs to us." So, I maybe even unconsciously kind of dipped out of hip hop because I just wasn't able to relate to girls in heels and booty shorts pushing up on the man and in the back of the video. I'm like, "No, I want to be the centre stage." For the boys, "cool if you want to be in my music video, that's OK," but like no, I won't be second to centre, this is my show.

For Tara, there is an immediate sense of place-making and indignation around the gendering of roles that contributes to Othering women and removing them from a central role as creator, producer, and artist. The push towards women only engaging in supportive and highly sexualized performance deters Tara from an entire genre. This also speaks to the impact of role modelling and the power of being able to identify with those on stage discussed earlier in the chapter. Tara continues:

> I didn't really relate to the sexualization of hip hop and I mean, I did look up to Lauryn Hill, Missy Elliot, Foxy Brown, Lil' Kim, and I really do respect Foxy Brown and Lil' Kim as lyricists, but could you just put some clothes on when you do that. I feel like if that's what we're feeding to the younger generation, like look where we are now with music, like do these girls even know where twerking came from? Do you know about Miami Booty Bass? In 1992? It really hurts my head to see where things are at with music right now. And I do feel like it's our job, as women who have worked very hard to get where we are, to kind of break down those ideas of what hip hop is, or should be, or what it takes to be a dancer, or what it takes to be an MC, or even a writer. Because I feel like we're just fed so much media, and we don't really know how to kind of grasp reality with all the commercial bullshit that we're being fed. I think that kind of holds true to females not being able to garner that confidence, and "this is what you have to do, this is how you dress, this is how you have to look, and this is how you dance," and it is hypersexual.

This hypersexualization of women, although controversial even within feminist discourse, provides a particular kind of "looked-at-ness" that draws us back to Laura Mulvey's (1975) work, "Visual Pleasure and Narrative Cinema," in which she theorizes power through looking, and being looked at, within a media frame. From Kim's perspective as a dancer there is a lack of young women participating in forms of more "athletic" styles of dance that are still dominated by men. Similar to the gendering of genres, technologies, and industry roles, for example, women continue to be socialized towards particular forms and styles of dance. Kim makes the argument, "what I see going on in the schools and in the studios are females not confident in what they're doing, and I look into the class, and I'm like, 'Ooh Pussycat Dolls class, what's that one about?' and I'm like, 'Not for me! I'm going to be in my locking class over here.'" There is a disconnect for Kim as she tries to make sense of "what it means to be a strong female through movement and still being sexy but doing a craft." Moreover, she tries to find a way to mentor other girls/women "to figure that out for themselves so they don't have to just do something that they don't feel. I feel like I want to help people find their root to what they need to do to feel empowered."

JB's perspective and evolution within the hip hop industry does not fall outside of such trappings:

> There were times where I was just like, "I'm just a girl, like I'm a chubby Indian girl, no one wants to hear me." And it was my friend, he's from The Main Offenders, Cole B, Cole Brownstone, he's like, "You know what JB, you have a strong voice, people wanna hear your voice." … Then he's like, "Actually, look at this music video," and it was Shad K, Shad KeepShining, and I was like, "Wohoo! This is blowing my mind, he's a Vancouver artist and he's a Toronto artist and he has a whole song about women." He's like, "We're only getting half of the story, we need more women in rap so that they they can do that," and I was like, "OK, I'm ready to go here!" And it pushed my whole entire album … And it was all these men that came around me and encouraged me and said "We need your voice."

This desire to include JB's voice is not only linked to adding more members. JB views her role as providing an important contribution to conversations on colonization and decolonization, on what meaningful practices of reconciliation could look/sound like, and to voice the concerns of Indigenous women:

> So I look at our times, in the sense of the times that we live in and the times I live in as an Indigenous person from Canada, where I'm decolonizing and unlearning colonization and assimilation tactics. I understand that these assimilation tactics against our people, they're only gonna let those messages through that are gonna keep the people down. So, I flipped that and said, "I'm gonna be a person that pushes through all of that assimilation and flip it." So, my hip hop, my stories, they need to be heard, and I'm really excited that hip hop has really given me a space, because looking at First Nations women in Canada, a lot of the statistics are the negative statistics. And for me to be a representation of women and bring voice to First Nations women is so powerful and empowering because our voices are still being taken away through murder, through poverty, through addictions, … and [we need to be] breaking through residential school [legacies] and overcoming genocide. Hip hop has made me, has brought out that part of my voice – to overcome those things and to bring awareness.

Within the roundtable discussion, it was important for the participants and myself to avoid falling into the easy trap that gender discrimination and sexism are issues of "men against women" rather than presenting them as part of a more complex system. For the roundtable participants, there was an emphasis on being able to voice women's experiences within male-dominated fields, cultures, and practices. Moreover, all of the artists sought to challenge these hegemonic norms while holding both themselves and men acting within and supporting the culture accountable for the ways in which they participate and engage. Kia continues:

> Over the years I found that people would ask me, "Well, what's it like being a women in hip hop?" and I'm like, "Well, I don't know, I just do hip hop." And I developed the respect of the men in the community so I wasn't ever separated as a man or a woman. You just have the respect of the guys because you are good at what you do. And then I really realized, "OK, hang on a second, there are not a lot of women that are in this position of power, where we can see something, but we are also respected by people because we do it well." And, so, I realized that's something important to share.

The realization that it is important to continually be sharing and promoting something alternative is key for Tara as well: "At the same time, here we are – we are a panel of very strong women, we're dressed appropriately, no one is twerking and … we could twerk it out if you want to, but at the same time, we will continue to work in our fields, and we do what we do well." Tara continues to speak of what she feels is her and others' responsibilities to future generations of hip hop women: "I don't think that giving in to the industry is the way to go. I think it's our job to really vocalize that to the younger generation, our peers, or even peers in the industry."

CONCLUSION

> And I think most of us want to represent the world of the conscious community, empowering hip hop that gives people something other than television, and money, and image, and all the other things that go along with the sexualization of women in hip hop.
>
> Kia

In the first Raincity Rap Festival, the focus was on histories, and on thinking, writing, understanding, and knowing hip hop histories. And one of the things that I spoke about during my presentation at that first festival was the intersections of histories. Within a broader hip hop context, certain narratives, certain perspectives, are told repeatedly. Many of the people who are actually on the ground and doing grassroots organizing – the kinds of labour that we hear about in panels such as the one that is the subject of this chapter – are often excluded from those histories. To engage in open dialogue about lived experience and the many layers of these women's hip hop lives furthers knowledge about the impact of marginalized voices within a complex culture and its practices. With this chapter, and indeed this entire collection on hip hop in Canada, we strive to add to a reimagining of hip hop. Talking about the layers found in these women's hip hop lives enriches the picture of what hip hop is in Canada. Bringing us back full circle to Rose, if hip hop is indeed sick, I want to suggest that these women's stories are part of the antidote.

In sharing their experiences, these women ensured that a number of significant and common issues were exposed. However, within this discussion and their lives, they offer creative strategies that enable them to continue to move forward and to produce critically engaged work. Seeking out knowledgeable role models, as well as supportive peers, opened up various paths within hip hop for these women. In return, they have become the role models, sharing their knowledge with others and mentoring, often through youth-based programs. They assist communities with ongoing concerns about program sustainability, knowledge sharing, and collaboration. Participating in events like Raincity Rap encourages networking opportunities, ongoing forms of community building, and the fostering of ethical friendships based on shared experiences of oppression, celebration, and support. Indeed, an exciting by-product of this panel discussion was the networking that happened between the women before, during, and after the roundtable discussion. Events like these make room for women to voice their experiences publicly, and they allow for an engagement with thought-provoking, difficult questions – questions that will, I hope, connect to the activist in all of us so that we can better inform the work and arts practices we love. From this conversation we also derive a commitment to an integrated feminist and decolonizing hip hop framework.

These women are strong mentors in their communities; the narratives and stories they shared demonstrate their thoughtful and complex navigations of hip hop culture. But these stories do not come ready made: they require authorship and an ability to give meaning to events, thoughts, and feelings. Within the context of this roundtable discussion, these women have contributed to, and illuminated, the multifaceted, ever so complicated world of hip hop. The stories these women share demonstrate that there needs to be room for contradiction and, more important, that hip hop holds possibilities for women.

NOTES

I would like to acknowledge the creative energies of Elaine Carol, artistic director of Miscellaneous Productions and the creator of Rain City Rap, for the opportunities to participate in the festival. The research for the writing of this chapter was generously supported by the Social Sciences and Humanities Research Council as well as the Canada Council for the Arts.

1 The bios for these five participants have changed since the roundtable in 2013, and the most updated bios are presented here to acknowledge the evolution of the artists and what they have accomplished since then.

2 See JB the First Lady (n.d.).

3 "Kia Kadiri is one of Vancouver's most respected female vocalists in the Western Canadian hip hop community for almost 20 years! Her energetic performances and unique style, keep her in demand with the best musicians in Vancouver, and in festivals across British Columbia. Kia's passion for music, rap and poetry makes her extremely productive as a workshop leader. She works for a variety of non-profit organizations as an instructor and facilitator, working with and mentoring at risk youth. Her debut record "Feel This" received acclaim across the country for thought-provoking lyrics, excellent production, and blend of genres. From hip hop to soul, jazz to drum and bass, Kia's lightning speed raps, and articulate delivery when improvising lyrics, leave her in a class of her own!" (Streetrich Society n.d.).

4 See CoreDance (n.d.).

5 See Jane Blaze (2019).

6 See Warner (n.d.).

7 The panel participants for the 2011 inaugural event included: DJ Flipout, Rob the Viking, Moka Only, Red1, Ndidi Cascade, Jeet K, Sol Guy, Jonathan Simkin, Mill Miller, Martha Rans, Glen Lougheed, Ari Wise, Sarah Webster,

Chin Injeti, Discreet Da Chosen 1, JB the First Lady, and Emotionz (Eventbrite 2011).

8 In 1999, I wrote an entry on Club DJs for the *Encyclopedia of Women and Music in America since 1900* (Marsh 2002). The themes/issues that were addressed during Raincity Rap all these years later bore considerable resemblance to the three major issues I described for women Club DJs then: accessibility, promotion, and professional connections within the community.

9 *Yeezus* (2013).

10 Following this roundtable, I conducted public interviews with both Kinnie Starr and Chin Injeti. During these interviews I also asked this question of them, particularly trying to work through the issue that such questions are often asked of women but not of men. I think we need to be asking these questions more and more, to the people who are participating and are generally holding those powerful positions.

11 For example, see the 2008 documentary *Slingshot Hip Hop*, directed by Jackie Reem Salloum.

12 See Marsh (chapter 3), Przybylski (chapter 4), and Robinson (chapter 9) in this collection.

13 For more specific examples, see Marsh (2012a, 2012b, 2011, and 2009).

References

DISCOGRAPHY

50 Cent. 2003. Get Rich or Die Tryin.' Shady Records, Aftermath, Interscope.

A Tribe Called Red. 2016. We Are the Halluci Nation. Radicalized Records.

Alaclair Ensemble. 2013. Les maigres blancs d'Amérique du Noir. AMR.

Alaiz Crew. Participants in the Piu Piu movement.

DJ Atrak. 1997. DMC World Championship winner.

The Attitude Crew. Early Toronto hip hop group consisting of True Daley, Neesha Nee, Es-Gee, Kay Gee, and Royal T.

Azim. "Reason Why." Participant in Winnipeg Child project.

Baby Blue. Early Montreal female hip hop pioneer.

Justin Bieber. 2015. Believe. Island, RBMG, Schoolboy.

– 2012. Purpose. Def Jam, RBMG, Schoolboy.

Marie Belleau. 2014. Inuit folk singer appears on Samian. "Plan Nord." Enfant de la terre. 7eCiel.

Blondie B. Regarded as Montreal's first female emcee.

Boi-1da. 2016. Production credits include Rihanna ft. Drake. "Work." Anti. Westbury Road, Roc Nation.

Jully Black. 2005. This Is Me. Universal Music Canada.

Black-I. 2000. "Where I'm From." Real Recordings.

Black Union ft. Maestro. 2008. "Africville." Hate Crimes.

Brail Optiks. 2008. Member of Black Union, known for "Africville." Hate Crimes.

Buck 65. 2003. Talkin' Honky Blues. WEA.

Ndidi Cascade. 2003. "Jah Soulja." Front & Center Vol. 1. Tha Chamber Entertainment.

Care Crew. Early Halifax hip hop group.
Chin Injeti. 2009. Production credits include Drake's "Fear." So Far Gone. Young Money, Cash Money, Universal Motown.
Christie Charles. BC Indigenous hip hop artist involved with Beat Nation.
Classified. 2005. "Maritimes." Boy-Cott-In The-Industry. Halflife.
Cool G. Early Halifax hip hop artist.
DJ Cree Asian. Edmonton DJ and winner of 2011 Red Bull Thre3Style competition.
True Daley, *Masters at Work* radio show. 90.3FM CKUT Montreal Community Radio.
Dead Indians. Prominent Winnipeg hip hop group.
Devon. Early Toronto emcee.
D.L. Incognito. 2008. A Captured Moment in Time. URBNET Records.
DJ Dopey. 2003. World DMC champion.
Down By Law. 1988. "Let Me Get Funky."
Drake. 2011. Take Care. Young Money, Cash Money, Republic.
– 2016. Views. Young Money, Cash Money, Republic.
Dream Warriors. 1991. And Now the Legacy Begins. 4th and B'way, Island Recordings, Polygram,
Eekwol. 2004. "Apprento." Apprentice to the Mystery. Mils Productions.
El Cotola. Participant in the Piu Piu movement.
Emotionz. 2015. Psychedelic Boombox. Independent.
Eternia. 2005. It's Called Life. URBNET Records.
The Finesse Ladies. Early Halifax hip hop group.
Nelly Furtado. 2000. Whoa, Nelly! Dreamworks.
– 2006. Loose, Mosley Music Group, Interscope Records.
Ghetto Child. 2004. Fax of Life.
Grandmaster Flash and the Furious Five. 1982. The Message. Sugar Hill Records.
Haltown Projex. 1992–98. Pheelings. HMV.
Christos Hatzis. Canadian composer and winner of multiple Juno awards.
Angel Haze. 2013. Dirty Gold. Republic Recordings, Island Records.
High Klassified. 2011. "Snap." Brassures du Terroir. ABMTL.
Hip Club Groove. 1994. Trailer Park Hip Hop. Murderecords.
Illaztic. "What Does It Mean..." Participant in Winnipeg Child program.
Jam. Participant in the Piu Piu movement.
James Brown. 1969. "Black and Proud." Say It Loud I'm Black and I'm Proud. King Records.
Jazz Cartier. 2016. Hotel Paranoia. Independent.
JB and the Cosmic Crew. Early Halifax hip hop group.

JB the First Lady. 2014. Indigenous Girl Lifestyle. Independent. (See also: Jerilynn Webster.)
– 2017. Meant to Be. Independent.
– 2018. Righteous Empowered Daughter. Independent.
Jorun Bombay. 2005. Jorun's Way. Dead Beads.
K4CE. Early Toronto hip hop pioneer, credited as being the first to nickname Toronto the T-Dot.
K6A. 2014. KOSSÉÇA. Basslac Musique.
Kia Kadiri. 2004. Feel This. MMG/Maximum Music.
Kardinal Offishall. 2008. Not 4 Sale. KonLive, Geffen Records.
Kaytranada. 2016. 99.9%. XL Recordings.
KenLo. 2007. Noir. Independent.
Kid Kudi. 2009. "Day 'N Night." Man on the Moon: The End of the Day. Universal Records.
K'naan. 2005. "Soobax." The Dusty Foot Philosopher. Interdependent Media.
– 2009a. "Dayless Nights."
– 2009b. "Wavin' Flag." Troubadour. A & M, Octone.
Krayzee. Winnipeg Child rapper.
Tommy Kruise. Participant in Piu Piu movement.
Lady P. Regarded as Toronto's first female emcee.
LC Posse. Early Halifax hip hop group.
Lil' Jaz. Toronto-based turntablist.
Litefoot. 1996. Good Day to Die. Red Vinyl Records.
Logikal Ethix and Unknown Misery. Toronto hip hop duo.
Mandela. Winnipeg Child rapper.
Manik 1derful. 2013. Murder of Ravens. High Heat Entertainment.
MCJ and Cool J. 1990. So Listen. Capitol Records.
Michie Mee. 2000. The First Cut Is the Deepest. Koch Records.
Musoni. 2016. NIGGAS IS ALLERGIC. Independent.
Nas. 1994. "Represent." Illmatic. Columbia Records.
New Beginning. Early Halifax hip hop group.
Faith Nolan. 1986. Africville. MWIC Records.
Maestro Fresh Wes. 1989. Symphony in Effect. Attic/LMR Records.
– 1991. "Nothin' At All." The Black Tie Affair. Attic/LMR.
The Main Offenders. 2007. Depth Perception. House Hold Records.
Mark the Magnanimous. Montreal-based producer and Artbeat co-founder.
Mischievous C. Early Canadian female rapper.
Mod'rn World Thang. 1991. Faith in Our Music. DTK Records.
Mr. 902. Halifax rapper.

Ostwelve. Vancouver-based interdisciplinary artist and rapper.
P. Noompse. 2008. "Africville" with Black Union, Kaleb Simmonds, Maestro, Brail Optiks. Hate Crimes. Independent.
Papa Grand. Halifax rapper.
Public Enemy. 1991. "By the Time I Get to Arizona." Apocalypse 91… The Enemy Strikes Black. Def Jam, Columbia.
Rascalz. 1993. Really Livin'. Epic/Sony Canada.
Red1. Member of Rascalz hip hop group. Participant in Raincity.
Reddnation. 2008. "When I'm Gone." "This Is for My Doggz." "Truth Be Told." Now or Never. Independent.
– 2010. "Who I Am." Grown Folk Muzik. Zabulon Publishing, XL Productionz.
Skeena Reece. Indigenous Canadian interdisciplinary artist and vocalist.
Damien Robitaille. 2006. L'homme qui me ressemble. Audiogram.
MC Rumble. Member of Get Loose Crew. 1988. Get Loose Crew. East Park Productions.
Samian. 2012. "Plan Nord." Enfant de la terre. 7e Ciel.
Saukrates. 1999. The Underground Tapes. Capitol Hill Music.
Sev Dee. Montreal-based producer and Artbeat co-founder.
Shad. 2010. TSOL. BlackBox Recordings.
DJ SHE. First female DJ in Canada to compete in the Red Bull 3 Style competition in 2010. 2012 nominee for the Pioneer DJ Stylus Award for Female DJ of the Year.
The Sick Kids. 1990s Toronto DJ crew.
Sikh Knowledge. Montreal-based producer.
Kaleb Simmonds. 2008. "Africville" with Black Union, P. Noompse, Maestro, Brail Optiks. Hate Crimes. Independent.
Sixtoo. 2004. Chewing on Glass & Other Miracle Cures. Ninja Tune.
Slangblossom. 2004. "The Hate." Convulsions. Arbor Records.
Slum Village. 2000. Fantastic vol. 2. GoodVibe.
Smahh. Participant in Piu Piu movement.
Spekwon. 2016. Sofa King Amazing. Moor Records.
Spesh K. Early Canadian female rapper.
Kinnie Starr. 2003. Sun Again. Universal Music Canada.
Robin Thicke ft. Pharrell Williams and T.I. 2013. "Blurred Lines." Blurred Lines. Star Trak.
Tone Mason. 2010. Production Credits include Drake ft. Jay-Z. "Light Up." Thank Me Later. Aspire Music Group, Young Money. Cash Money, Universal Motown.
Turnstylez Crew. 1990s Toronto DJ crew.
Turntable Monks. 1990s Toronto DJ crew.

Two Young. Winnipeg Child rapper.
Uniacke Square Posse. Early Halifax hip hop group.
V-LOOPER. Quebec City-based Piu Piu producer.
DJ Vekked. Seven-time World DJ Championship winning turntablist.
War Party. 2001. "Feeling Reserved." The Reign. Independent.
The Weeknd. 2015. Beauty Behind the Madness. XO, Republic.
WondaGurl. 2015. Production Credits include Rihanna. "Bitch Better Have My Money." Westbury Road, Roc Nation.

INTERVIEWS

Belleau, Marie. 2013. Interview by Liz Przybylski. 27 March.
Charles. 2011. Interview by Alexandrine Boudreault-Fournier and Laurent K. Blais, 16 November.
Gizmo and Flex of Bag of Trix. 2007. Interview by Mary Fogarty.
Mark the Magnanimous. n.d. on Art Beat Montreal. Viewed 18 November 2012.
– 2011. Interview by Alexandrine Boudreault-Fournier and Laurent K. Blais, 3 November.
Musoni. 2011. Interview by Alexandrine Boudreault-Fournier and Laurent K. Blais, 16 November.
Samian. 2010. Interview by Stefan Christoff. "Cultural Crossroads: Algonquin Hip-Hop Artist Samian – Indigenous Rap."
Sev Dee. 2011. Interview by Alexandrine Boudreault-Fournier and Laurent K. Blais, 3 November.
– 2012a. Interview by Alexandrine Boudreault-Fournier and Laurent K. Blais, 2 December.
– 2012b. Interview by Alexandrine Boudreault-Fournier and Laurent K. Blais, 29 November.
Sikh Knowledge. 2011. Interview by Alexandrine Boudreault-Fournier and Laurent K. Blais, 1 December.
Tania Willard. 2014. Conversations with Charity Marsh, Summer.
Tremblay, Samuel. 2012. Interview by Liz Przybylski, 4 December.
Williams, Odario. 2008. Interview by Mark V. Campbell, 17 September.

VIDEOGRAPHY

Benzo: Bag of Trix. n.d. Promotional DVD.
Brown, Bobby, prod. 2011. Love, Props and the T. Dot: Toronto's Hip Hop History. CBC.

Dickerson, Ernest R, dir. 1992. Juice. United States: Paramount Pictures.
Hall, Stuart, dir. 2002. Representation and the Media. Media Education Foundation.
Hudlin, Reginald, dir. 1990. House Party. USA: New Line Home Video. DVD.
Jackson, George and Doug McHenry, dir., 1991. House Party 2. USA: New Line Cinema.
Klymkiw, Joe, dir. 2012. Hip Hope Eh. Joi Productions.
Meza, Eric, dir. 1994. House Party 3. USA: New Line Cinema.
Munger, Andrew, dir. 1994. Make Some Noise! Canada: Ultramagnetic.
Salloum, Jackie Reem, dir. 2008. Slingshot Hip Hop.
Spirer, Peter, dir. 1997. Rhyme & Reason. United States: Miramax.
Wiggles, Mr, dir. n.d. Break Away Video Magazine. Vol. 3.Underground b-boy video. DVD.

PUBLISHED WORKS

Aboriginal Affairs and Northern Development Canada. 2007. Aboriginal Demography: Population, Household, and Family Projections 2001–2026. http://www.aadncaandc.gc.ca/DAM/DAMINTERHQ/STAGING/textetext/ai_rs_pubs_sts_ad_ad_1309454434736_eng.pdf (page discontinued at time of publication).
– 2008. Backgrounder - Urban Reserves. http://www.aadncaandc.gc.ca/eng/1100100016331/1100100016332.
About bboy. 2012. "bboy: bboy dyzee explain about 'Canadian Thread Style.'" http://akadope.blogspot.ca/2012/07/bboy-dyzee-explain-about-canadian.html.
Ahmad Ali, Mehrunnisa. 2010. "Second Generation Youth's Belief in the Myth of Canadian Multiculturalism." *Canadian Ethnic Studies* 40 (2): 89–107.
Aive, Marhi. 2012. "Defending the Land: Indigenous Women's Resistance to Plan Nord and Community Violence." Coop média de Montréal, 1 October.
Alaclair Ensemble. n.d.a. "Glossaire." http://alaclair.com/glossaire/ (page discontinued at time of publication).
– n.d.b. "Post-rigodon." http://alaclair.com/postrigodon/ (page discontinued at time of publication).
Alfred, Taiaiake. 2001. "From Sovereignty to Freedom: Towards an Indigenous Political Discourse." *Indigenous Affairs* 3: 23–8.
Allen, Aaron. 2012."Ecomusicology: Bridging the Sciences, Arts, and

Humanities." In *Environmental Leadership: A Reference Handbook*, vol. 1, ed. Deborah Rigling Gallagher, 373–81. London: Sage.

Alim, H. Samy. –. 2002. "Street-Conscious Copula Variation in the Hip Hop Nation." *American Speech* 77 (3): 288–304.

– 2009. "Straight Outta Compton, Straight aus München: Global Linguistic Flows, Identities, and the Politics of Language in a Global Hip Hop Nation." In *Global Linguistic Flows: Hip Hop Cultures, Youth Identities, and the Politics of Language*, ed. H. Samy Alim, Awad Ibrahim, and Alastair Pennycook, 1–22. New York: Routledge.

Alim, H. Samy, and Alastair Pennycook. 2007. "Glocal Linguistic Flows: Hip hop Culture(s), Identities, and the Politics of Language Education." *Journal of Language, Identity, and Education* 6 (2): 89–100.

Althusser, Louis. 2006. "Ideology and Ideological State Apparatuses (Notes towards an Investigation)." *The Anthropology of the State: A Reader* 9 (1): 86–98.

Anderson, Benedict. 2006 [1983]. *Imagined Communities: Reflections on the Origin and Spread of Nationalism*. London: Verso.

Anderson, Mark Cronlund, and Carmen L. Robertson. 2011. *Seeing Red: A History of Natives in Canadian Newspapers*. Winnipeg: University of Manitoba Press.

Anti-Capitalist Convergence Montreal. 2012. "Anti-Colonial Forum against the Plan Nord for a Sharing of Resistance to Plan Nord and Colonization," 30 August.

Appadurai, Arjun. 1996. *Modernity at Large*. Minneapolis: University of Minnesota Press.

Art Beat Montreal. n.d. https://Artbeatmontreal.org (page discontinued at time of publication).

Bal, Mieke. 1999. "Introduction." In *Acts of Memory: Cultural Recall in the Present*, ed. Mieke Bal, Jonathon Crewe, and Leo Spitzer. Hanover: University Press of New England.

Ball, David P. 2012. "Beat Nation Showcases Indigenous Artists from across the Continent through a Hip Hop Lens." Vancouver Observer, 23 May. http://www.vancouverobserver.com/blogs/artsbeat/2012/05/23/beat-nation-showcases-indigenous-artists-across-continent-through-hip-hop.

Banes, Sally. 1985. "Breaking." In *Fresh: Hip Hop Don't Stop*, ed. Nelson George, Sally Banes, Susan Flinker, and Patty Romanowski. New York: Random House.

Bannerji, Himani. 2000. *The Dark Side of the Nation: Essays on Multiculturalism, Nationalism and Gender*. Toronto: Canadian Scholars' Press.

Bauman, Richard, and Charles Briggs. 1990. "Poetics and Performance as Critical Perspectives on Language and Social Life." *Annual Review of Anthropology* 19: 59–88. doi: 10.1146/annurev.an.19.100190.000423.

BBoy North. n.d. "Toronto Hip Hop Originals: Bboy Lego." http://bboynorth.com/521/toronto-hip-hop-originals-bboy-leg-o/ (page discontinued at time of publication).

BBoy World. n.d. "Origami Footworks and Threading." Forums. http://www.bboyworld.com/forum/showthread.php?86416-Origami-Footworks-and-threading.

Beat Nation. n.d. www.beatnation.org.

Benjamin, Walter. 2002. *The Arcades Project*. New York: Belknap Press.

Berdichewsky, Bernardo. 1994. *Racism, Ethnicity and Multiculturalism*. Vancouver: Future Publications.

Berger, Harris, and Giovanna Del Negro. 2004. *Identity and Everyday Life: Essays in the Study of Folklore, Music, and Popular Culture*. Middletown, CT: Wesleyan University Press.

Berkes, Howard. 2004. "Hick-Hop: Hip-Hop Meets the Hollow." National Public Radio, 27 March. http://www.npr.org/templates/story/story.php?storyid=1794557.

Berry, John W., and Jean A. Laponce, eds. 1994. *Ethnicity and Culture in Canada: The Research Landscape*. Toronto: University of Toronto Press.

Bhabha, Homi K. 2004 [1994]. *The Location of Culture*. London: Routledge.

Black, Simon. 2011. "Remixing Urban Education." Star (Toronto), 30 January. https://www.thestar.com/opinion/editorialopinion/2011/01/30/remixing_urban_education.html.

Blackburn, Carole. 2009. "Differentiating Indigenous Citizenship: Seeking Multiplicity in Rights, Identity, and Sovereignty in Canada." *American Ethnologist* 36 (1): 66–78.

Bolick, Cheryl Mason. 2006. "Digital Archives: Democratizing the Doing of History." *International Journal of Social Education* 21 (1): 122–34.

Born, Georgina. 1993. "Afterword: Music Policy, Aesthetic and Social Difference." In *Rock and Popular Music: Politics, Policies, Institutions*, ed. S. Frith, T. Bennett, L. Grossberg, J. Shepherd, and G. Turner, 266–93. London: Routledge.

– 2013. "Introduction – Music, Sound and Space: Transformations of Public and Private Experience." In *Music, Sound and Space: Transformations of Public and Private Experience*, ed. Georgina Born, 1–69. Cambridge: Cambridge University Press.

Born, Gerogina, and David Hesmondhalgh, ed. 2000. *Western Music and Its*

Others: Difference, Representation, and Appropriation in Music. Berkeley: University of California Press.

Bouchard, Gérard. 2011. "What Is Interculturalism?/Qu'est ce que l'interculturalisme?" *McGill Law Journal* 56 (2): 435–68.

Bradley, Adam. 2009. *Book of Rhymes: The Poetics of Hip Hop*. New York: Basic Books.

Brave Heart, Maria Yellow Horse, and Lemyra M. DeBruyn. 1998. "The American Indian Holocaust: Healing Historical Unresolved Grief." *American Indian and Alaska Native Mental Health Research* 8 (2): 60–82.

Braziel, Jana Evans, and Anita Mannur, eds. 2003. *Theorizing Diaspora: A Reader*. Oxford: Blackwell.

Brennan, Timothy. 2008. *Secular Devotion: Afro-Latin Music and Imperial Jazz.* London: Verso.

Bricks69. 2006. "Ghetto Originals (RockSteady Crew in Toronto, Canada 1994)." YouTube video. https://www.youtube.com/watch?v=qb1I_uFItM0.

Broadacres Junior High. 2012. "Hip Hop Dance Workshop." Toronto District School Board. http://schoolweb.tdsb.on.ca/broadacres/LearninginAction/HipHopDanceWorkshop.aspx (page discontinued at time of publication).

Bruckert, Chris, and Frédérique Chabot. 2010. "Challenges: Ottawa Area Sex Workers Speak Out." Power Ottawa. https://www.powerottawa.ca/wp-content/uploads/2019/03/POWER_Report_Challenges.pdf

Buffam, Bonar. 2011. "Can't Hold Us Back! Hip-hop and the Racial Motility of Aboriginal Bodies in Urban Spaces." *Social Identities* 17 (3): 337–50. doi:10.1080/13504630.2011.570973.

Burman, Jenny. 2002. "Remittance; or, Diasporic Economies of Yearning." *Small Axe* 6 (2): 49–71.

Butler, Judith. 1993. *Bodies That Matter: On the Discursive Limits of "Sex."* New York: Routledge.

Cairns, Alan, and Cynthia Williams, eds. 1986. *The Politics of Gender, Ethnicity and Language in Canada.* Toronto: University of Toronto Press.

Campbell, Mark V. 2014. "Scratch, Look and Listen: Improvisation and Digital DJ Interfaces." *Journal for Critical Studies in Improvisation* 10 (1): 1–10.

Campbell, Mark V., and Maya Stitski. 2018. "Archival Activism: Deciphering State-Sanctioned Histories and Reporting of Canadian Hip Hop." *Journal of World Popular Music* 5 (2): 229–49.

Canadian Council on Social Development. 2003. Social Challenges: The Well-Being of Aboriginal People. http://www.ccsd.ca/cpsd/ccsd/c_ab.htm (page discontinued at time of publication).

Cardinal, Linda. 2012. "L'identité en débat: Repères et perspectives pour l'étude du Canada français." *International Journal of Canadian Studies* 45 (6): 55–68.

Carment, David, Frank P. Harvey, and John F. Stack, eds. 2001. *The International Politics of Québec Secession: State Making and State Breaking in North America.* Westport, CT: Praeger.

CBC. n.d. "Pierre Trudeau's Washington Press Club speech." CBC video. https://www.cbc.ca/player/play/1797537698.

– 1990. "Maestro Fresh-Wes Chats about Rap in 1990." CBC Digital Archives, 27 February. https://www.cbc.ca/archives/entry/maestro-fresh-wes-chats-about-rap-in-1990.

Chalifoux, Éric, et al. 2011. "Dossier Plan Nord." *Recherches Amérindiennes au Québec* 41 (1): 33–95.

Chamberland, Roger. 2001. "Rap in Canada: Bilingual and Multicultural." In *Global Noise: Rap and Hip Hop Outside the USA*, ed. Tony Mitchell, 306–26. Middletown, CT: Wesleyan University Press.

Chandler, Michael J., and Christopher E. Lalonde. 1998. "Cultural Continuity as a Hedge against Suicide in Canada's First Nations." *Transcultural Psychiatry* 35 (2): 191–219.

– 2008. "Cultural Continuity as a Moderator of Suicide Risk among Canada's First Nations." In *Healing Traditions: The Mental Health of Aboriginal Peoples in Canada*, ed. Lawrence J. Kirkmayer and Gail G. Valaskakis, 221–48. Vancouver: UBC Press.

Chang, Jeff. 2005. *Can't Stop. Won't Stop. A History of the Hip Hop Generation.* New York: Picador.

– 2007. *Total Chaos: The Art and Aesthetics of Hip-Hop*. New York: Basic Civitas Books.

Chew, May, Susan Lord, and Janine Marchessault, eds. 2018. Archives/Counter Archives of Public: Art/Culture/Ideas, special issue (Summer): 57.

Christensen, Erik. 2012. "Revisiting Multiculturalism and Its Critics." *Monist* 95 (1): 33–48.

Citizenship and Immigration Canada. 2012. Annual Report on the Operation of the Canadian Multiculturalism Act, *2010–2011*. Gatineau, QC: Minister of Public Works and Government Services Canada.

Clarke, George Elliott. 1997. "White Like Canada." *Transitions* 73: 98–109.

Clifford, James. 1997. *Routes: Travel and Translation in the Late Twentieth Century.* Cambridge, MA: Harvard University Press.

Cole, Desmond. 2016. "Documentary about Dixon Unfair to Somali Residents." *Toronto Star*, 9 June. https://www.thestar.com/opinion

/commentary/2016/06/09/documentary-about-dixon-unfair-to-somali-residents-cole.html.

Collins, Patricia Hill. 2006. *From Black Power to Hip Hop: Racism, Nationalism, and Feminism.* Philadelphia: Temple University Press.

Condry, Ian. 2007. *Hip Hop Japan: Rap and the Paths of Cultural Globalization.* Durham, NC: Duke University Press.

Connerton, Paul. 1989. *How Societies Remember.* Cambridge: Cambridge University Press.

CoreDance. n.d. "Kim Sato." https://coredance.ca/faculty/kim-sato/.

Cousineau, Sophie. 2012. "What's the Plan for PQ's Plan Nord?" *Globe and Mail.* 19 September. http://www.theglobeandmail.com/report-on-business/industry-news/energy-and-resources/whats-the-plan-for-pqs-plan-nord/article4552488/.

Crossing Communities Art Project. n.d. http://www.crossingcommunities.org/.

Daily Motion. n.d. "K'Naan Calls Out Gangsta Rap + Performs 'What's Hardcore?' Acapella." http://www.dailymotion.com/video/xiazjx_k-naan-calls-out-gangsta-rap-performs-what-s-hardcore-acapella_music.

Darnell, Regna. 2000. "Canadian Anthropologists, the First Nations and Canada's Self-Image at the Millennium." *Anthropologica* (Reflections on Anthropology in Canada/Réflexions sur l'anthropologie au Canada) 42 (2): 165–74.

Davis, Angela. 1994. "Afro Images: Politics, Fashion, and Nostalgia." *Critical Inquiry* 21 (1): 37–9, 41–3, 45.

Day, Richard J.F. 2000. *Multiculturalism and the History of Canadian Diversity.* Toronto: University of Toronto Press.

De Coninck, Danielle. 2004. Portrait du quartier St-Michel par le groupe de travail sur les quartiers Villeray, St-Michel et Parc Extension. Montréal: Ville de Montréal and Corporation de développement économique communautaire Centre-Nord.

Dei, George Jerry Sefa. 1997. *Reconstructing "Dropout": A Critical Ethnography of the Dynamics of Black Students' Disengagement from School.* Toronto: University of Toronto Press.

De Kosnik, Abigail. 2016. *Rogue Archives: Digital Cultural Memory and Media Fandom.* Cambridge, MA: MIT Press.

Demers, Joanna. 2003. "Sampling the 1970s in Hip-Hop." *Popular Music* 22 (1): 41–56.

Derrida, Jacques. 1995. *Archive Fever: A Freudian Impression.* Chicago: University of Chicago Press.

Diamond, Beverley, Denis Crowdy, and Daniel M. Downes, eds. 2008. *Post-*

Colonial Distances: The Study of Popular Music in Canada and Australia. Newcastle: Cambridge Scholars.

Diamond, Beverly, and Robert Witmer, eds. 1994. *Canadian Music: Issues of Hegemony and Identity.* Toronto: Canadian Scholars' Press.

DiCola, Peter, and Kembrew McLeod. 2011. *Creative License: The Law and Culture of Digital Sampling.* Durham, NC: Duke University Press.

DMC World DJ Championships. n.d. www.dmcdjchamps.com.

Durand, Alain-Philippe, ed. 2002. *Black, Blanc, Beur: Rap Music and Hip Hop Culture in the Francophone World.* Oxford: Scarecrow Press.

Dussel, Inés. 2009. "Education and the Production of Global Imaginaries: A Reflection On Teachers' Visual Culture." *Yearbook of the National Society for the Study of Education* 108 (2): 89–110. doi:10.1111/j.1744-7984.2009.01163.x

Eichhorn, Kate. 2014. "The Archival Turn in Feminism: Outrage in Order." *Afterimage* 42 (2): 33.

Ekos Research Associates Inc. 2011. *Rethinking the Top of the World: Arctic Security Public Opinion Survey.* Ottawa: Ekos Research Associates. Ellis, Clyde, Luke Eric Lassiter, and Gary H. Dunham, eds. 2005. Powwow. Lincoln, NE: BisonBooks.

Environics Institute. 2010. Urban Aboriginal People's Study. http://www.cbc.ca/news/ pdf/uaps-report-april5.pdf (page discontinued at time of publication).

Enwezor, Okwui, ed. 2008. *Archive Fever: Uses of the Document in Contemporary Art.* Durham, DE: Steidl/Edition7L.

Erfurt, Jürgen. 2010. "Canada's Domestic French-Speaking Groups and the International Francophonie Compared." In *Canadian Language Policies in Comparative Perspective*, ed. Michael Morris, 206–40. Montreal and Kingston: McGill-Queen's University Press.

Esses, Victoria M., and Robert C. Gardner. 1996. "Multiculturalism in Canada: Context and Current Status." *Canadian Journal of Behavioural Science/ Revue canadienne des sciences du comportement* 28 (3): 145–52.

Eventbrite. 2011. "Raincity Rap: The History of Hip Hop in Vancouver." https://www.eventbrite.com/e/raincity-rap-the-history-of-hip-hop-in-vancouver-tickets-2175490952#.

Fanon, Frantz. 1963. *The Wretched of the Earth.* Translated by Constance Farrington. New York: Ballantine Books.

Fat Laces TV. 2012. "Break In & Out: The Canadian Rise and Fall of Breaking, Toronto 1983 1985 - Toronto B-boys." Vimeo video. https://vimeo.com/54738331.

Feld, Steven. 2000. "A Sweet Lullaby for World Music." *Public Culture* 12 (1): 145–71.

Flanagan, Thomas. 2000. *First Nations? Second Thoughts.* Montreal and Kingston: McGill-Queen's University Press.

Fogarty, Mary. 2006. "'What Ever Happened to Breakdancing?': Transnational B-boy/b-girl Networks, Underground Video Magazines and Imagined Affinities." MA thesis, Brock University. https://dr.library.brocku.ca/bitstream/handle/10464/2826/Brock_Fogarty_Mary_2007.pdf?sequence=1&isAllowed=y.

– 2011. "Dance to the Drummer's Beat: Competing Tastes in International B-Boy/B-Girl Culture." PhD diss., University of Edinburgh. https://www.era.lib.ed.ac.uk/handle/1842/5889.

– 2012a. "Breaking Expectations: Imagined Affinities in Mediated Youth Cultures." *Continuum: Journal of Media and Cultural Studies* 26 (3): 449–62, DOI: 10.1080/10304312.2012.665845.

– 2012b. "Each One Teach One: B-Boying and Ageing." In *Ageing and Youth Cultures: Music, Style and Identity*, ed. Andy Bennett and Paul Hodkinson, 53–65. Oxford: Berg.

– 2014a. "Gene Kelly: The Original, Updated." In *The Oxford Handbook of Dance and the Popular Screen*, 83–97, ed. Melissa Blanco Borelli. New York: Oxford University Press.

– 2014b. "Music Creates Opportunity: A New Creation. Interview with Crazy Smooth." *Centre Stage*, Spring, 30–2.

– 2015. "Breaking Bad: The New B-Girls." *Dance Current*, March/April.

Forman, Murray. 2002. *The 'Hood Comes First: Race, Space, and Place in Rap and Hip Hop.* Middletown, CT: Wesleyan University Press.

– 2004. "'Represent': Race, Space, and Place in Rap Music." In *That's the Joint! The Hip-Hop Studies Reader*, ed. Murray Forman and Mark Anthony Neal, 201–22. New York: Routledge.

– 2008. "'Represent': Race, Space, and Place in Rap Music." In *Cultural Studies: An Anthology*, ed. Michael Ryan and Hanna Musiol, 880–903. Oxford: Blackwell.

Foster, Cecil. 1996. *A Place Called Heaven: The Meaning of Being Black in Canada.* New York: Harper Collins.

Foucault, Michel. 1969. *The Archaeology of Knowledge.* New York: Routledge.

Frood, Peter. 1999. "Foreword." In *Urban Indian Reserves: Forging New Relationships in Saskatchewan*, ed. F. Laurie Barron and Joseph Garcea, xiii-xiv. Saskatoon: Purich.

Gainer, Aspen. 2012. "DJ CreeAsian Hosts a Hip Hop Event Every Thursday Evening." *Edmonton Examiner*, 4 June. http://www.edmontonexaminer.com/2012/06/04/dj-creeasian-hosts-a-hip-hop-event-every-thursday-evening.

Garcea, Joseph, Anna Kirova, and Lloyd Wong. 2008. "Introduction: Multiculturalism Discourses in Canada." *Canadian Ethnic Studies* 40 (1): 1–10.

Garneau, David. 2016. "Imaginary Spaces of Conciliation and Reconciliation: Art, Curation, and Healing." In *Arts of Engagement: Taking Aesthetic Action in and Beyond the Truth and Reconciliation Commission of Canada*, ed. Dylan Robinson and Keavy Martin, 21–42. Waterloo, ON: Wilfrid Laurier University Press.

Gates, Henry Louis. 1988. *The Signifying Monkey: A Theory of African American Literary Criticism*. Oxford: Oxford University Press.

George, Jane. 2009. "Aglukkaq to Steer Language Law through Commons." *Nunatsiaq News*, 3 April. http://www.nunatsiaqonline.ca/archives/2009/904/90403/news/nunavut/90403_2037.html (page discontinued at time of publication).

Giddens, Anthony. 1984. *The Constitution of Society*. Berkeley: University of California Press.

Gilroy, Paul. 1991a. "'It Ain't Where You're From, It's Where You're At...': The Dialectics of Diasporic Identification." *Third Text* 5 (13): 3–16.

– 1991b. "Sounds Authentic: Black Music, Ethnicity, and the Challenge of a 'Changing' Same." *Black Music Research Journal* 11 (2): 111–36.

– 1993. *The Black Atlantic: Modernity and Double Consciousness*. London: Verso.

– 2004. "It's A Family Affair." In *That's the Joint! The Hip hop Studies Reader*, ed. Murray Forman and Mark Anthony Neal, 87–94. New York: Routledge.

– 2010. *On the Moral Economies of Black Atlantic Culture*. Boston: Harvard University Press.

Glissant, E. 1992. *Caribbean Discourse: Selected Essays*. Charlottesville: University of Virginia Press.

Goertzen, Chris. 2001. "Powwows and Identity on the Piedmont and Coastal Plains of North Carolina." *Ethnomusicology* 45 (1): 58–88.

Goodwin, Andrew. 1990. "Sample and Hold: Pop Music in the Digital Age of Reproduction." In *On Record: Rock, Pop, and the Written Word*, ed. Simon Frith and Andrew Goodwin, 258–73. New York: Pantheon Books.

Gouvernement du Québec. 2011. Faire le nord ensemble: Le chantier d'une génération.

– 2012. Building Northern Québec Together: The Project of a Generation. http://plannord.gouv.qc.ca (last updated July 2012).

Grace, Sherrill. 2001. *Canada and the Idea of North.* Montreal and Kingston: McGill-Queen's University Press.

Grande, Sandy M.A. 1999. "Beyond the Ecologically Noble Savage: Deconstructing the White Man's Indian." *Environmental Ethics* 21 (3): 307–20.

Grossberg, Lawrence. 1984. "Another Boring Day in Paradise: Rock and Roll and the Empowerment of Everyday Life." *Popular Music* 4: 225–58.

Hager, Steven. 1984. *Hip Hop: The Illustrated History of Break Dancing, Rap Music and Graffiti.* New York: St Martin's Press.

Hall, Stuart. 1990. "Cultural Identity and Diaspora." In *Identity: Community, Culture, Difference*, ed. Jonathan Rutherford, 222–37. London: Lawrence and Wishart.

– 1996. "Cultural Identity and Diaspora." In *Contemporary Postcolonial Theory: A Reader*, ed. Padmini Mongia, 110–21. New York: St Martin's Press.

Hallett, Darcy, Michael J. Chandler, and Christopher E. Lalonde. 2007. "Aboriginal Language Knowledge and Youth Suicide." *Cognitive Development* 22: 392–9.

Hatzis, Christos. 1999."Footprints in New Snow: Postmodernism or Cultural Appropriation?" Presentation, St John's, NL. http://homes.chass.utoronto.ca/~chatzis/footpaper.htm.

Heller, Monica. 1999. "Alternative Ideologies of la francophonie." *Journal of Sociolinguistics* 3 (3): 336–59.

– 2004. "Réimaginer la francité: La construction communicative locale d'une transformation identitaire." In *Discours et constructions identitaires*, ed. D. Vincent and D. Deshaies, 77–94. Québec: Presses de l'Université Laval.

– 2011. *Paths to Post-Nationalism: A Critical Ethnography of Language and Identity.* Oxford: Oxford University Press.

Heller, Monica, and Normand Labrie, eds. 2003. *Discours et identités: La francité canadienne entre modernité et mondialisation.* Cortil-Wodon: Éditions modulaires européennes.

Henderson, Errol A. 1996. "Black Nationalism and Rap Music." *Journal of Black Studies* 26 (3): 308–39.

Hess, Mickey. 2007. *Is Hip Hop Dead? The Past, Present and Future of America's Most Wanted Music.* Westport, CT: Greenwood.

– 2009. "It's Only Right to Represent Where I'm From: Local and Regional Hip Hop Scenes in the United States." In *Hip Hop in America: A Regional Guide*, ed. Mickey Hess, vii-xxx. Santa Barbara: ABC-CLIO.

Hesse, Barnor, ed. 2000. *Un/settled Multiculturalisms: Diasporas, Entanglements, "Transruptions."* New York: St Martin's Press.

Hill, Juniper. 2007. "'Global Folk Music' Fusions: The Reification of Transnational Relationships and the Ethics of Cross-Cultural Appropriations in Finnish Contemporary Folk Music." *Yearbook for Traditional Music* 39: 50–83.

Hip Hop Franco. n.d. "Alaclair Ensemble." http://www.hiphopfranco.com/forum/hip hop-quebecois/80009-alaclair-ensemble-ouin.html (page discontinued at time of publication).

Historica Canada. n.d. "Heritage Minutes." https://www.historicacanada.ca/content/videos.

Hobsbawn, Eric. 1991. *Nations and Nationalism since 1780: Programme, Myth, Reality.* Cambridge: Cambridge University Press.

Hoefnagels, Anna, and Beverley Diamond, eds. 2012. *Aboriginal Music in Contemporary Canada: Echoes and Exchanges.* Montreal and Kingston: McGill-Queens University Press.

Horowitz, Steven J. 2012. "Copyright's Asymmetric Uncertainty." *University of Chicago Law Review* 79 (1): 331–85.

Howard-Hassmann, Rhoda E. 1999. "'Canadian' as an Ethnic Category: Implications for Multiculturalism and National Unity." *Canadian Public Policy/Analyse de Politiques* 25 (4): 523–37.

Huijgh, Ellen. 2012. "S'ouvrir Aux Publics Etrangers." *Québec Studies* 52: 137–52.

Ibrahim, Awad. 1999. "Becoming Black: Rap and Hip-Hop, Race, Gender, Identity, and the Politics of ESL Learning." *TESOL Quarterly* 33 (3): 349–69.

– 2009. "Takin Hip Hop to a Whole Nother Level: Métissage, Affect, and Pedagogy in a Global Hip Hop Nation." In *Global Linguistic Flows: Hip Hop Cultures, Youth Identities, and the Politics of Language*, ed. Samy H. Alim, Awad Ibrahim, and Alastair Pennycook, 231–48. New York: Routledge.

ichkuro. 2012. "Boogie Brats Just to Prove a Point Vol. 1." YouTube video. https://www.youtube.com/watch?v=scN8PC-L2BU.

Innu Power. 2011. "Petition Contre Le Plan Nord," 31 May.

Intini, John. 2005. "A War-Weary Rapper with More Street Cred than 50 Cent." *Maclean's*, 31 October.

Ipsos Reid. 2008. "Canada and the Arctic: True North Strong and Ours?" 18 August. http://www.ipsos-na.com/news-polls/pressrelease.aspx?id=4039 (page discontinued at time of publication).

James, Carl E. 2001. "The Distorted Images of African Canadians: Impact, Implications and Responses." In *Globalization and Survival in the Black*

Diaspora: The New Urban Challenge, ed. Charles Green, 307–30. New York: State University of New York Press.

Jane Blaze. 2019. http://www.janeblaze.ca.

JB the First Lady. n.d. https://www.jbthefirstlady.ca.

Jeanaro. 2010. "Megas aka Vengeance (Boogie Brats) Trailer." YouTube video. https://youtu.be/LG6b9ZoiPdA.

Johnson, Imani Kai. 2015. "Hip Hop Dance." In *The Cambridge Companion to Hip Hop*, ed. Justin A. Williams, 22–31. Cambridge: Cambridge University Press.

Jones, LeRoi (Amiri Baraka). 1971. "The Changing Same (R&B and New Black Music)." In *The Black Aesthetic*, ed. Addison Gayle Jr, 112–25. New York: Anchor/Doubleday.

Jones, Vanessa E. 2004. "Old-School Attitude? Denied Tenure at Harvard, Marcyliena Morgan Leaves Critics behind and Takes Her Mission – to Ease Hip-Hop Scholarship's Transition into Academia – to Stanford." *Boston Globe*, 24 December. http://archive.boston.com/news/globe/living/articles/2004/12/21/old_school_attitude/.

Kalyan, Rohan. 2006. "Hip-Hop Imaginaries: A Genealogy of the Present." *Journal for Cultural Research* 10 (3): 237–57. doi:10.1080147975806008 48070.

Kashmere, Brett. 2010. "Cache Rules Everything around Me." Incite# 2 Counter-Archive.

Keillor, Elaine. 1995. "Indigenous Music as a Compositional Source: Parallels and Contrasts in Canadian and American Music." In *Taking a Stand: Essays in Hounour of John Becwith*, ed. Elaine Keillor and Timothy J. McGee, 182–218. Toronto: University of Toronto Press.

– 2006. *Music in Canada: Capturing Landscape and Diversity*. Montreal and Kingston: McGill-Queen's University Press.

– 2008. "Le rababou au Québec: Passé, présent et futur (essai sur la culture musicale québécoise)." *Les Cahiers de La Société québécoise de recherche en musique* 10 (1): 39–46.

Kinew, Wab. 2012. "Evolution in the Revolution." Wab Kinew Blog, 22 November. http://wabkinew.ca/evolution-revolution/ (page discontinued at time of publication).

King, Kendra A., and Renee S. King. 2009. "For Us, By Us: Marginalized Groups Need to Take Back Hip Hop." http://www.polity.co.uk/minoritypol/african/pdf/for_us_by_us_bydr_king_r_king.pdf (page discontinued at time of publication).

Kirmayer, Laurence J., Gregory M. Brass, Tara Holton, Ken Paul, Cori Simpson, and Caroline Tait. 2007. Suicide among Aboriginal People in Canada. Ottawa: The Aboriginal Healing Foundation. http://www.douglas.qc.ca/uploads/File/2007-AHF-suicide.pdf.

Kitwana, Bakari. 2005. *Why White Kids Love Hip Hop: Wankstas, Wiggers, Wanabes, and the New Reality of Race in America.* New York: Basic Civitas Books.

Knight, Lindsay. 2015. "Rhyming Out the Future: Reclaiming Identity through Indigenous Hip Hop." Decolonization: Indigeneity, Education and Society, 31 March. https://decolonization.wordpress.com/2015/03/31/rhyming-out-the-future-reclaiming-identity-through-indigenous-hip-hop/.

Koganometry. 2011. "Ron Nelson Pt.2 – CKLN Saturday Afternoon Hip Hop Alumni Edition." YouTube video. https://www.youtube.com/watch?time_continue=198&v=GyDN_PM6b-o.

Krims, Adam. 2000. *Rap Music and the Poetics of Identity*. Cambridge: Cambridge University Press.

– 2007. *Music and Urban Geography.* New York: Taylor and Francis Group.

Labelle, Micheline. 2008. "Les intellectuels québécois face au multiculturalisme: Hétérogénéité des approches et des projets politiques." *Canadian Ethnic Studies* 40 (1): 32–56.

LaCapra, Dominick. 1987. *History and Criticism.* New York: Cornell University Press.

Laipply Judson. 2006. "Evolution of Dance.: YouTube video, viewed 6 June 2016. https://www.youtube.com/watch?v='dMH)bHeiRNg.

Lalonde, Christopher E. 2006. "Identity Formation and Cultural Resilience in Aboriginal Communities." In *Promoting Resilience in Child Welfare*, ed. Robert J. Flynn, Peter M. Dudding, and James G. Barber, 52–71. Ottawa: University of Ottawa Press.

Landzelius, Kyra. 2006. "Introduction: Native on the Net." In *Native on the Net: Indigenous and Diasporic Peoples in the Virtual Age*, ed. Kyra Landzelius, 1–42. London: Routledge.

La Presse canadienne. 2011. "Plan Nord: Des Députés Indepéndants Veulent Une Commission Parlementaire." *Le Devoir*, 1 December. http://www.ledevoir.com/politique/quebec/337363/plan-nord-des-duptes-independants-veulent-une-commission-parlementaire .

– 2012. "Plan Nord: Charest sévèrement critiqué à Rio." *Le Devoir*, 18 June. http://www.ledevoir.com/politique/quebec/352730/plan-nord-charest-severement-critique-a-rio.

Lashua, Brett. 2006. "Just Another Native? Soundscapes, Chorasters, and Borderlands in Edmonton, Alberta, Canada." *Cultural Studies, Critical Methodologies* 6 (3): 391–410. doi:10.1177/1532708605285735.

Lashua, Brett, and Karen Fox. 2006. "Rec Needs a New Rhythm Cuz Rap Is Where We're Livin." *Leisure Science* 28 (3): 267–83. doi:10.1080/01490400600598129.

Lassiter, Luke Eric. 2001. "From Here on, I Will Be Praying to You": Indian Churches, Kiowa Hymns, and Native American Christianity in Southwestern Oklahoma." *Ethnomusicology* 45 (2): 338–52.

Lawrence, Bonita. 2003. "Gender, Race, and the Regulation of Native Identity in Canada and the United States: An Overview." *Hypatia* 18 (2): 3–31.

– 2004. *"Real" Indians and Others: Mixed-Blood Urban Native Peoples and Indigenous Nationhood.* Vancouver: UBC Press.

LeBlanc, Marie-Nathalie, Alexandrine Boudreault-Fournier, and Gabriella Djerrahian. 2007. "Les jeunes et la marginalisation à Montréal: La culture-hip-hop francophone et les enjeux de l'intégration." *Diversité urbaine: Revue du Groupe de recherche ethnicité et société* 7 (1): 9–30.

Leman, Marc. 1999. *Canadian Multiculturalism.* Ottawa: Library of Parliament.

Lévis, Ludovic Hirtzmann. 2011. "Le Plan Nord Déchire Les Québécois." *Le Temps*, 13 May.

Lewis, George. 1996. "Improvised Music after 1950: Afrological and Eurological Perspectives." *Black Music Research Journal* 16.1: 91–122.

Library and Archives Canada. 1920. RG 10, vol. 6810, file 470-2-3, Evidence of D.C. Scott to the Special Committee of the House of Commons Examining the Indian Act Amendments of 1920, 55 (L-3) and 63 (N-3).

Low, Bronwen Elisabeth. 2001. "Spoken Word: Exploring the Language and Poetics of the Hip Hop Popular." PhD diss., York University. ProQuest (NQ66356).

Low, Bronwen, Mela Sarkar, and Lise Winer. 2009. "'Ch'us mon propre Bescherelle': Challenges from the Hip Hop Nation." *Journal of Sociolinguistics* 13 (1): 59–82.

Lyonais, Sheena. 2013. "Literacy through Hip Hop Provides At-Risk Youth with More Than Education." Yonge Street, 24 April. http://www.yongestreetmedia.ca/features/LTHH042413.aspx.

Maaka, Roger, and Augie Fleras. 2005. *The Politics of Indigeneity: Challenging the State in Canada and Aoteara New Zealand.* Dunedin, NZ: University of Otago Press.

MacDowell, Deborah E. 1995. *The Changing Same: Black Women's Literature, Criticism and Theory.* Bloomington: Indiana University Press.

MacKenzie Art Gallery. n.d. "Exhibitions: Beat Nation," http://www.mackenzie

artgallery.ca/engage/exhibitions/beat-nation (page discontinued at time of publication).

Mackey, Eva. 1999. *The House of Difference: Cultural Politics and National Identity in Canada.* London: Routledge.

Mancini Billson, Janet and Kyra Mancini. 2007. *Inuit Women: Their Powerful Spirit in a Century of Change.* Lanham, MD: Rowman and Littlefield.

Manning, Erin. 2000. *Ephemeral Territories: Representing Nation, Home, and Identity in Canada.* Minneapolis: University of Minnesota Press.

Marsh, Charity. 2002. "DJ Club." *Women and Music in America Since 1900: An Encyclopedia*, ed. Kristine H. Burns, 158–9. Westport, CT: Greenwood Press.

– 2006. "In & Out of the Classroom: Reflections on Identity, Technology, and the Radio Project." *Intersections: Canadian Journal of Music* 26 (2): 81–96.

– 2009a. "'Don't Call Me Eskimo': Representation, Mythology, and Hip Hop Culture on Baffin Island." *MUSICultures: The Canadian Journal for Traditional Music* 36: 110–29.

– 2009b. "Interview with Saskatchewan Hip Hop Artist Lindsay Knight (a.k.a. Eekwol)." *Canadian Folk Music* 43 (1): 11–14.

– 2011. "Keepin' It Real? Masculinity, Race, and Media Representations of (Gangsta' Rap in) Regina." In *Making It Like a Man: Canadian Masculinities in Practice*, ed. Christine Ramsay, 149–70. Waterloo, ON: Wilfrid Laurier University Press.

– 2012a. "Bits and Pieces of Truth: Storytelling, Identity, and Hip Hop in Saskatchewan." In *Perspectives on Contemporary Aboriginal Music in Canada*, ed. Anna Hoefnagels and Beverley Diamond, 346–71. Montreal and Kingston: McGill-Queen's University Press.

– 2012b. "Hip Hop as Methodology: Ways of Knowing." *Canadian Journal of Communication* 37 (1): 193–203.

– 2012c. "You Can't Stop the Hip-Hop: Charity Marsh at TEDxRegina." YouTube video, filmed 20 June, TEDx Regina. http://www.youtube.com/watch?v=VpYnwDJYAm4.

Marsh, Charity, and Sheila Petty. 2011. "Globalization, Identity, and Youth Resistance: Kenya's Hip Hop Parliament." *MUSICultures: The Canadian Journal for Traditional Music* 38 (1): 132–47.

Martinez, Theresa A. 1997. "Popular Culture as Oppositional Culture: Rap as Resistance." *Sociological Perspectives* 40 (2): 265–86.

Maxwell, Ian. 2001. "Sydney Stylee: Hip Hop Down Under Comin' Up." In *Global Noise: Rap and Hip Hop Outside the USA*, ed. Tony Mitchell, 259–79. Middletown, CT: Wesleyan University Press.

– 2003. *Phat Beats, Dope Rhymes: Hip Hop Down Under Comin' Upper.* Middletown, CT: Wesleyan University Press.

Mbembe, Achille. 2002. "The Power of the Archive and its Limits." In *Refiguring the Archive*, ed. Carolyn Hamilton, Verne Harris, Jane Taylor, Michele Pickover, Graeme Reid, and Razia Saleh, 19–27. Cape Town: New Africa Books.

McAllester, David P. 1949. *Peyote Music.* New York: Viking Fund.

McGuire, Michael. 2011. "How the East Coast Rocks: A History of Hip Hop in Halifax: 1985 – 1998." MA thesis, Dalhousie University.

McKittrick, Katherine. 2002. "'Their Blood Is There, and They Can't Throw It Out': Honouring Black Canadian Geographies." *Topia: Canadian Journal of Cultural Studies* 7: 27–37.

McNamara, Rea. 2007. "The Youth Program That Worked." *Eye Weekly*, 8 November.

Meunier, Martin, and Joseph Yvon Thériault. 2008. "Que reste-t-il de l'intention vitale du Canada français?" In *L'espace francophone en milieu minoritaire au Canada: Nouveaux enjeux, nouvelles mobilisations*, ed. Joseph Yvon Thériault, Anne Gilbert, and Linda Cardinal, 205–40. Montréal: Fides.

Middleton, Richard. 1990. *Studying Popular Music.* Buckingham: Open University Press, 1990.

Miller, Jimmothy. 2011. "Lyrics Case Study: K'Naan." Toronto District School Board, 21 December. http://www.tdsb.on.ca/wwwdocuments/programs/gender_based_violence_prevention__gbvp_/docs/lyrics%20case%20study%20%20violence%20and%20young%20people.pdf (page discontinued at time of publication).

Mills, Sherylle. 1996. "Indigenous Music and the Law: An Analysis of National and International Legislation." *Yearbook for Traditional Music* 28: 57–86.

Ministère du Tourisme. 2011. Québec Tourism Strategy North of the 49th Parallel: Cultures and Wilderness to Discover. http://www.tourisme.gouv.qc.ca/strategie49

Mitchell, Tony, ed. 2001a. *Global Noise: Rap and Hip Hop Outside the USA.* Middletown, CT: Wesleyan University Press.

– 2001b. "Another Root-Hip hop Outside the USA." In *Global Noise: Rap and Hip Hop Outside the USA*, ed. Tony Mitchell, 1–38. Middletown, CT: Wesleyan University Press.

Mitchell, Terry L., and Dawn T. Maracle. 2005. "Healing the Generations: Post-Traumatic Stress and the Health Status of Aboriginal Populations in Canada." *Journal of Aboriginal Health* 2 (1): 14–24.

Mooney, Annabelle, and Betsy Evans, eds. 2007. *Globalization: The Key Concepts*. New York: Routledge.

More or Les, and Jill Murray. 2006. "E=emcees²: Toronto Rappers Buddy Up to Solve the Riddle of the Missing Infrastructure." In *The State of the Arts: Living with Culture in Toronto*, ed. Alana Wilcox, Christina Palassio, and Jonny Dovercourt, 186–91. Toronto: Coach House Books.

Morelli, Sarah. 2001. "Who Is a Dancing Hero? Rap, Hip Hop and Dance in Korean Popular Culture." In *Global Noise: Rap and Hip Hop Outside the USA*, ed. Tony Mitchell, 248–58. Middletown, CT: Wesleyan University Press.

Morissonneau, Christian. 1978. *La terre promise: Le mythe du Nord.* Montréal: Hurtubise HMH.

MTV Network. n.d. "The Next Best Thing to Being at Low End Theory, Los Angeles." http://www.mtviggy.com/blog-posts/the-next-best-thing-to being-at-low-end-theory-los-angeles/ (page discontinued at time of publication).

Mulvey, Laura. 1975. "Visual Pleasure and Narrative Cinema." *Screen* 16 (3): 6–18.

Nadasdy, Paul. 2005. "Transcending the Debate over the Ecologically Noble Indian: Indigenous People and Environmentalism." *Ethnohistory* 52 (2): 291–331.

Nattiez, Jean-Jacques. 1999. "Inuit Throat-Games and Siberian Throat Singing: A Comparative, Historical, and Semiological Approach." *Ethnomusicology* 43 (93): 399–418.

Neal, Mark Anthony. 2013. *What the Music Said: Black Popular Music and Black Public Culture.* London: Routledge.

Nelson, Jennifer Jill. 2009. *Razing Africville: A Geography of Racism.* Toronto: University of Toronto Press.

Nelson, Sarah. 2012. "Challenging Hidden Assumptions: Colonial Norms as Determinants of Aboriginal Mental Health." National Collaborating Centre for Aboriginal Health. http://www.nccahccnsa.ca/Publications/Lists/Publications/Attachments/70/colonial_norms_EN_web.pdf (page discontinued at time of publication).

Newhouse, David, and Evelyn Peters. 2003. Not Strangers in These Parts: Urban Aboriginal Peoples. Publications of the proceedings from the Aboriginal Policy Research Conference. Ottawa: Policy Research Initiative. http://www.urbancentre.utoronto.ca/pdfs/elibrary/Canada_Urban-Aboriginal-Peo.pdf.

Newman, Michael. 2009. "'That's All Concept: It's Nothing Real': Reality and Lyrical Meaning in Rap." In *Global Linguistic Flows: Hip Hop Cultures,*

Youth Identities, and the Politics of Language, ed. H. Samy Alim, Awad Ibrahim, and Alastair Pennycook, 195–212. New York: Routledge.

Noble, Safiya. 2018. *Algorithms of Oppression.* New York: NYU Press.

Northside Hip Hop Archive. 2018. www.nshharchive.ca.

Okin, Susan Moller. 1999. *Is Multiculturalism Bad for Women?* Princeton, NJ: Princeton University Press.

"On se met au point avec Samian." 2012. L'essentiel de la musique indie Canadienne, 22 October. http://brbr.tfo.org (page discontinued at time of publication).

Payette, Jean-François, and Stephane Roussel. 2011. "The Other Sovereignties: Québec and the Arctic." *International Journal* 66 (4): 939–55.

Pennycook, Alastair. 2007. *Global Englishes and Transcultural Flows.* New York: Routledge.

Peoples, Whitney A. 2008. "Under Construction: Identifying Foundations of Hip Hop Feminism and Exploring Bridges between Black Second-Wave and Hip Hop Feminisms." *Meridians: Feminism, Race, Transnationalism* 8 (1): 19–52.

Perry, Imani. 2004. *Prophets of the Hood: Politics and Poetics in Hip Hop.* Durham, NC: Duke University Press.

Philip, Marlene NourbSe. 1992. *Frontiers: Selected Essays and Writings on Racism and Culture, 1984–1992.* Stratford, ON: Mercury Press.

Porcello, Thomas. 1991. "The Ethics of Digital Audio-Sampling: Engineers' Discourse." *Popular Music* 10 (1): 69–84.

Potter, Russell. 1995. *Spectacular Vernaculars: Hip-Hop and the Politics of Postmodernism.* New York: State University of New York Press.

Pough, Gwendolyn D. 2004. *Check It While I Wreck It: Black Womanhood, Hip Hop Culture and the Public Sphere.* Lebanon, NH: University Press of New England.

The Power Plant. 2014. "Beat Nation: Art, Hip Hop and Aboriginal Culture," 15 December 2012 – 5 May 2013. http://www.thepowerplant.org/Exhibitions/2012/2012_Winter/Beat-Nation.aspx.

Price, Emmett. G. 2006. *Hip Hop Culture.* Santa Barbara: ABC-CLIO.

Prince, David J. 2010. "How K'naan's Song Became Coca-Cola's World Cup Soundtrack." Billboard.com, 9 June.

Proulx, Craig. 2010. "Aboriginal Hip Hoppers: Representin' Aboriginality in Cosmopolitan Worlds." In *Indigenous Cosmopolitans*, ed. Maximilian C. Forte, 39–61. New York: Peter Lang.

Proulx, Craig, and Heather Ann Howard, eds. 2011. *Aboriginal Peoples in Canadian Cities: Transformations and Continuities.* Waterloo, ON: Wilfrid Laurier University Press.

Puplampu, Korbla P., and Wisdom J. Tettey. 2005. "Ethnicity and the Identity of African Canadians: A Theoretical and Political Analysis." In *The African Diaspora in Canada: Negotiating Identity and Belonging*, ed. Wisdom J. Tettey and Korbla P. Puplampu, 25–48. Calgary: University of Calgary Press.

Rees, Helen. 2003. "The Age of Consent: Traditional Music, Intellectual Property and Changing Attitudes in the People's Republic of China." *British Journal of Ethnomusicology* 12 (1): 137–71.

Ristock, Janice, Art Zoccole, and Jonathan Potskin. 2011. Aboriginal Two-Spirit and LGBTQ Migration, Mobility and Health Research Project. Vancouver, Final Report. http://www.2spirits.com/PDFolder/2011%20Vancouver%20full%20report%20final.pdf.

Robinson, Dylan. 2012. "Listening to the Politics of Aesthetics: Contemporary Encounters between First Nations/Inuit and Early Music Traditions. In *Perspectives on Contemporary Aboriginal Music in Canada*, ed. Anna Hoefnagels and Beverley Diamond, 222–48. Montreal and Kingston: McGill-Queen's University Press.

Rodgers, Tara. 2003. "On the Process and Aesthetics of Sampling in Electronic Music Production." *Organised Sound* 8 (3): 313–20.

– 2010. *Pink Noises: Women on Electronic Music and Sound.* Durham, NC: Duke University Press.

Rodriguez, Louie F. 2009. "Dialoguing, Cultural Capital, and Student Engagement: Toward A Hip Hop Pedagogy in the High School and University Classroom." *Equity and Excellence in Education* 42 (1): 20–35.

Rose, Tricia. 1994. *Black Noise: Rap Music and Black Culture in Contemporary America.* Middletown, CT: Wesleyan University Press.

– 2008. *The Hip Hop Wars: What We Talk about When We Talk about Hip Hop – and Why It Matters.* New York: Basic Books.

Rudin, Jonathan. 2005. "Aboriginal Peoples and the Criminal Justice System." Research paper commissioned by the Ipperwash Inquiry. Toronto: Ipperwash Inquiry. http://www.archives.gov.on.ca/en/e_records/ipperwash/policy_part/research/pdf/Rudin.pdf.

Samian. n.d. "Determination Film." http://pmm.qc.ca/determinationfilm/site/eng/samian.htm (page discontinued at time of publication).

Sarkar, Mela, and Dawn Allen. 2007. "Hybrid Identities in Quebec Hip-Hop: Language, Territory, and Ethnicity in the Mix." *Journal of Language, Identity and Education* 6 (2): 117–130. http://dx.doi.org/10.1080/15348450701341253.

Scales, Christopher. 2007. "Powwows, Intertribalism, and the Value of Competition." *Ethnomusicology* 51 (1): 1–29.

Schloss, Joseph. 2004. *Making Beats: The Art of Sample-Based Hip-Hop*. Middletown, CT: Wesleyan University Press.

– 2009. *Foundation: B-boys, B-girls, and Hip-Hop Culture in New York*. New York: Oxford University Press.

Scott, James C. 1990. *Domination and the Arts of Resistance: Hidden Transcripts*. New Haven, CT: Yale University Press.

Scramblelock. 2012. "Bag of Trix on MuchMusic – Rap City." YouTube video. http://www.youtube.com/watch?v=p8mnRo5wna4.

Seeger, Anthony. 1996. "Ethnomusicologists, Archives, Professional Organizations, and the Shifting Ethics of Intellectual Property." *Yearbook for Traditional Music* 28: 87–105.

Sewell, John. 1993. *The Shape of the City: Toronto Struggles with Modern Planning*. Toronto: University of Toronto Press.

Shadd, Adrienne. 1994. "Where Are You Really From? Notes of an 'Immigrant" from North Buxton, Ontario." In *Talking about Difference: Encounters in Culture, Language and Identity*, ed. Carl E. James and Adrienne Shadd, 9–15. Toronto: Between the Lines.

Shapiro, Ari. 2016. "Somali Rapper K'Naan Schools American MCs," Morning Edition, 6 January 2009. Academic OneFile. http://go.galegroup.com/ps/i.do?id=GALE%7CA191542473&v=2.1&u=rpu_main&it=r&p=AONE&sw=w&asid=7057007e416f7e9693cabac5c570a6bc.

Smitherman, Geneva. 1977. *Talkin and Testifyin: The Language of Black America*. Detroit: Wayne State University Press.

Snc1Generation. 2012. "Supernaturalz (Ghetto Creations) 1st Generation (Stripes & Lego) feat. Dyzee, Megas, & JRebel." YouTube video. http://www.youtube.com/watch?v=ZhIDvZj7mEo.

Spence, Lester. 2015. *Knocking the Hustle: Against the Neoliberal Turn in Black Politics*. Goleta, CA: Punctum Books.

Srikanth, H. 2012. "Multiculturalism and the Aboriginal Peoples in Canada." *Economic and Political Weekly* 47 (23): 17–21. https://www.researchgate.net/publication/287909089_Multiculturalism_and_the_aboriginal_peoples_in_Canada.

Statistics Canada. 2006. Aboriginal Peoples in Canada in 2006: Inuit, Métis and First Nations. *2006 Census*. http://www12.statcan.ca/census-recensement/2006/as-sa/97-558/p3-eng.cfm.

Stokes, Martin. 1994. *Ethnicity, Identity and Music: The Musical Construction of Place*. Oxford: Berg.

– 2004. "Music and the Global Order." *Annual Review of Anthropology* 33: 47–72. DOI: 10.1146/annurev.anthro.33.070203.143916.

Stolen from Africa. 2013. "About." http://stolenfromafrica.com/about.

Stoler, Ann Laura. 2010. *Along the Archival Grain: Epistemic Anxieties and Colonial Common Sense.* Princeton, NJ: Princeton University Press.

Straw, Will. 1991. "Systems of Articulation, Logics of Change: Communities and Scenes in Popular Music." *Cultural Studies* 5 (3): 368–88.

Streetrich Society. n.d. "About Kia Kadiri." https://streetrich.ca/board/about-kia-kadiri/ (page discontinued at time of publication).

Strife TV. 2012. "Dyzee/Strife.Tv/Toronto Style," YouTube video. http://www.youtube.com/watch?v=uG4LfqmQWSk.

Studio XX. n.d. http://www.studioxx.org.

Tate, Greg, Vijay Prashad, Mark A. Neal, and Brian Cross. 2006. "Got Next: A Roundtable on Identity and Aesthetics after Multiculturalism." In *Total Chaos: The Art and Aesthetics of Hip Hop*, ed. Jeff Chang, 33–51. New York: Basic Books.

Tennant, Paul. 1990. *Aboriginal Peoples and Politics: The Indian Land Question in British Columbia, 1849–1989.* Vancouver: UBC Press.

Tettey, Wisdom, and Korbla P. Puplampu, eds. 2005. *The African Diaspora in Canada: Negotiating Identity & Belonging.* Calgary: University of Calgary Press.

Thompson, Carmen R,. and Elon D. Johnson. 2001. "Native Tongues: American Indian MCs Are Coming on Strong with Their Skills and Messages." *Vibe* 48: 46.

Toprockcity. 2011. "Mr. Wiggles Spider Man Footwork Style." YouTube video. https://www.youtube.com/watch?v=yIpVfgzFLfE.

Toronto District School Board. 2010. "Wes Williams Motivates TDSB Students to Achieve Success!" 24 September. http://www.tdsb.on.ca/about_us/media_room/Room.asp?show=allNews&view=detailed&self=26507.

Treanor, Brian. 2009. "What Tradition, Whose Archive? Blogs, Googlewashing, and the Digitization of the Archive." *Analecta Hermeneutica* [S.l.], (1): ISSN1918-7351. http://journals.library.mun.ca/ojs/index.php/analecta/article/view/17.

Tulk, Janice E. 2008. "Our Strength Is Ourselves: Identity, Status and Cultural Revitalization among the Mi'kmaq in Newfoundland." PhD diss. Memorial University.

Valiquet, Patrick. 2012. "Music, Digitization, Mediation – Fieldwork Report." Unpublished ms., University of Oxford.

Verán, Cristina, Darryl Thompson, Litefoot, Grant L. Saunders, Mohammed Yunus Rafiq, and JAAS. 2006. "Hip-Hop's Global Indigenous Movement." In *Total Chaos: The Art and Aesthetics of Hip Hop*, ed. Jeff Chang, 278–90. New York: Basic Civitas Books.

Vincer, Mary Pamela. 2008. "A History of Marginalization – Africville: A Canadian Example of Forced Migration." MA thesis, Ryerson University.

Wade, Peter. 2000. *Music, Race, and Nation.* Chicago: University of Chicago Press.

Walcott, Rinaldo. 2001. "Caribbean Pop Culture in Canada; Or, the Impossibility of Belonging to the Nation." *Small Axe* 5 (1): 123–39.

– 2005. "Emerging Diaspora Consciousness among African-Canadians in Toronto." In *Encyclopedia of Diasporas: Immigrant and Refugee Cultures around the World*, 438–45, ed. Melvin Ember, Carol R. Ember, and Ian Skoggard. New York: Springer.

– 2006. "Salted Cod." In *Reading the Image: Poetics of the Black Diaspora – Deanna Bowen, Christopher Cozier, Michael Fernandes, Maud Sulter*. Exhibition catalogue, Canada Council for the Arts, Ottawa.

– 2010. "Towards a Methodology for reading Hip Hop in Canada." In *Ebony Roots, Northern Soil: Perspectives on Blackness in Canada*, ed. Charmaine A. Nelson, 238–53. UK Cambridge Scholars' Press.

Waldram, James B. 2004. *Revenge of the Windigo: The Construction of the Mind and Mental Health of North American Aboriginal People.* Toronto: University of Toronto Press.

Warner, Andrea. n.d. http://www.theandreawarner.com/.

Warner, Remi. 2006. "Hiphop with a Northern Touch!? Diasporic Wanderings/Wonderings on Canadian Blackness." *TOPIA: Canadian Journal of Cultural Studies* 15: 45–68.

Warren, Jean-Philippe. 2003. "The History of Québec in the Perspective of the French Language." In *Linguistic Conflict and Language Laws*, ed. Pierre Larrivée, 57–86. New York: Palgrave Macmillan.

Warsame, K'naan. 2012. "Censoring Myself for Success" *New York Times*, 9 December.

Watkins, Craig S. 2001. "A Nation of Millions: Hip Hop Culture and the Legacy of Black Nationalism." *Communication Review* 4: 373–98.

Weheliye, Alexander G. 2005. *Phonographies: Grooves in Sonic Afro-Modernity.* Durham, NC: Duke University Press.

Wesley-Esquimaux, Cynthia C., and Magdalena Smolewski. 2004. *Historic Trauma and Aboriginal Healing.* Ottawa: Aboriginal Healing Foundation. http://www.ahf.ca/downloads/historic-trauma.pdf

Whitfield, Harvey Amani. 2005. "The Development of Black Refugee Identity in Nova Scotia, 1813-1850." *Left History: An Interdisciplinary Journal of Historical Inquiry and Debate* 10 (2): 9–31.

Winnipeg Child Program. 2009. Winnipeg: Crossing Communities Art Project, 3 and 4 April.

Williams, Jonathan D. 2007. "The Realness: In Search of Hip Hop Authenticity." College Undergraduate Research Electronic Journal. http://repository.upenn.edu/curej/78.

Wilson, Daniel, and David MacDonald. 2010. *The Income Gap between Aboriginal People and the Rest of Canada.* Ottawa: Canadian Centre for Policy Alternatives. http://www.policyalternatives.ca/sites/default/files/uploads/publications/reports/docs/Aboriginal%20Income%20Gap.pdf.

Wolfe, Patrick. 2006. "Settler Colonialism and the Elimination of the Native." *Journal of Genocide Research* 8 (4): 387–409.

Yeats, William Butler. 1936. "Introduction." In *The Oxford Book of English Verse*, ed. W.B. Yeats. London: Oxford University Press.

Yon, Daniel. 1995. "Identity and Difference in the Caribbean Diaspora: A Case Study from Metropolitan Toronto." In *The Reordering of Culture: Latin America, the Caribbean and Canada in the 'Hood*, ed. Cecilia Taiana and Alvina Ruprecht, 479–98. Ottawa: Carleton University Press.

Young, Jasmin A. 2008. "Get in Where You Fit in: Hip-Hop's Muted Voice on Misogyny." Northridge: California State University.

Zemp, Hugo. 1996. "The/An Ethnomusicologist and the Record Business." *Yearbook for Traditional Music* 28: 36–56.

Contributors

LAURENT K. BLAIS is a freelance journalist and researcher in Montreal, Quebec.

ALEXANDRINE BOUDREAULT-FOURNIER is an associate professor at the University of Victoria. She is a visual anthropologist interested in sound and creative practices. She conducts research on media infrastructure and digital media consumption and circulation in Cuba and in Canada. She co-edited (with Martha Radice) the volume *Urban Encounters: Art and the Public* (2017, McGill-Queen's University Press) and the volume *Audible Infrastructures: Music, Sound, Media* (co-edited with Kyle Devine) is under contract with Oxford University Press. Her manuscript *Aerial Imagination in Cuba: Above the Rooftops* was published in 2019 (Routledge). She directed the film *Golden Scars* (2010), in part funded by the National Film Board of Canada, about the life and fears of two rappers from Santiago de Cuba, and co-directed Fabrik Funk (2015), an ethno-fiction about funk musick in the periphery of São Paulo. Two of her films, entirely shot in Cuba, *La Tumba Mambi* and *Guardians of the Night*, are currently in post-production.

MARK V. CAMPBELL is a DJ, scholar, and curator. His research explores the relationships between Afrosonic innovations and notions of the human. Mark is co-founder of the *Bigger Than Hip Hop* radio show (1997–2015) and is a founder of the Northside Hip Hop Archive. Since 2010 the archive has partnered with major cultural institutions such as the Royal Ontario Museum, the McMichael Art Collection, the Toronto Public Library, and the Ryerson University Archives to celebrate and preserve hip hop in Canada. From 2010 to 2013, Mark curated the *T-Dot Pioneers* Trilogy of exhibitions, *Mixtapes: Hip Hop's Lost Archive* in 2016, *I Was There! Steel City Edition* in 2017, and ...*Everything Remains Raw: Photographing Toronto Hip Hop Culture from Analogue to Digital* in 2018 as part of the Contact Festival. In 2019, Mark co-curated *For the Record – An Idea of the North* exploring and documenting Toronto's history of Soundsystems, DJ crews, and Turntablists. Mark has published widely, with articles appearing in the *Southern Journal of Canadian Studies*; *Critical Studies in Improvisation*; *Souls: A Critical Journal of Black Politics*; *Culture and Society*; and the CLR *Journal of Caribbean Ideas*. Dr Campbell is assistant professor of music and culture in the Department of Arts, Culture and Media at the University of Toronto Scarborough.

CHARLOTTE FILLMORE-HANDLON is a 2019 graduate of the Humanities Doctoral Program housed in the Centre for Interdisciplinary Studies in Society and Culture at Concordia University. Her dissertation focuses on the phenomenon of Leonard Cohen as an entry point to explore the dynamism of celebrity discourse in Canada over the past sixty years.

MARY FOGARTY is associate professor of dance at York University, Toronto. She is co-editor of *The Oxford Handbook of Hip Hop Dance Studies* with Imani Kai Johnson (forthcoming) and *Movies, Moves and Music: The Sonic World of Dance Films* (2016) with Mark Evans. She has chapters in *The Routledge Reader on the Sociology of Music* (2015), *The Oxford Handbook of Dance and the Popular Screen* (2015), and *Ageing and Youth Cultures* (2012) among other publications. Fogarty has collaborated with neuroscientists to scan expert b-boy brains (*Neurocase* 2014), written about the struggles of independent dance artists featured in EQ *Magazine* (danceequity.com), and addressed the experiences of b-girls for Canada's national *Dance Current Magazine* (2015). Her arts collective, KeepRockinYou, founded by Toronto's own Judi Lopez, has hosted multiple seasons of the Toronto B-Girl Movement, a program to empower women through hip hop dance.

CHARITY MARSH, PhD, is associate professor in interdisciplinary studies and creative technologies, and held the Canada Research Chair in Interactive Media and Popular Music from 2007 to 2019 in the Faculty of Media, Art, and Performance at the University of Regina in

Saskatchewan, Canada. Dr Marsh is founder and director of the Interactive Media and Performance (IMP) Labs, which include the Centre for Indigenous Hip Hop Cultures and Community Research, the Popular Music and Mobile Media Labs, an electronic beat-making lab, and an interactive DJ lab. She has published extensively in the areas of hip hop cultures in Canada, women in popular music, gender and technology, queering music, interactive media and performance, and community arts-based education and programs. She is also the producer and director of the documentary *I'm Gonna Play Loud: Girls Rock Regina and the Ripple Effect* (2020).

LIZ PRZYBYLSKI is assistant professor of ethnomusicology at the University of California, Riverside. Her recent publications include "Customs and Duty: Indigenous Hip Hop and the US-Canada Border" in the *Journal of Borderlands Studies*; "Popular Music and (R)evolution of the Classroom Space: Occupy Wall Street in the Music School" in *The Routledge Research Companion to Popular Music Education* (co-authored with Nasim Niknafs); "Horizontal Networking and the Music of Idle No More" in the *Civic Media Project*; and "Indigenous Survivance and Urban Musical Practice" in *Revue de recherche en civilisation américaine*.

SALMAN A. RANA (YLOOK) is a member of Toronto's hip hop community and is a founding member of the artist collective, the Circle, along with artists Kardinal Offishall, Saukrates, and Choclair et al. The Circle is largely credited with having globalized Toronto's hip hop sound throughout the 1990s and the first decade of the 2000s. Salman is a doctoral candidate at McGill University's Faculty of Law, where his work explores the intersection of youth subcultures, law, and normativity in both state and non-state/unofficial contexts. He is a graduate of Osgoode Hall Law School, McGill University, and the University of Oxford. As a lawyer, Salman works in the cultural industries representing artists, musicians, and writers. He has lectured on youth cultures, the sociology of law, law and social change, legal research methodology, and cultural studies of law. His broader legal research interests intersect with his interests in civil society and legal education, critical legal pluralism, subcultures, childhood studies, Islam, and international human rights law. Before graduate work, Salman articled with the Ministry of The Attorney General's Office of The Children's Lawyer (Ontario) and was a field researcher in Kampala with the Ugandan Law Society. He has also worked with children and educators in Istanbul, Turkey.

MARGARET ROBINSON is a two-spirit L'nu scholar from Eskikewa'kik, Nova Scotia, and a member of the Lennox Island First Nation. Dr Robinson holds a Tier 2 Canada Research Chair in Reconciliation, Gender, and Identity, and is currently leading research on the Indigenous New Wave, on off-reserve and non-status Indigenous identities in the Wabanaki region, and on Mi'kmaw language resurgence. She is an assistant professor cross-appointed in the Department of English and the Department of Sociology and Social Anthropology at Dalhousie University, and is an affiliate scientist at the Centre for Addiction and Mental Health in Toronto. Her work has explored how two-spirit people understand and maintain mental health, how bisexual women in Canada and the US experience aggression and acceptance, and how work by Mi'kmaw filmmakers supports cultural continuity.

JESSE STEWART is a composer, percussionist, visual artist, researcher, and educator. His music has been documented on over twenty recordings including Stretch Orchestra's self-titled debut album, which was honoured with the 2012 Instrumental Album of the Year Juno award. He has performed and/or recorded with musical luminaries, including Pauline Oliveros, Hamid Drake, William Parker, Joe Mcphee, David Mott, Dong-Won Kim, and many others. His music has been performed at festivals throughout Canada, Europe, and the United States, and he has been widely commissioned as a composer and artist. His writings on music and art have appeared in such journals as *American Music*, *Black Music Research Journal*, *Contemporary Music Review*, *Intermedialities*, and in numerous edited anthologies. He is a professor of music in Carleton University's School for Studies in Art and Culture and an adjunct professor in the Visual Arts Program at the University of Ottawa. In 2013, he received Carleton University's Marston LaFrance Research Fellowship, the Faculty of Arts and Social Sciences senior research award. In 2014, he was named to the Order of Ottawa. He has also received numerous teaching awards, including a Carleton University Teaching Achievement Award, the university's highest honour in recognition of teaching excellence. In 2017, he was one of five educators in the world honoured with the D2L Innovation Award in Teaching and Learning.

Index